PLEASE ENTER ON LOAN SLIP:

AUTHOR: STEWART

TITLE: AT A LOSS

ACCESSION NO:

To Patrick and Penelope
and
To all families who have
suffered the death of a
baby or who have lost
all hopes of having one.

At a Loss
Bereavement Care when a Baby Dies

Alison Stewart
BSc, RGN, MSc, RM, RHV
Lecturer in Nursing and Midwifery
Otago Polytechnic, Dunedin, New Zealand.
Formerly Avon Infant Mortality Study
Co-ordinator, University of Bristol

Ann Dent
SRN
National Bereavement Co-ordinator
Bereavement Project
Department of Child Health
University of Bristol
St Michael's Hospital
Bristol, UK

Baillière Tindall

LONDON   PHILADELPHIA   TORONTO   SYDNEY   TOKYO

<u>Baillière Tindall</u> 24–28 Oval Road
WB Saunders   London NW1 7DX

The Curtis Center
Independence Square West
Philadelphia, PA 19106–3399, USA

Harcourt Brace & Company
55 Horner Avenue
Toronto, Ontario, M8Z 4X6, Canada

Harcourt Brace & Company, Australia
30–52 Smidmore Street
Marrickville
NSW 2204, Australia

Harcourt Brace & Company, Japan
Ichibancho Central Building
22–1 Ichibancho
Chiyoda-ku, Tokyo 102, Japan

A catalogue record for this book is available from the British Library

ISBN 0–7020–1682–9

Typeset by J&L Composition Ltd, Filey, North Yorkshire
Printed and bound in Great Britain by
Mackays of Chatham PLC, Chatham, Kent

Contents

List of Appendices

Acknowledgements

Joint Acknowledgements

Firstly we would like to acknowledge all the individuals and families who have shared either feelings or experiences of the death of their baby with us, as part of our practice or as part of writing this book. To have listened, shared time together and been with someone who is grieving, who is in pain, sadness, silence, emptiness or hope is an experience that can leave no-one untouched. Where the experiences of individuals have been described, we honour and acknowledge their permission to share their feelings with an unknown audience. We also note that any names that have been used are fictitious.

We would also like to thank all the health workers who have been colleagues at different times in our lives. For those who have supported us, challenged us, guided us and contributed the ideas that make us the practitioners we are today.

Finally, we wish to acknowledge the support of our publishers at Baillière Tindall, particularly of Sarah James, who offered us the chance to write this book and believed in this project when we were struggling with the additional unexpected demands of home and work. We celebrated the birth of Sarah and Jerry's son during the time of this book and had the care of Karen Gilmour whilst Sarah was away.

We thank all those who have been with us during the writing of this book. To Jenni Thomas, who was with us until she moved into other areas where she has done some tremendous work. To Carol Baxter and Carol Simpson for their energy and efforts in collaborating in this book.

Alison Stewart's Acknowledgements

Firstly, I wish to acknowledge the patience and dedication of Ann, continuing with this project when I decided to settle in New Zealand, 12 000 miles from her. It meant faxes, letters, phone calls and belief in each other. I would like to recognise the impact Bristol Maternity Hospital (now St Michael's Hospital, Bristol) had on my ideas of bereavement issues: firstly, working in the Neonatal Intensive Care Unit as a staff midwife, where families were bereaved of the expectation of a normal, term, healthy baby; then in the Avon Infant Mortality Study (AIMS), with families bereaved by cot death. In particular I wish to thank Peter Fleming for sharing his knowledge, supporting new ideas and challenging existing practices. Other members of AIMS who made me reconsider events of life and death were Yehu Azaz and Ruth Wigfield. To all the families I met during my time in bereavement support and research I owe an unpayable debt for having opened doors to new places, feelings and ideas.

In the past year of settling in New Zealand, to a new life and job, I would like to thank all the friends who have been patient when I have disappeared from meetings or not accepted invitations, because 'I was writing'. I look forward to our reacquaintance in 1994. To my parents, Phil and Judy Baker, who have constantly helped track down information and send it to me in New Zealand, before they too emigrated here. Finally, my biggest thank you is to John, my husband, who has seen his house turn upside down in the process and has always grinned.

Ann Dent's Acknowledgements

We have talked frequently in this book about the need for support. Without it this book would not have been finished. I recognise and appreciate the calm and willing help that I have received from my husband, Richard, over the months and, in a different way, the inspiration that has come from my little granddaughter, Carragh, and my three lovely children.

I would also like to thank the many families with whom I have worked over the years, who have shared their sadness with me and helped my growth, development and knowledge.

My thanks also go to the many professionals who have openly and honestly shared their feelings, their expertise and their anxieties. Lastly, without Alison, this book would never have been written. I thank her for her dedication, for her perseverance and for her loving support and encouragement which has kept me going.

Formal Acknowledgements

We also gratefully acknowledge permission to print or reprint the following:

Leslie, the mother of a baby who died as a cot death, gave her drawings to Cot Death Research and with the permission of Jo and Jim MacDonald we have used some of them.

Excerpts from the following:

SANDS, *Miscarriage, stillbirth, neonatal death: guidelines for professionals*
BAAF, Chennells P, *Explaining adoption to your child.*
Baby Check, Cambridge, UK
Susan Hill, *Family* (1989)
Ann Oakley, Ann Roberts and Helen McPherson, *Miscarriage* (1990)

Contributing Authors

Carol Simpson is Family Care Midwife at St Michael's Hospital, Bristol, UK.

Carol Baxter is an independent consultant primarily concerned with equal opportunities, and service research within the public and voluntary sectors.

Foreword

The title of this book is particularly appropriate – we as professional carers can so often feel 'at a loss'.

The level of emotional care that we all need around loss is frequently undervalued. It is impossible to separate medical and emotional care; both are concerned with our basic needs as human beings. In the past, most people died at home, in a familiar environment, surrounded by their family; death and grieving were seen as a more natural part of life than is now the case. Today, most births and deaths occur in hospital, in surroundings that are unfamiliar to the families who may often feel disorientated and isolated. Also, we all have high expectations of medical science and death is harder to accept – both for families and health professionals – and particularly when the tragic and untimely death of a baby occurs. Many of us do not know how to behave when faced with loss, and typical reactions include denial, avoidance or feelings of inadequacy and uncertainty. All parties, both the professional carers and the bereaved families need help and support.

This important book reflects a growing realisation among the general public and professional carers of the need to recognise and acknowledge the grieving process and allow it to happen. It breaks new ground in that it dares to address many of the very difficult emotional issues around grieving which we must all face at some time in our lives, but which we prefer not to look at. It uses the leading research work in the field as a framework within which to discuss the critical issues, and offers practical advice and exercises to assist all parties in being honest with and loving to themselves and others in facing their truth.

The process of grieving is complex in that it involves the feelings of all who have contact with the loss. Without emotions real understanding is impossible. Our greatest asset in bereavement work is our own essential humanity; we need to be in contact with this and to be 'real' people in our response to others while maintaining a professional approach. To support a grieving family, the professional carer must allow the family to feel their loss, which in turn necessitates a high level of self-awareness as to our own feelings around loss. Professional carers may often be seen as the 'experts' by their clients; the reality is that in handling sensitive emotional situations, none of us is more 'expert' in being human and the professional and client have to work together in a trusting partnership. Professionals may not act as a resource in some areas, e.g. around medical information while clients can act as a resource in areas where the professional does not have the knowledge, e.g. their expectations around grieving and loss. The task of the professional in breaking down preconceived role stereotypes, establishing and maintaining a trusting relationship with their client, while managing their own feelings is not easy.

There are various ways in which this book will help the professional carers address these questions. The availability of honest information at all stages so that families know what to expect is critical in helping them to feel involved in crucial decisions during pregnancy. As medical technology improves, so the variety of choices available increases. To make informed choices, families have to be informed, and as the choices are inevitably emotional in nature, professional carers need a high level of emotional competence and counselling skills in order to be able to communicate effectively with the families. This book offers a great deal of information about what may happen at different stages of pregnancy, after the birth, and how to deal with the remains of a baby in the event of a death at any gestational age. It also helps professionals communicate with their clients in a sensitive manner by helping them to understand more about the grieving process. It recognises the need that professionals themselves will have for support, and offers some practical suggestions as to how they may find this. It acknowledges and legitimises the potential personal costs of being alongside people who are grieving. I particularly like the unusual approach of explicitly recognising that professional carers themselves need emotional support if they are to give of their best to their clients.

My work with grieving families over a number of years both as a nurse on a Special Care Baby Unit and as a counsellor has given me an acute awareness of the problems faced by professionals in supporting bereaved families in these very difficult circumstances. I passionately believe in the importance of professionals receiving the training, support and care they need, recognising the pressure they are working under, in order that they in turn have the inner resources to offer the best possible care to their clients. I have recently established a national charity, The Child Bereavement Trust, to take this work forward, and to enable the professionals to understand their own feelings, and communicate with families in such a way that they in their turn can support and help each other. I celebrate the fact that the theme throughout this book is about support both for the professional carers and the families they care for.

I believe this book will be of tremendous value to those learning how to work with loss in a loving, responsive, and caring way. It is clearly apparent that despite the practical difficulties Alison and Ann must have faced in writing this book together from different sides of the globe they have produced a book which is written from the heart with a real understanding of the painful realities they describe. Their approach is sensitive, practical and thoughtful and I commend this book as essential reading to anyone working in this field.

Jenni Thomas
The Director – of The Child Bereavement Trust, UK.

Foreword

This is a book for those committed to 'making it better', for both the bereaved parent and themselves.

For parents, in the dim dark, often urgent times of miscarriage, perinatal and infant mortality, the role of the health care worker is critical. The offer of helpful supportive care and options can make the difference between needless months (perhaps years) of recriminations or a healthy working through of issues leading to learning to live with a changed life because of the death of a child or the potential of becoming a parent.

As both a worker in this industry and a mother who has suffered miscarriages, a cot death and become an adopting parent I found this book to be a breath of fresh air.

As well as practical descriptive text, there are key points, summaries, check-lists, resources and references in an easy to read fashion. In an emergency the reader can 'dip' into stand alone chapters and quickly pick up salient points. It is essential reading for doctors and others in the health care area.

For so long the roles of those in health care, counselling and support have been seen as providing 'band aids' without due recognition of the importance of that old saying, prevention is better than cure.

This sensible book which openly explores health care workers' feelings, the importance of family, in particular grandparents and siblings, friends and the individual needs of both mothers and fathers should help fill a demand in our community.

Kaaren Fitzgerald
Executive Director
Sudden Infant Death Research Foundation,
Melbourne, Australia

Chairman
SIDS Global Strategy Task Force

Introduction

It all started on a wet windy day in Bristol in the winter of 1991 when Sarah James from the publishers Baillière Tindall met with Alison to discuss the possibility of writing a book on issues surrounding the death of a baby. Since then Alison has moved to New Zealand, making communication more difficult and costly! Consequently there have been times when we almost gave up the struggle, but our commitment to the task has kept us going and with hindsight we are pleased that we have completed what we set out to do.

We both come from different professional and personal backgrounds, first meeting in 1990 at a workshop that Ann was running on dying children. At this time there was an increased awareness of bereavement issues facing families who had experienced the death of a child or baby. Alison has come from a midwifery background, going on to provide bereavement care for families whose baby had died suddenly and unexpectedly in Avon. The support and questions from families and other health workers created a thirst for information, which in time developed into resources such as newsletters, leaflets, study days and support groups. Ann's background has been in Macmillan Nursing, both in adult and paediatric care, setting up new paediatric initiatives in different parts of the country as well as offering workshops nationwide to health professionals. She has also been very involved with the work of CRUSE.

In the 1980s practices that had existed over the previous 30 years were being questioned, such as removing a stillborn baby from the parents to avoid 'upsetting them'. Practitioners in the field began to realise that this was a sensitive area requiring certain skills. Some developed an interest and expertise, while others felt inadequate and incompetent. Many believed that their pre- and postgraduate training had not dealt with these issues. Any training had concentrated on definitions, incidence, epidemiology, pathology, causal mechanisms and practical management of the situation. Only a few hours were devoted to subjects related to bereavement of a baby or child, such as infertility, adoption, abortion, stillbirth, cot death or preterm delivery. In addition, although we are beginning to understand something of the wider issues of bereavement, we are products of the society we live in, which still considers many bereavement issues as invisible.

In the 1980s hospitals began to develop policies to care for families who suffered a stillbirth or cot death. The value of policies is to provide a framework for practice that can prevent aspects of care being forgotten. The risk is that policies and checklists can be seen as a recipe for success for all bereavement situations, when in reality each situation is different and unique. Training programmes for health workers need to include opportunities for us all to examine our own thoughts on loss and to improve our existing skills, remembering that we all have something to offer bereaved families.

Our joint experience, different as it is, has enabled us to combine our knowledge to produce this book, which we acknowledge does not seek to be an authoritative guide on each specific situation of bereavement. Each one has had whole books written on them! However, we both share the same philosophy and the belief that spreading information and ideas, and being reflective in our practice, will hopefully produce better care for affected families.

Common themes run through each chapter. All share the need for tangible memories, for information and space to share feelings, not only for the families we care for but also ourselves. We have sought to raise issues that are often omitted in training, such as setting boundaries for our care, knowing when to refer, ethical issues and the need to assess and care for ourselves.

It is our sincere wish that in 1994 'The Year of the Family' this book will bring reassurance, hope and some understanding to its readers, so that those families who are bereaved, in whatever way, may receive our sensitive, imaginative and individual care.

Most of the information in this book is applicable to any country in which health workers practice. However, some of the legislation may be specific to the UK and you will need to clarify any differences in the country where you are working. Many of the resources which refer to organisations at the end of the same chapters give details of UK agencies. The last appendix in the book has details of organisations in the USA, Australia and New Zealand.

Chapter One

Understanding Loss and Bereavement

Education is an admirable thing, but it is well to remember from time to time that nothing that is worth knowing can be taught.

(Oscar Wilde)

Within this chapter

1. The effect of change within a family
2. Needs basic to us all
3. The importance of self-awareness
4. The effects of loss
5. Attachment and separation
6. Bereavement as a series of phases as identified by Bowlby, Worden and Parkes

---

Families

It is true to say that most of us come from families! Throughout our lifetime we will be striving to maintain some sort of balance between attachment and intimacy, and between separation and independence of that family and its members, depending on our age, development and circumstances. There will be times when being part of a family unit will be important, but other times when we will want to be on our own as individual human beings. No two families are the same. Each will have its own dynamics, standards, rules, secrets, strengths and weaknesses.

For all of us in our professional work we will be endeavouring to help individuals who are part of a family. Sometimes we will be involved with several members of the same family. Today the word 'family' takes on different meanings. No longer can a family be defined as the nuclear unit. Divorce and remarriage mean that overnight the 'family' can grow to double its size with an increasing number of different relationships and dynamics – or that one or several of its members are no longer part of the original family unit.

Marriage, although still popular, does not always feature as being a prerequisite to having children, but the parents and children are still seen as a 'family'. Increasingly, parents are bringing up children single-handed, without the father or mother being part of the family – perhaps the mother or father now belonging to a different family.

Walrond Skinner (1988) defines the family as:

> A dynamic, interdependent psychological unit, made up of individuals and the interactions between them, a nucleus of whom form a household over time and may be related by either blood or law in addition to their emotional bonds. Whilst a family will evolve and change through the course of its life-cycle, its members will retain crucial emotional significance for one another of both a positive and negative kind.

Whatever way our family is made up, there are important questions that will affect each member's life within that family.

- Each person has a feeling of worth, positive or negative – which is it?
- Each communicates – how, and what happens as a result?

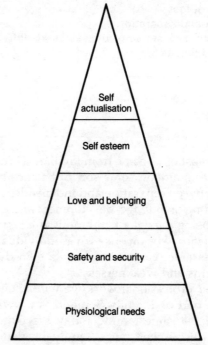

Figure 1.1 Maslow's hierarchy of needs.

- Each of us follows rules – but what kind and how well do they work for us?
- We are all linked to society – but how, and what are the results?

Although most of us belong to families and are therefore part of a whole, we are also individuals with our own unique identities and lives. However, for each of us there are certain factors common to us all for survival and development. It is worth remembering Maslow's (1968) hierarchy of needs (Fig. 1.1).

Physiological needs

The greatest need is for our physical needs to be met. This will encompass the basic functions of life such as eating, sleeping, exercising, our body being at the right temperature and being physically well. Without these elements we will eventually die.

Safety and security needs

It is important for all of us to feel free from fear. Our basic instinct is to protect ourselves and those we love from any threat to our survival.

Love and belonging needs

As human beings we need to love as well as to be loved. It is important for us to give and to receive caring, affection, warmth, support and appreciation. None of us enjoys the feeling of isolation or separation, and so we need to feel accepted as part of a family and/or community.

Esteem needs

We all like to understand as well as to be understood. We like to know the reasons for what is going on around us and within us and feel that other people can comprehend what we are trying to express to them. We also need to choose and to be chosen, to be able to take part in decisions affecting our lives so that we feel in control, but we also need to be chosen as someone special because of our particular qualities and abilities.

Self-actualisation

This is at the top of the pyramid, where we find our identity and feel a 'complete' human being. We will have used our creative talents, feel that we are fulfilled, but also recognise our limitations and accept them.

These needs are inherent in all of us. However, if these needs are not met, then the reaction of one or several members will inevitably change the dynamics of the family unit.

> Every part of a system is so related to its fellow parts that a change in one part will cause a change in all of them and in the total system. That is, a system behaves not as a simple composite of independent elements but coherently as an inseparable whole.
>
> (Watslavick *et al.*, 1967)

The loss through death of one of the family's members is therefore bound to have severe repercussions, affecting the whole family for quite some time.

Understanding Loss and Bereavement

Fortunately, today, the death or parting from a baby or child is rare, but its rarity means that we, as professionals, are faced with a situation where we have little experience or expertise. It is therefore understandable that we may initially be overwhelmed by feelings of inadequacy and uncertainty as to how best to help parents and other members of the family.

We are faced with a situation where we will be expected as professionals to fulfil a certain role with sensitivity and, at the same time, cope with our own emotions of sadness, injustice, anger and sometimes revulsion. Kennedy (1977) has stated that 'a conflict arises between acquiring disciplined skills and being oneself; between trying to do something correctly and doing the right thing spontaneously'. Unlike a physical procedure, there is no book to consult to tell us what to say and how to behave. What is right for one bereaved person may be totally inappropriate for another, so it is easy to see how we could become overwhelmed and confused.

In bereavement care it is not sufficient to look at identified models, useful as they are for giving us a framework. This is an area of caring where we must consider ourselves as the most important tool, leaning on our innate humanness and being aware of our own feelings. We need to be 'real' people responding at a deep level to people's pain, using our sensitivity and empathy whilst still maintaining a sense of professionalism. It is not an easy task, one requiring much from us as professionals as well as human beings. We will all make mistakes, but this should not prevent us from trying. We learn by doing, and doing teaches us, although this can be a painful experience. Alternatively, by maintaining a purely professional role we may be seen as cold and uncaring. Nurse (1980) has said that 'when we are at our place of work occupying a particular position in a social structure, it is all too easy to take refuge in our professional role as tutor, midwife or whatever it may be, and to use that role as a means of protecting ourselves or as a substitute for effectiveness'.

It is more likely that by being ourselves, touched by someone else's pain, we give what is required. However, we may come away wondering if what we have done and said was right, wondering if we should have shown emotion or not, and hoping that we have not made matters worse.

We will be affected by others' pain, perhaps in ways we least expected. Giving time to look at our feelings about death and dying may prevent our own personal feelings getting in the way of those of our clients. Tschudin (1987) believes that 'how we deal with another person may lie in a deeper understanding of ourselves and our world, and a willingness to use this understanding with the client'. When we increase our self-understanding we extend our capacity to be sincere.

Over the last 15 years I have worked with many professionals and bereavement counsellors, eager to learn more about helping grieving people. I have learnt that time spent on examining our own attitudes and feelings to death and dying is an important, indeed vital, component before working with the bereaved. Like our clients, we, too, are mortal human beings, bringing our own list of life experiences and possible vulnerabilities. We are not robots, just programmed to help bereaved people. If we bring our own unresolved grief experiences to someone else's bereavement, we are likely to respond in several ways. To protect ourselves from our own pain we may use considerable energy in containing it, pushing it deeper within ourselves. Consequently we may not hear what the bereaved person is saying and therefore we do not respond spontaneously. Conversely, our own grief may be nearer the surface so that faced with someone else's pain, ours is released. We may therefore cry inconsolably, which will certainly not help the client, and may cause us deeper distress and feelings of failure. There is nothing wrong in crying with the client, but the tears should be for their pain and suffering, not ours. Each of us needs to take responsibility for our feelings and deal with them appropriately.

I have used the following format to focus our own thoughts on death and dying in the many workshops I have run. For those of you reading this chapter on your own I would suggest that you do this exercise with a trusted colleague sharing your thoughts together. If you attempt it in isolation, it may end up by being a paper exercise, masking any deeper feelings that could emerge at a later date when helping others. It is important for your own confidence and well-being to know where *you* stand in relation to past losses.

For use in a workshop (8–12 participants)

It is important that this exercise is done within a trusting group, preferably as part of a day course to allow members to relax beforehand and to debrief following it. It should not be rushed, so participants need to go at their own pace. At the beginning of the workshop, time should be allowed to talk about how the group will deal with someone who gets upset.

1. Participants are asked to fill in the form (Fig. 1.2) on their own. Make sure all members have finished before moving on. (You may find that someone in the group may not wish to complete it. This is rightly their

THOUGHTS ON DYING AND DEATH

1. How often do you think of your own death?
   Daily . . . .   Occasionally . . . .   Never . . . .

2. When did you first learn about death?
   . . . .

3. How did it affect you?
   . . . .

4. How many deaths of family or friends have you experienced since then?
   . . . .

5. How did these affect you?
   . . . .

6. When you think about dying, how do you feel?
   . . . .

7. What concerns you most about dying? (the time before death)
   . . . .

8. If you had a choice how would you like to die?
   . . . .

9. At what age would you like to die?
   . . . .

10. Have you made a Will?
    . . . .

11. How would you like your body disposed of when you die?
    . . . .

12. How would you want your friends and relatives to react once you have died?
    . . . .

13. What does death mean to you?
    . . . .

If you have been doing the exercise with a colleague, do give yourselves time to withdraw, after looking at the further questions on page 7, and spend a few minutes describing an object in detail, so that you are not dwelling on death when you leave each other.

Figure 1.2

choice but do make time to approach that person sensitively, to allow them to share feelings in private if they choose.)
2. Ask the group to choose a partner with whom to discuss their thoughts. With an odd number the group leader should also join in. After about 15–20 minutes return to the larger group.

Having completed the exercise, consider the following:

1. *What concerns you most about dying?*
   I have found that many people are frightened of pain, of being isolated, of being dependent, of losing control (physically and mentally) and not being allowed to make choices.
2. *Where would you like to die?*
   Most people prefer to die in their own homes, some in hospices and a very few in hospital (usually to relieve the relations of any nursing care).
3. *Is sudden death preferable to a long-term deteriorating illness?*
   Many people respond initially by wanting a quick and sudden demise, but, in discussion, worry about not saying goodbye to family, of not sorting out their affairs and decide therefore they would prefer to have some short time for preparation of their death.
4. *Would you choose euthanasia for yourself?*
   Many people would choose this, but when asked if they would take the final step to end one of their own family's life, find that perhaps others in the family could not help them to cause their own death.
5. *Would you choose burial or cremation?*
   Most people would prefer cremation. Some are concerned about being buried alive but would not want their bodies burned.
6. *Have you told anyone of your preference?*
   I found that most younger people have not discussed this with their nearest and dearest. Older members on the whole had shared it.
7. *How would you want your friends and relations to react once you have died?*
   In discussion, most wanted some outward show of emotion, to demonstrate that they were missed and that their lives had meant something. They realised the importance of grieving, but did not wish the relatives to suffer endlessly.
8. *What does death mean to you?*
   For some it was the end, for some a new beginning. Many were uncertain. For most, dying was more frightening than death itself.
9. *How has the death of friends or family affected you?*
   I have never asked this in group discussion. I feel this is private and can only be shared with the partner if it feels safe. What I do stress is the importance of being honest with ourselves, asking, if we have suffered a significant loss, whether we have recovered from it or still need to grieve about it. Only you, the reader, can draw conclusions about yourself. If you have discovered that you have unburied a deep pain from some previous loss, do find someone you can share this with. It

may be necessary to seek professional help, or it may be sufficient to share your feelings further with a friend.

I have learnt from the workshops that:

- There is no 'right' way to think about death and dying.
- Many of us share the same fears and anxieties, especially about dying.
- All of us want to be able to make choices.
- Death, which still remains a mystery for many of us, is a necessary part of life, although it is hard to accept both for ourselves and those we leave behind.

What is Loss?

When we think of loss we tend to think of the loss through death of people we love. However, from the time we are born until we die, our lives will be made up of many losses, not necessarily associated with death. Loss is a constantly recurring theme from which we adapt and change – it is part of life. 'It is a necessary part of the human experience which helps us to grow and develop' (Viorst 1989).

Some losses will be pleasant, e.g. getting married, when we lose our single status and learn to live with someone else. It may require change and adaptation. Similarly, giving birth to a baby changes one's whole mode of life. We have lost the freedom to do what and when we like. Each loss brings its own reactions, which will vary depending on the severity or change in our lives. We can measure the effect loss has on us by using a scale from 1 to 10. For each of us different losses will have different effects, so different numbers on the scale will apply. The ultimate loss surely must be the death of someone close who has become part of our lives. It follows therefore that this will rate as 10 for many people.

Whether the loss is small or great, there is a process that must be experienced in order to recover fully. The greater the loss, the deeper the intensity of feelings and the longer the recovery.

To illustrate the loss process, think of a time when you lost your purse or wallet. It is likely that at first you will disbelieve that it has happened. This will give way to panic and perhaps confusion as to what to do. You will no doubt search for it and feel angry with yourself. You may then blame someone else and think 'if only I had or hadn't'. For a short while you will be caught up in the inconvenience. Eventually the situation will be resolved either in finding the purse with great relief or recovering from the loss. Your life has been temporarily upset. It is worth taking a few minutes to remember the feelings you experienced, how you coped and how you feel about the loss now.

As children, we have all experienced losses and experienced or suppressed various reactions according to our role model. Feelings of anger, despair, isolation, guilt, panic and confusion are familiar to us at an early age as a result of loss and stay with us throughout our lives. It is important to recognise this, especially when we are dealing with children's grief. These feelings don't just appear when we come of age!

Much of how we cope with loss throughout our lives will be determined by the model we have learnt from our parents. Society, too, plays its part by deciding what is acceptable or unacceptable behaviour, which in turn affects parents. For example, it is still common practice to say to little boys who are upset, 'Come on, don't cry, you're a big boy now.' Consequently boys grow into men believing that crying is weak and wrong.

At the age of 26 my first husband died suddenly and unexpectedly. I had been brought up to believe that to exhibit painful feelings was unacceptable behaviour. I therefore bottled up what I felt and put a brave face on the world. This lasted for over 2 years until I suffered a minor loss when all the pent-up feelings came to the surface. It took many months thereafter, with considerable help, to come out of deep depression. How much better if I could have talked about those feelings after my husband's death. I followed the model I had learnt as a child from my parents and also believed that society expected me to get on with life, without complaining or giving in to painful feelings.

What is Bereavement?

Even if we have not been bereaved it is possible to understand something of the grieving process in relation to our own experience of loss. Bereaved people will go through the same pattern but in a much deeper and more painful way. Instead of having a temporary inconvenience it will turn their lives upside down so that recovery can take several years.

However, we need to go a stage further when we lose someone from death, as we need to consider attachment and all that it implies.

Attachment and separation anxiety

Bowlby's attachment theory (Bowlby, 1980) helps us to understand why human beings make strong bonds with others. He explains that our need for security and safety develops from an early age, relying on just a few people to provide them. As small children, we look to our parents for security and safety so that attachment starts from birth. As we develop we can leave our parents for longer periods, knowing that they will be there to return to. If for some reason that parent disappears, our response will be one of intense anxiety and strong protest. Rutter (1981) reinforces this theory in his work on child/parent separation. Both Bowlby and Rutter agree that if the parent doesn't return, withdrawal, apathy and despair will follow.

Forming attachments with other human beings is natural not only for children but also for adults. When we lose someone in adulthood through death, then the feelings we had as children will still be there. Although adults are not children, within each of us is the child, still needing safety and security, as Maslow's hierarchy of needs has shown. Our response to a separation, like the young child, will be to withdraw, to despair and be apathetic.

> As we get more confident and learn more about the world and how to handle it, we can cope with more and more stress before having to go back for support. But the potential need continues all our lives. *All* of us in sufficiently stressful situations will need looking after, and that 'looking after' very much corresponds to what babies and children get – mothering. (Skynner 1983)

In the last 40 years much work has been done in identifying grieving as a process, putting different feelings into different stages. This work has helped us greatly to understand better, but there is a risk that we may expect too much from our clients, get confused when they don't conform to the patterns and be too rigid in our approach.

Bowlby (1980) sees mourning in four phases:

- a phase of numbing that lasts from a few hours to a week and may be interrupted by outbursts of extremely intense distress and/or anger;
- a phase of yearning and searching for the lost figure, lasting some months and sometimes for years;
- a phase of disorganisation and despair;
- a phase of greater or lesser degree of reorganisation.

For those who have studied bereavement, all would agree that grieving is necessary. Worden (1983) states that there are certain tasks of mourning that must be accomplished for equilibrium to be re-established and for the process of mourning to be completed. He likens mourning to child growth and development and quotes Havighurst (1953) by saying that if a child does not complete a task on a particular level, then the child's adaptation is impaired when trying to complete tasks on a higher level. The four tasks of mourning that he sees as essential are:

- accepting the reality of the loss;
- experiencing the pain of grief;
- adjusting to an environment in which the deceased is missing;
- withdrawing emotional energy and reinvesting in another relationship.

He sees grief as hard work and a process that will take several years.

Parkes (1972) talks about the bereavement process being 'the cost of commitment'. In other words, the idea that life is about balance between the negative and positive; by allowing ourselves to be happy we are also vulnerable to pain and unhappiness. Parkes similarly sees bereavement as a series of stages or phases:

- shock, numbness and panic;
- feelings of fear, anger, guilt and resentment, yearning and searching for the dead person;
- aimlessness and apathy;
- hope leading to recovery.

We will look at these models in more depth in another chapter.

All three approaches are concerned with moving through stages. They all have similarities. They give us a framework with which to work and understand better. Bereaved people do not necessarily move through each stage in turn, sometimes going backwards and forwards, sometimes getting 'stuck' in one stage, which we will consider in Chapter 10.

Theoretical frameworks are very important, but unless we base them on something that we can relate to, there is a risk that they will be learned by rote. Consider the symptoms of a physical illness. We can all learn them from a book, but if we remember a particular patient whom we have cared for, it is much easier to relate them to a real illness of a real person. Similarly, I believe that if we can remember our reactions to a loss, then we have a far better understanding of what happens to a bereaved person than trying to remember all the theoretical points others have made.

Key points
- Each family is different
- Each member of a family unit will have different needs at different times
- As caring helpers, it is important to be aware of our own personal losses and deal with them appropriately, if necessary
- Each of us can identify with loss by using our own experience. It is not necessary to have been bereaved to understand the grieving process
- Death, although universal, will have different meanings for each of us, all of which are right
- A significant death in our lives takes time to recover from. There is a broad pattern of painful feelings to be experienced before recovery takes place

References

Bowlby J. *Attachment and loss*, Vol I. New York: Basic Books, 1969
Bowlby J. *Attachment and loss*, Vol III., *Loss, sadness and depression*. London: Hogarth Press, 1980
Havighurst R. *Developmental tasks and education*. New York: Longman, 1953
Kennedy E. *On becoming a counsellor*. Dublin: Gill & Macmillan, 1977
Maslow A. *Motivation and personality*. New York: Harper & Row, 1968
Nurse G. *Counselling and the nurse*, 2nd edn. Aylesbury: HM&M, 1980
Parkes CM. *Studies of grief in adult life*. Harmondsworth: Penguin, 1972
Rutter M. *Maternal deprivation reassessed*. Harmondsworth: Penguin, 1981
Skynner R. *Families and how to survive them*. London: Mandarin, 1983
Tschudin V. *Counselling skills for nurses*. London: Baillière Tindall, 1987
Viorst J. *Necessary losses*. London: Simon and Schuster, 1989
Walrond Skinner S. *Family matters*. London: SPCK, 1988
Watslavick P, Beam J, Jackson D. *The pragmatics of human communication*. New York, WW Norton, 1967
Worden JW. *Grief counselling and grief therapy*. London: Tavistock, 1983

Chapter Two

Lost Beginnings: When Pregnancy Ends Before Birth

Wandering between two worlds, one dead. The other powerless to be born.

(Matthew Arnold, *The Grande Chartreuse*)

Within this chapter

1. Society's view of grieving after miscarriage, therapeutic termination and abortion
2. What does miscarriage, therapeutic termination and abortion mean to women and families?
3. What are the particular aspects of grief for fathers, siblings and grandparents?
4. A reflection on our own attitudes to miscarriage, therapeutic termination and abortion
5. How can health workers, family and friends help at the time of the ending of the pregnancy?
6. What long-term bereavement care extending to future pregnancies can be offered to individuals and families?

Introduction

Pregnancy, once confirmed, can change the feelings and plans of a woman and a man – they are now a mother, father and potentially a family. Pregnancy changes the role from an individual to a creator and nurturer, bringing with it a whole range of hopes, fears and dreams. Current technology in Western society means we can have a positive pregnancy test and see a developing embryo on an ultrasound scan (USS) at a point when our grandmothers might not have known that they were pregnant. Equally, technology means that we can detect fetal abnormalities and terminate pregnancies. What does it mean for women and families, whose pregnancy ends when life is only just beginning?

There are different reasons for the ending of a pregnancy: *involuntary* as a miscarriage; or *voluntary* as a termination of pregnancy for either therapeutic reasons (maternal health, fetal abnormality) or psychosocial reasons (rape, incest, feeling unable to care for the baby). Whilst miscarriage and abortion, the terms in everyday usage, may seem far apart, there are similarities in that both are the ending at the beginning of life. The pregnancy was probably not visible or announced to friends and family, leaving no tangible memories as evidence that there *was* a baby and that there *is* a reason to mourn.

Our society is only just beginning to appreciate the invisible losses or life changes that we all experience and then validate these as sufficient reason to be full of feelings such as 'sad, glad, mad or bad'. Traditionally, only *visible* events that maintain the stability of society, such as the birth of a live baby or the funeral of a child or adult, have received the attention and support of family and friends. Losses such as miscarriages, termination of pregnancy, birth of a handicapped child, divorce and adoption have received scant attention and have been placed as *'invisible'* by ignoring them. Whilst we make a claim for these families' right to visible loss and grief, we need to acknowledge that families from different cultures and social groups will place a different meaning on the loss and may not see a need to grieve (see Chapter 9).

What do these individuals and families face when their pregnancy ends? How can we help them? We will look at families first in different situations of loss and then draw together the common threads of care that we can offer. Whilst any reason for the ending of a pregnancy can result in bereavement, I have divided the following sections in to the three different situations: *miscarriage; therapeutic termination* for maternal physical illness or fetal abnormality; and *abortion* for psychosocial reasons. In this chapter we use a range of words such as pregnancy, fetus, products of conception, body tissue and baby – with families we always need to be conscious of using words that are suited to what this loss *means* to the mother or parents.

Miscarriage

What is miscarriage?

The word is poignant and descriptive, derived from the 'mis-carrying' of pregnancy. In medical terms it is a 'spontaneous abortion' (expulsion of products of conception before viability), which is distinct from an 'induced abortion' where the pregnancy is terminated by medical means (surgical or pharmaceutical). This overlap of terms can be very painful to parents who desperately wanted this baby. A mother cited in Oakley et al. (1990) said:

> I wish the medical term 'abortion' wouldn't be used when it is a natural miscarriage. I found that very upsetting as I felt that I had in some way killed the baby. (p. 10)

The layman's term 'miscarriage', which existed prior to the advent of the medical term abortion, is more acceptable, widely understood and the one that we should use with families. In legal terms, miscarriage applies to pregnancies that end before 24 weeks. This was revised, from the limit of 28 weeks' pregnancy, in the Stillbirth Definition Act (1992). It means that a pregnancy miscarrying at less than 24 weeks gestation does not have to be registered as a birth or death. This can cause confusion and distress for parents whose perfectly formed baby born dead at 23 weeks is termed a miscarriage, without formal, administrative recognition with a birth and death certificate. Miscarriage is an umbrella term that covers a variety of experiences, according to the *time* of the miscarriage (first or second trimester), and the *type* of miscarriage (spontaneous, threatened, complete, incomplete, recurrent) and *events* preceding the miscarriage (amniocentesis, previous miscarriage, ectopic pregnancy). A detailed list of these terms is included in the glossary at the end of the book.

Miscarriages, in all circumstances, represent a huge human loss and weight of sadness, and are a frequent outcome of pregnancy. Oakley et al. (1990) estimated that in the UK there were at least 426 000 miscarriages in comparison to 640 000 births annually. The general figure, cited by textbooks and professionals, is that between 15 and 20% of pregnancies end in miscarriage. Any figure is likely to be an underestimate, because many miscarriages pass unrecognised as a late heavy period, without the woman even appreciating she is pregnant. The frequency with which miscarriage is perceived as occurring can create the expectation by health workers, family and friends that miscarriage is 'normal' and the couple will 'just have another one'. Whilst it is generally true that subsequent pregnancies are successful, it is a denial of what the pregnancy and the baby that miscarried, represented. Susan Hill highlighted what this felt like for her:

> 'Oh pooh, miscarriages,' an acquaintance said to me recently, 'miscarriages are nothing – everybody's had a miscarriage.' And yes, so they have – what are the statistics? One in five of all pregnancies? I scarcely know a married woman who has not had one at some point in her child-bearing years . . . . Nevertheless, I take issue with that woman's dismissive attitude, for the misery and grief one suffers at a miscarriage and the depression afterwards, are out of all proportion to the seriousness of the event and bear no relation to it. Nearly every-

one I have ever talked to about it and who has suffered one says the same. (Excerpt from Hill 1989, p. 111)

The experience of miscarriage

Loss of a wanted pregnancy is a poignant and tragic event for an individual or a family whether at 6 or 19 weeks of pregnancy. We know from our own lives that grief is unique in its intensity and does not reflect quantifiable things such as age, size or length of relationship. Pepper and Knapp (1980) point out that unlike many of the views held in our society, there is no hierarchy of grief that correlates to gestation of the baby. If there were a hierarchy, it would mean that grief for a baby who miscarried would be less than for a stillbirth, which would be less than for an infant dying or an adult. We need to remember that grief reflects what the pregnancy, fetus or baby represented to the woman and her family.

For the woman the psychological bereavement is tied to her own physical state. It means death of part of herself and not a separate person, which means that despite the absence of tangible loss the experience of miscarriage may be profound. I remember one mother, whose baby miscarried at 8 weeks, said that the only place she had known her baby was in her own body, which was a 'bittersweet' memory. It was a reminder of having nothing to share with others and not even the 'bump' of a growing baby, yet her body felt different and told her that she had been briefly a mother.

Part of healthy grieving is often anger. The anger can centre around 'Why did this happen to me?', sometimes with resentment towards health workers and other families who have pregnancies and babies. Following miscarriage, anger can become compounded into guilt and self-recrimination in a search for a cause over months and years (Jones 1990). This is, in part, the need to establish control and identify a method to prevent miscarriage recurring. It may also be a religious (Christian or pagan) legacy of seeing retribution to self for misdemeanour (Oakley et al. 1990). A common explanation of miscarriage given to parents is that there was something 'abnormal' about the developing fetus and that the mother's body recognised this and expelled it as 'nature's way' of ensuring that normal, healthy babies are born. This explanation is cruel, leaving parents grieving for something imperfect that they created; their self-esteem may fall to zero. If a definite or probable cause can be given to parents it can ease their grieving by offering some answer to the question 'Why?' However, no matter how thorough the answer, it still does not prevent the pain of loss. With no reason for the miscarriage, individuals and couples are left with constant nagging doubts, such as 'Was it because I ran for the bus?' or recriminations such as 'It was your fault, you lifted that table.'

The duration of grieving is often not appreciated. A survey of women in the UK, who had experienced a total of 219 miscarriages, noted that 4 weeks after the miscarriage 50% of women said that they had high levels of distress (Oakley et al. 1990). Other studies have confirmed that there tend to be recurrent themes including: concentrating on the miscarriage event; dealing with the loss; interacting with outsiders; and facing the future (Bansen and Stevens 1992; Hutti, 1988; Swanson-Kaufman, 1984). A major issue for all families is to have their feelings acknowledged and valued – not denied or expected to be resolved in 2–3 weeks.

There is a desperate need for families to receive recognition and support from health workers. In a survey of members by the UK Miscarriage Association, 80% of women felt angry and bitter after their miscarriage and 65% felt that the medical care was inadequate with no information, counselling or advice (Jones 1990). For many families, parent-for-parent groups such as the Miscarriage Association are the only place for their grief (see Chapter 7 for a wider discussion of these grieving feelings).

Issues specific to the circumstances of the miscarriage

The particular circumstances of the miscarriage can present different grief issues.

1. A woman having an *early* miscarriage may be alone and afraid at home. For one family I cared for, the worst part of the experience was having what represented their baby pass down the toilet and yet not knowing what else to do. Afterwards they questioned whether they should have kept the blood clots and pieces of tissue that were their child. They could have then planted them in the garden, as a complete ending for their baby, rather than the unvoiced thoughts of their 'baby' in the sewage system.
2. A woman having a *threatened* miscarriage, with intermittent bleeding, can be in a time of limbo lasting days or weeks with feelings of confusion, anger and powerlessness to stop it. The woman may be going for repeated ultrasound scans to confirm the fetus is still alive. For some families this is a time of anticipatory grieving; perversely, this can make it hard to adjust if the threatened miscarriage stops and the pregnancy continues.
3. If the miscarriage is *incomplete*, the woman generally needs to have a dilatation of the cervix and curettage of the uterus (D&C) to remove retained products of conception. It is a surgical procedure needing admission to hospital and an anaesthetic. For the woman, it may bring both feelings of loss of control, loss of her 'baby' to a suction machine and admission to a gynaecology ward where she may meet women having a termination of pregnancy by the same surgical method. It is only recently that there is an awareness that 'women are dissatisfied with standard management, reporting that they seemed to be a routine case for junior medical staff' (Henshaw et al. 1993).

4. For a woman who has a *missed* abortion, where the fetus has died without being expelled, there can be the sense of worry that things are not 'quite right'. For example, her breasts may not be so tender as several weeks earlier. Alternatively, she may have gone for a routine antenatal check to find that the uterus is not growing at the expected rate. An ultrasound scan and pregnancy test may confirm that the baby has been dead whilst the mother has continued thinking that she was pregnant. The shock at the mismatch between her body and her dreams can contribute to sadness and fear of having 'missed' some vital sign that would have saved her baby. For her, too, there may be the terrible feeling of being a 'walking coffin' until medical treatment is organised, in the next few hours or day, to remove the dead fetus.

5. In the *second trimester*, a miscarriage can involve cramping uterine pains of labour and delivery. It can be an unexpected shock to the family, who may expect that the baby will 'slip out'. This can compound the grief and anger at suffering a labour with no live baby at the end of it. There can also be the poignant surprise, which precipitates sorrow, at seeing their perfectly formed baby at the age of 15 or 16 weeks of pregnancy. A woman who miscarried at 18 weeks said:

> She was so fragile and so perfect, I could not believe she was mine and had been inside me. Then the beauty of her made the pain that she was dead, so strong.

Fathers' feelings

Fathers have received little attention in studies of the meaning of miscarriage for parents (see Chapter 7). Experience in practice supports the view that they are often marginalised in having the opportunity to share their feelings. Borg and Lasker (1981) found that there were marked differences in the grieving of mothers and fathers after miscarriage. The woman tended to focus on the loss of the baby and the father focused on his partner. This may in part be due to the expectation in Western society that men will be 'strong' and do not visibly grieve, and this can make it especially hard for the father to adjust to the loss (Oakley et al. 1990). The strain on relationships, of grieving differently, can be severe. One mother who miscarried at 8 weeks said:

> I felt so sad afterwards, I wanted to do nothing but cry. Ian went to work and I stayed at home. When I wanted to talk he was busy and when I cried I wanted him to cry too. When he didn't I used to go into the bathroom to cry in private, because I felt that he was getting frustrated with me; a watering can.

Grandparents' feelings

The miscarriage can bring pain at the loss of their anticipated grandchild and pain for their own child's suffering. For many grandmothers it may raise memories of their own miscarriages. The differences over a 50-year period with the advent of accessible contraception can mean that miscarriage has different meanings, and even a mismatch of feelings, for mothers and grandmothers. For the current generation of childbearing women, the use of contraception has created expectations that pregnancies can be planned and organised to perfection – miscarriage is not part of the plan. For grandmothers and great-grandmothers, miscarriage was often sought as a welcomed outcome to a pregnancy that was unplanned and unpreventable with the lack of access to reliable contraception. It can mean grandparents grieve for their child, their grandchild and for themselves in the past – a mixture of losses compounded into one (see Chapter 7 for a discussion about grandparents' grieving). We can appreciate, from working through Chapter 1, the impact that loss can have on the whole family.

What if the pregnancy was twins?

Parents are in an ambiguous and bewildering situation when ultrasound scans reveal a twin pregnancy, where one twin has died. They may not have even realised that it was a twin pregnancy, or may have just had the confirmation to have it taken away again. The rest of the pregnancy can be spent worrying about losing the remaining twin without mourning for the fact that they had a 'special' pregnancy with two children. At the birth of the live, healthy baby there are 'contradictory processes' of mourning and celebration in the one event (Lewis and Bryan 1988). It can be very hard to hold these two sets of conflicting feelings and achieve a balance. For some families it can mean pretending that it was not a twin pregnancy by denying the one that died. Alternatively, they may mourn the death of one twin to the exclusion of the surviving twin.

Termination of Pregnancy: Induced Abortion

What is it?

Abortion, a practice that has existed over the centuries, is currently regulated in England and Wales by the Abortion Act of 1967, which states that a pregnancy can be terminated by a registered medical practitioner, if two medical practitioners are of the opinion that:

1. continuing the pregnancy will involve risk to life of the pregnant woman, or injury to the physical or mental health of the woman or

her existing children which is greater than if the pregnancy was terminated; or

2. there is substantial risk that if the child is born it would suffer physical/ mental abnormalities as to be seriously handicapped.

In 1991, the Human Fertilisation and Embryology Act clarified some of the uncertainties relating to late abortions. It confirmed that the upper gestation limit for abortion is generally defined as the end of the 24th week of pregnancy except in situations such as risk to the life of the woman, e.g. renal disease, or evidence that the child would be seriously handicapped. In practice, many gynaecologists and the British Pregnancy Advisory Service use 22 weeks as the upper limit for termination, because it is the age of potential fetal viability in some neonatal intensive care centres.

The term 'therapeutic termination/abortion' has been used in situations where the pregnancy is either a risk to the life or physical health of the mother or there is a risk of fetal abnormality. The term 'abortion', in common lay usage, generally refers to termination on the grounds of risk to mental health of mother or existing children.

We can all appreciate that the *reasons* for the termination and the *timing* of the termination can have a very different impact on grieving. We will look at therapeutic terminations of pregnancy and then terminations referred to as 'abortion' in common usage.

Therapeutic termination

Families' experience

The decision to have a therapeutic termination is one of the saddest and most poignant encountered with the loss of a child. Parents are faced with an often intolerable dilemma, and then decision, to end the life of the child they have been waiting for. The termination is based on the parents' 'choice' to have an abortion on the basis of their own beliefs and interpretation of medical advice about risks to health. The pregnancy is generally a wanted child and the decision to end the pregnancy is often in the second trimester when the reality of the baby is becoming concrete with the baby's movements starting to be felt, plans made and names chosen. It is hard to prevent or avoid the situation arising so late in pregnancy. The damaging effects of the pregnancy on maternal health may have been unanticipated in the first trimester, and the prenatal diagnosis (PND) of fetal abnormality has, until recently, been dependent on tests completed at around 16–18 weeks gestation. Recently, the advent of chorionic villus sampling (CVS) for some genetic disorders at 8–9 weeks gestation has meant that decisions can be made earlier in pregnancy. However, regardless of the point in time when the specimen is taken, there is a time delay as the specimens are sent away for laboratory tests. The parents have to wait 1–3 weeks, until contacted by either a midwife or obstetrician with the results. In the case of a positive result to the alphafetoprotein (AFP) blood test, which is routinely offered to women at 16 weeks gestation to test for neural tube defects (NTDs), an amniocentesis may be recommended. This means a further wait of 2–3 weeks for results that may confirm that the baby is normal or has an NTD such as spina bifida. During that time of waiting some parents are grieving the loss of a normal, happy pregnancy others appear oblivious to the risks and choices.

One mother I cared for, who had a therapeutic termination for spina bifida, said:

> The worst time was the waiting after the amnio, I did not want to be pregnant, I did not want to eat and make the baby grow, I did not want to sleep. I wanted everything to stop until I knew the results and then when they came I could not believe them and asked for it in writing.

As health workers, we need to recognise that many families have a different perception to ours of the offer of routine tests such as an ultrasound scan and AFP blood test. The parents' group, Support Around Termination for Abnormality (SAFTA), notes in an information sheet:

> The majority of parents see screening as a confirmation of the health of their baby. Few expect to be told that their baby has a severe abnormality and are therefore unprepared for the consequences of such screening.

Parents are certainly not prepared that it may be the beginning of choices, death of their child and long-term feelings of shock and devastation. In addition, performing PND tests such as CVS or amniocentesis carries risks such as miscarriage and damage to the fetus.

In the case of maternal ill-health the decision to have a termination is based on values of maternal life versus potential infant life. One specific situation that we are seeing increasingly is a consequence of the widespread use of ultrasound scans early in pregnancy, which detect an ectopic pregnancy. This can result in therapeutic termination of the pregnancy before it reaches the life-threatening point of maternal tubal rupture.

In many maternity units, even after discussions with an obstetrician and/or paediatrician that result in a family's decision to terminate the pregnancy, there is still a delay in organising admission for the termination. The mother may have to wait another 24 hours with the agonising knowledge that her child is still growing and still alive within her (Adler and Kushnick 1982).

This assumes that agreement can be reached. Sometimes parents do not reach a consensus on issues of the mother's health or the extent of the baby's handicap and sometimes they change their decision, or they may decide to continue with the pregnancy. Some of the bereavement issues related to having a baby with developmental disabilities are discussed in

Chapter 6. No part of the process to termination or to continue with the pregnancy is easy, nor is it what the parents expected when they set out on the pregnancy. All the expectations and norms of pregnancy are shattered.

The termination, depending on gestation, may involve surgical aspiration, curettage, or use of vaginal or intravenous prostaglandins. Any method is an invasion of both the pregnancy and privacy. At the end there is only a dead baby. How the family is cared for at this time can have a crucial impact on their grieving (see Chapter 7). One mother decided to come and share her experience at one of our study days for health workers. She had had a termination for fetal abnormalities 5 years previously. For her, one of the hardest things had been the feeling during the termination that she had no place as a mother; that the procedure was like a 'clean out' rather than the death of her baby. It took her 2 years to talk about this with her family, and when she did, she used the medical term 'therapeutic termination' and not the words 'my baby'. She dealt with the pain by immersing herself in her career as a place she could organise and keep control of her life.

For many families the shock of what is happening can have a nightmarish, numbing quality which is sufficient to carry them through the time of the termination. It is afterwards that there may be questions and guilt. This may be compounded with loss of maternal health or with fetal abnormality and the sense of imperfection. The sense of failure may be strengthened by family and friends who isolate the parents or make no reference to what has happened. Sometimes parents are even told 'it is best forgotten', which leaves no place to talk about what has happened.

Bereavement brings questions that reflect both anger and guilt, 'Why me? . . . Why us?', which are discussed in more detail in Chapter 7. Sometimes, there are recriminations from one partner to another: 'It was because you did . . .'. Whilst it might be expected that parents would feel relief at not having a disabled child or risking the life of the mother, the reality is not that simple. For many families it takes time to reach this acceptance. Many women experience a severe grief after the termination (Lloyd and Laurence 1985), which may be damaging and long term. A study by White-Van Mourik et al. (1992) of 152 parents, visited 2 years after termination for fetal abnormality, found that in the first year after the termination most parents had felt emotional turmoil. The relationship between many of the parents had been strained, largely as a result of 'lack of synchrony in grieving' – men and women grieved differently in terms of style and time. Most importantly, they found that the main difficulty in coming to terms with the loss of the baby was not the abnormality of the baby but pre-existing stressors in the parents, e.g. lack of communication and immaturity. Whatever the loss (baby, child or adult), we all come with our lives and personalities, which, as we discussed in Chapter 1, have a major effect on how we grieve.

Siblings' and grandparents' feelings

The feelings of other family members are discussed further in Chapters 7 and 8; we will only briefly look at them here. The power of parents' feelings can affect other family members such as siblings who can become unsettled and upset (Furlong and Black 1984). Explaining the termination of a baby for abnormality can be very hard – children have their own views on it. One little boy asked his mother if the baby (terminated for anencephaly) was a monster like ET. Whilst most parents have the same questions in their heads, it can be devastating to be asked it by your child. Yet avoiding telling children only has the effect of making them upset and fearful because they do not fully know what is going on.

For grandparents there may be a revisiting of their own personal griefs of death of a baby or child in their own lives. They may also question and seek a 'cause' for the maternal ill-health or the fetal abnormality, which sometimes can result in protecting the image of perfection of their own family and recriminations against the partner who is not their own child.

Abortion

Feelings of the mother

Grieving is generally assumed to be the response to the loss of something that one values (see Chapter 1). It might be expected that with an abortion on the grounds of a threat to mental health of the woman or her existing children, the woman or her family would not particularly grieve over the loss of something they wanted to lose. This is the reality for many women, who have a sense of relief and happiness after abortion, which confirms that they have made the right decision (Broome 1984). However, for others there can be confusion and pain.

Whatever the reasons for the abortion, the very fact of being pregnant brings a change to the woman's or couple's perceptions of their fertility. This change, when it ends with abortion, still needs acknowledgement to self and sometimes to others as a part of one's life. In terms of opportunities to acknowledge change or to grieve, there are similarities between abortion and that of the relinquishing mother in the adoption process – both clients may be perceived by others to have voluntarily chosen to bereave themselves. As a consequence the woman may feel that she is not offered or entitled to any space to grieve or be upset.

Women may feel that they are 'expected' to be glad or grateful to have an abortion, which means feelings, changes and dreams are denied. One day, with no warning, a nurse I had worked with for several years said how sad she was when she saw mothers going home from hospital with their babies to realise that she did not have her child. Six years previously she had had an abortion and felt that it was the 'right thing to do'. She had even felt that she should be grateful to the nurses and doctors who gave her the opportunity to 'shelve' her parental responsibilities and to continue as a single person. The reality was that she still had the grief hidden and buried inside her, and she still marked dates such as when her child would have been starting to talk or going to school.

The fact that abortion in the first trimester can be completed on a day-patient basis can perpetuate the view that it is 'all over and done with' quickly. It makes it a socially neat procedure. The message to the woman may be that the abortion is over and that she has no 'rights' or 'need' to grieve, talk about or cry over her pregnancy or baby. In addition, research has found that gynaecological nurses may condemn women with the attitude that they are having an abortion 'just because it is convenient' (Webb 1985). This view often reflects the high workload of nurses who have no specialist training and no understanding of the journey to reach the decision to have an abortion. In practice it means that women may feel judged and unsupported during their abortion.

The difficulties that some women have long term in accepting an abortion as part of their life is often a reflection of their emotional state prepregnancy, rather than the effect of the actual abortion (David 1978). Women who are vulnerable emotionally include teenagers and women who are pressured to have an abortion, when it is not their clear choice. This may be explicit: 'If you have that baby I will leave you', or it may be implicit: 'Do you think *you* can cope with a baby?' Celia's story of having abortions in the USA highlights both the vulnerability of teenagers and the fact that the rest of life may be spent trying to make sense of the choice.

> The first time I had an abortion was when I was about fifteen and a half . . . At the time I don't think I was really in touch with any feelings, I was just like a robot. I felt like I was a little girl and the big people were in charge of me and they were telling me what I needed to do. When I told my folks, they said 'Yeah, you have to have this abortion'. And I said, Okay, I'll have this abortion . . . My folks were very distant from me. They didn't give me any permission to feel and didn't create any space at least with me to express what they were feeling. ('Everytime I had sex I got pregnant', in Townsend and Perkins 1991, p. 174)

Having an abortion in the second trimester of pregnancy, when the baby is growing and visible, may leave experiences and feelings that can be more difficult to resolve. Kaltreider (1973) pointed out that by the second trimester many women talk about the fetus as a 'baby', whereas in the first 12 weeks they talk about a 'pregnancy'. The perception of the baby as a person, the sense of sharing one's body with another being, can make it very hard to accept afterwards the choice to empty out that space in one's body.

For women who have difficulty resolving their grief and accepting the abortion as part of their lives, the long-term effects can cause profound anger (towards themselves and others) and depression based on fears of having further children or being in another relationship. We need to recognise that this grief is often compounded by other stresses such as rape, unemployment, abuse or low self-esteem (see the sections in Chapters 7 and 10 on difficulty in grieving). To keep this in perspective, there are many women who are happy with their choice, accept the place that it has in their lives and move forwards to other experiences.

Fathers' feelings

We have said little about the feelings of fathers after abortion; little support or research has been focused on their role. Some will have been part of the decision-making process, some will not have been told by their partner that she is pregnant and some will have pressured the woman. Inevitably, as Raphael-Leff (1991) points out, there are tensions within a relationship where 'she' is pregnant and 'he' is apparently unscathed. This was illustrated in the popular TV series 'Casualty' in 1993, when Staff Nurse Ashe did not support his partner Nicky in the idea of having a baby as a result of an unplanned pregnancy. She terminated the pregnancy and then left him. Only then did he begin to realise and regret what he had lost.

What can Health Workers do to Help?

This section is for health workers in hospital or community, caring for these women and families. There is no expectation that care will involve in-depth grief counselling; instead we focus on some of the practical points we all need to remember. We also recognise that whilst families are referred to frequently in this book, there are many situations where the mother is alone in her grief or adaptation to change. Chapter 7 discusses in detail caring for the bereaved, including assessing needs, short- and long-term care, what to say and do and using a contract of care. In this chapter we focus on what we need to do specifically in situations of miscarriage and abortion. There are both similarities and differences in the care needed and we have highlighted these for the reader.

The aim of our care

The principles of our bereavement care are based on:

- *Honesty* to ourselves and to the women and families.
- *Being there* when the woman or family need us.
- *Valuing individuals* with different needs and griefs based on cultural, social and personal differences.

- *Being confident* we have something to offer, even if it is only the fact that we care about the person.

As we discussed in Chapter 1, we cannot assume a professional facade and fulfil a checklist to provide the ideal bereavement care in situation X, Y, Z; we ourselves are part of the situation and need to be 'real' people. We have to recognise that each individual brings their own resources and views to the experience (Fig. 7.1) and that we cannot grieve for them. In particular we need to be sensitive to cultural aspects of grieving, which are discussed further in Chapter 9. We need to know the local names of community workers who will act as interpreters if needed.

Our care has two roles: information-giving and support. It has two time periods: at the time of the miscarriage/termination and long term extending into future pregnancies and babies. Table 2.1 sums up briefly what not to do (see also the section in Chapter 7, 'What helps bereaved parents most/least').

Self-awareness

If you have read Chapter 1 you will have explored something of yourself and your losses. Most health workers feel vulnerable, humble and sometimes threatened by caring for a family during miscarriage or termination of pregnancy. Some may object and refuse to care for women during termination of pregnancy on ethical and religious grounds. For the

Table 2.1 Some don'ts when caring for women and families after miscarriage, therapeutic termination or abortion

---

- **Do not** assume that the experience of one person or of a research study applies to all people undergoing the same event – grief is individual.
- **Do not** try to 'make it better' – you can only make it 'not worse' for a family whose pregnancy has ended.
- **Do not** send parents or a woman home without:
  information of what to expect physically and emotionally
  a contact name for support and information.
- **Do not** feel the need to be 'professional' to avoid sharing emotion and feelings if you want to. The caregivers, who are valued by parents, are those who gave them a hug or smiled or said they were 'sorry'.
- **Do not** leave parents, having a miscarriage or therapeutic termination, alone in a single room or ward to 'quietly get on with it' with a call-bell at hand.
- **Do not** rush through information and procedures to get away from the discomfort of the parents – grieving takes time and shock means that information and choices need to be repeated. In years to come the time spent on this may be invaluable for the parents.
- **Do not** assume that parents will **not** want the opportunity to see or keep their baby or pregnancy, whether a fetus or only indeterminate body tissue.
- **Do not** leave the parents after a miscarriage or therapeutic termination with the comment, 'Never mind you can have another'.

---

majority, we tentatively offer care to these families and feel in some way responsible for the lack of a 'perfect' pregnancy and frightened by the strength of pain and distress that families may have. It is easy to hide behind a professional facade. 'It is not always easy to manage miscarriage. It can draw one into the very heart and soul of a sometimes tremendously hurting person, a setting in which too many physicians feel unfamiliar and uncomfortable' (Wells 1991).

This comment applies to all health workers and all situations of bereavement. What can we do? Firstly, it means that we need to be self-aware and honest about our own feelings towards both abortion and death. We need to use the *cues* from the woman and her family as to how they think of the therapeutic termination, abortion or miscarriage. To us the miscarriage may represent the end of a pregnancy or death of a fetus, but to the woman it may be her 'baby'. Conversely, the woman having an abortion may not want to personalise the experience and refer to 'ending the pregnancy' or 'getting rid of it'. The choice of words and labels influences parents' view of their child; think about the difference between saying 'an anencephalic baby' as opposed to 'a baby with anencephaly'.

At the Time of the Termination or Miscarriage

Organisational issues

These have to be addressed by all hospitals and practitioners – where should these families be cared for? It has frequently been proposed that women who are miscarrying or having a therapeutic termination should have the option to go to a maternity unit and receive the care of midwives, who are trained to deliver babies. It has been argued that gynaecological wards have staff who are excellent in their care, but are not trained in childbirth, and that women are amongst patients admitted for a variety of medical and surgical treatments. Whatever the setting, the environment needs to be private and comfortable with options such as a double bed during therapeutic termination, telephones, tea and coffee. As with all patients we need to be sensitive to issues of privacy, dignity and ensure that all women and families have a named and identified health worker.

Information during miscarriage or termination

In all situations discussed in this chapter the need for information is urgent. This means a full explanation and preparation for whatever is happening or likely to happen. As Raphael-Leff (1991) points out, the grief at the loss of a baby can be compounded and cause panic when there is a loss of control over one's own body.

What are the decisions and choices?

Bereavement is about adjustment to change; to be able to adjust we need to have some part and some ownership in the process. Information is one tool for achieving this. With regard to miscarriage a woman needs to know what is happening to her pregnancy. If she is having a threatened miscarriage, is it likely to stop or fully miscarry? She needs clear *boundaries* of what she can do to protect her baby and when to seek help, e.g. contact the doctor if the blood loss becomes heavier. If it is an abortion, the decision must be the client's and she will need information about the procedure, the risks, future contraception options and alternatives to abortion (Broome 1984). The client will need time to go away and think about her decision before making a final choice. If a family is facing the option of a therapeutic termination they need the opportunity to discuss, with a person who is able to explain, findings of any results, the implications of handicap or survival of the baby, the options for continuing or ending the pregnancy and an explanation of the procedure of termination.

What about during the event?

Once committed to a course of action such as D&C or suction aspiration of pregnancy, the woman and family need detailed knowledge about the procedure, the anaesthetic, how long it will take, what analgesia is available and when she can go home. Appreciating cultural differences and the need for an interpreter may be fundamental to offering care to women who have come to the UK for an abortion from places such as Italy or Spain. At the ending of the pregnancy, women and families may want to have detailed information about their baby/pregnancy, e.g. what their baby looks like in terms of size or shape, which if we are *honest* we will provide. Consider using a set of cardboard cutouts to illustrate the size or shape of their baby (Fig. 2.1) or the book by Lennart Nilssen, *A Child is Born*, (Nilssen, 1977) which has photographs of developing fetuses. A miscarriage or termination at 9 weeks is a few lumps of tissue and blood clots; at 18 weeks it is a perfectly formed baby. If the pregnancy is terminated for fetal abnormality the family may need time to find out what their baby will really look like. For example, a baby with anencephaly is a beautifully formed baby to the level of the forehead. Talking about the reality of the abnormality is rarely, if ever, worse than the imagination of the parents, who are often surprised at how beautiful their baby actually looks.

What happens to their pregnancy or baby?

For many women and families there is also the need to plan or know about seeing their pregnancy and how it may be disposed of. After abortion

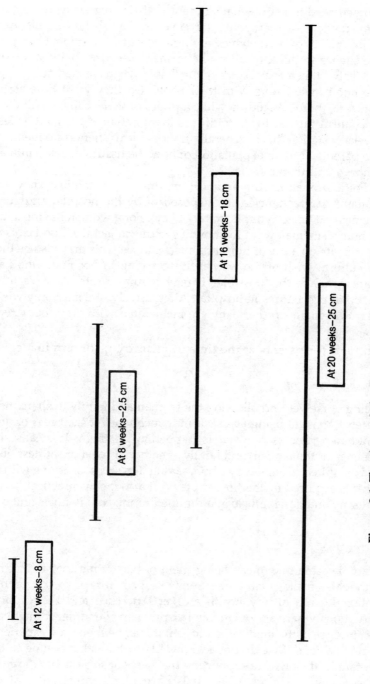

At 16 weeks—18 cm

At 20 weeks—25 cm

At 8 weeks—2.5 cm

At 12 weeks—8 cm

At 4 weeks—1 cm

Figure 2.1 The size and shape of the developing embryo and fetus.

women need to know what happens to their pregnancy. A woman who has a miscarriage or therapeutic termination may deliver an identifiable fetus or just pieces of tissue which are products of conception. She needs to have the chance to think whether she wishes to see the 'baby' at delivery, have the 'baby' taken away or have the 'baby' when cleaned and wrapped. Will the family want time with their baby? Do they want time alone or with someone there? Would they like a photo of their 'baby'? Will they want us to confirm the sex for them if it is identifiable? If the baby is less than 15 weeks gestation this is generally impossible. If there is no identifiable body the parents need an explanation of how the tissues develop into a placenta, embryo and then a fetus.

For a woman having an abortion, this may mean just knowing that the remains of pregnancies are disposed of by the hospital and generally are incinerated (check your hospital policy). For a woman having a miscarriage at home, she may want to know if she can collect the blood clots and tissue to cremate on a fire or bury in a special place. This may also be the personal or cultural wish of the woman miscarrying in hospital, who has a D&C. Can we make this possible? It may require a rethink of vacuum suction disposal procedures in hospital. Alternatively, she may only wish to know that the remains of her baby are incinerated with other body tissues.

Support for parents at the time of miscarriage or termination

Showing we care

Being ourselves and allowing the woman and family to share their feelings safely is part of being *honest*. It may mean facing their fear or anger at the unknown process of what is happening to them. It means sharing the feelings of the woman and family, whether of relief or sadness, in whatever way is suited to ourselves: a hug, saying 'I'm sorry' or crying with the family. This is explored further in Chapter 7. It also means practical, physical care: offering analgesia, music in a dimmed room, cool flannels and drinks.

Being quiet

Part of caring may mean being silent or just sitting to listen to the family's thoughts, feelings and questions. Respect for privacy and dignity are integral parts of any health worker's practice and they apply in these situations where a woman has her pregnancy ending. It may be a routine occurrence in the medical world, but it may be their only experience of such pain and fear. If we do not acknowledge what is happening to the woman or family, then we are supporting the views of society that the ending of the pregnancy is a hidden loss. It is particularly important that we do not isolate or fail to visit families, either by not visiting their homes or placing them in far-flung single rooms on a ward.

Figure 2.2 Wrapping a baby with anencephaly.

Making memories

Having something to remember after the pregnancy has ended is important for families who have wanted their baby. This means giving parents choices to see and hold their baby or the products of conception. How we hold and touch the baby, with tenderness and dignity, will give memories and cues to the parents for grieving for their child. Depending on the gestation and fragility of the baby it may be possible to wrap the baby in a piece of lightweight cloth (e.g. cotton muslin) in a manner to highlight the perfect features of the face or hands, especially important with a baby who has a congenital abnormality such as anencephaly (Fig. 2.2). For a tiny, fragile fetus of 12–13 weeks gestation, the only option may be to place them in as near a natural body position as possible and hold them in the palm of the hand or on a small piece of cloth, which, if firm, may help to support the baby's gelatinous skin and body structure.

We need to think carefully about where to place the baby. If it is of very early gestation, the palm of the hand or a small basket may be best suited to the size of the baby. For example, a small doll's carry cot suitably padded and lined is in proportion to a tiny baby.

Other mementos for parents that may be appropriate, depending on the gestation and physical development of the fetus, are discussed in more detail in Appendix 1 and are placed in the context of caring for the bereaved in Chapter 7. Options include:

- photos – polaroid and a complete 35 mm roll to be offered to all parents (Appendix 2);
- footprints and handprints (try having a pair);
- a lock of hair if the parents agree;

- wrapping or dressing the baby;
- keeping something (blanket) that has been touched or worn by the baby;
- having a copy of the records of the pregnancy.

Some parents, following miscarriage or therapeutic termination at any gestation, may wish for a ceremony to bless the pregnancy or name the baby with a name that is gender neutral (e.g. Robin) unless the sex of the baby is known. We need to suggest this to families and organise to contact any person that they request to perform this type of ceremony.

After the Event

Information

What to expect

The process of having a pregnancy end, or a baby die, brings a physical change for the woman and emotional changes for the whole family. Generally, families have no previous experiences against which to chart their progress in terms of what to expect as part of normal grieving. All women, before they are left alone or go home, need to have clear discussion and written information about:

- what has happened, to be aware that miscarriage or termination is a physical stress;
- what to expect in the next few days, e.g. vaginal bleeding, signs of infection;
- who to contact for:
  medical care, e.g. General practitioner (GP)
  professional support – an identified person, e.g. social worker, nurse, midwife or counsellor
  parent-to-parent support (such as, in the UK, Miscarriage Association, SATFA, local post abortion group);
- when to expect contact from a health worker; this should include a fixed follow-up appointment at approximately 6 weeks.

A discussion of physical changes that occur at the end of pregnancy is important for all women after miscarriage, therapeutic termination and abortion, commenting on uterine bleeding (how much is normal, signs of infection), lactation suppression (breast support and Panadol) and general tiredness. For families who have had a wanted pregnancy end, there needs to be discussion about what they may experience emotionally, and this is discussed in detail in Chapter 7. For example, they may feel upset, angry, guilty and even hallucinate with the feeling of the baby still inside them. These are all normal feelings and by preparing parents we are trying to minimise the confusion and fear of the unknown. A handout, personalised to suit the local area, practitioners and the specific reason for the loss, can be an invaluable resource. Some are supplied by voluntary agencies such as the Miscarriage Association, others can be developed, such as altering the handout shown in Appendix 3, which was written for women after miscarriage.

Postmortems and funerals

Most of this section applies particularly to families after miscarriage or therapeutic termination. However, we should remember that some of these points about remembrance and goodbyes may at some point be important to some women after abortion.

Postmortem

Sometimes it is suggested that parents consider a postmortem to try to establish the cause of miscarriage or fetal abnormality, which may have implications for future pregnancies if the cause is genetic. Whilst parental consent for postmortem is only required legally for babies born dead after the age of viability (24 weeks), the Polkinghorne report (1989) recommended that all parents should have the opportunity to consent to, or refuse, a postmortem on their child. If parents consent, they need to sign a consent form and have a copy of it. The information they need in order to be able to give informed consent includes:

- why the postmortem is being performed;
- what is involved in a postmortem (check your hospital practice and see Appendix 4 for the explanation we give to families in Avon, UK);
- what are the benefits and risks of the postmortem – with babies of early gestation, repair following a postmortem may be impossible (check your hospital practice);
- when they can expect to receive the results of the postmortem.

The new UK Department of Health leaflet, *'Guide to the postmortem examination – brief notes for families who have lost a baby in pregnancy or early infancy'*, should be given to all parents and used for discussion.

No registration of birth and death

An important part of mourning a dead baby is recognition that the baby lived and died. If a baby is born dead before 24 weeks, none of the existing forms for registration of birth and death are completed. Particularly in the second trimester, where there may be a fully formed baby, parents emotionally need a formal acknowledgement of their baby's life and death. Midwives or obstetricians who attend the delivery of such a baby need to provide parents with some evidence, either a letter or an individually designed certificate. Figure 2.3 shows an option proposed by SANDS in their *'Miscarriage, stillbirth, neonatal death: guidelines for professionals'* (1991).

Certificate for a baby born dead before the legal age of viability

This is to certify that

_____

was born to _____ (mother)

and _____ (father)

on _____

after _____ weeks gestation

and showed no signs of life.

Signed _____

Name _____

Registered qualifications _____

Date _____

Figure 2.3 Example of a certificate used in Scotland for pregnancies that end before the age of viability. (Reproduced by kind permission of The Stillbirth and Neonatal Death Society from *Miscarriage stillbirth and neonatal death: guidelines for professionals*, London: SANDS, 1991.)

It is a certificate used in Scotland for babies born dead at less than 20 weeks. A certificate can act as permission for parents to feel that they are allowed to grieve. It also is a requirement of any funeral director who conducts a burial or cremation for the baby.

Funerals

There are no legal requirements to bury or cremate a baby born dead before the age of viability (24 weeks). The parents may choose to make their own arrangements, or if hospital care has been provided, the hospital will offer to organise disposal. Parents need to consider:

- what will happen to their 'baby'
- do they want a burial or cremation?
- what are the costs?
- would they like a remembrance service?

Information about these choices is discussed in Appendix 5 and summarised in Table 2.2. Appendix 6 is a leaflet for parents about these choices, which can be adapted to suit individual circumstances and was originally used with families after cot death. You should read through the SANDS booklet by Nancy Kohner, '*A dignified ending*' (1992), which has recommendations for good practice for disposal of babies born before the legal age of viability.

Particularly after the distress of late miscarriage or therapeutic termination, it is very important that families know that they have time to make those choices and that their baby may stay in the hospital mortuary until they make their decision.

There are two points to note if parents want a burial. Firstly, families who have only remains of their 'baby', e.g. miscarrying at 8 weeks, may feel more comfortable with the idea of burying their 'baby' themselves, often in the garden or a special place. In this instance, consideration needs to be given to practicalities of burial sufficiently deep that children and dogs are unable to unearth the remains and that there are no hygiene risks involved. It is also important to balance burial in the garden against the emotional tie this may have if the family then moves house. Secondly, if the parents prefer burial in a public burial place, each cemetery and churchyard has their own policy regarding burial of babies before the age of viability. Local funeral directors can advise on this.

Caring is about administration and liaison

Finally, care is about avoiding additional distress to any woman whose pregnancy has ended as miscarriage or termination. This includes detailed and accurate documentation:

Table 2.2 Checklist of points for health workers to discuss with parents organising
a funeral or remembrance service

Would you like your child buried or cremated?
Where would you like a service?
Who will take the service?
What type of service would you like?
What would you like your baby to wear?
Would you like special items to be with your baby in the coffin?
What mementos do you want to keep of your baby?
Will your other children go to the funeral?
Who will look after your other children if they go to the funeral, so that you can
   be free to say your goodbyes?
Do you want to see your child before the funeral?
Do you want to see family and friends after the funeral?
Do you want people to give flowers or money?
Do you want a memorial?
Do you want to keep some flowers from the funeral to press?
Do you want to make an inscription in a Book of Remembrance?
Do you want to plant a tree for your child?

(These points are included in the booklet *The importance of goodbyes* for parents to read at
leisure, see Appendix 6.)

- labelling the baby or products of conception with the mother's name and
  hospital number;
- recording on the notes what has happened and why (for women having
  an abortion, it may be helpful for nurses caring for them to have
  sufficient notes to appreciate particular reasons or beliefs in reaching
  that decision, to avoid perceiving women as 'another abortion');
- contacting the appropriate agencies to stop further routine antenatal
  appointments being sent or a home visit from the midwife.

Having a checklist adapted to the local area, such as the one devised for
SANDS (Fig. 2.4), can be invaluable. This is not to advocate that care can be
reduced to checklists, but to a practitioner caring infrequently for these
women and families, it can be an aid to feel confident and competent to
care.

Support for families who want to see their baby again

We may be involved with families after miscarriage and therapeutic termination whose 'baby' (identifiable or unidentifiable form) remains in the
hospital mortuary prior to postmortem, going home or collection by the
funeral director. Parents may want to see their baby again, or see their baby
for the first time. An important part of grieving is having the time and the
opportunity to make a reality of death – seeing their baby is one way of
doing this. The issues we need to consider include: access times, the place,

the people and the contact arrangements. These are discussed fully in Appendix 7.

Long-term Information and Support

Purpose of visiting

Grief or recognition of change in our lives goes on for weeks and months and sometimes years. We cannot do the grieving for the bereaved, it is a 'do-it-yourself' job and we can only provide some of the tools in our visits. Chapter 7 gives detailed information about our role in long-term bereavement care and the importance of planning care, and Chapter 10 refers to ending visiting and recognising grief that has become 'stuck'. The following are points to consider if we care for individuals or families after miscarriage or termination.

- Exploring how the individual and couple feel and how they view the time since the ending of the pregnancy.
- Strategies for anger and guilt management, e.g. sports activities to release angry energy and rationalisation exercises to consider events that cause guilt.
- Discussing the differences between men and women grieving and accepting that there is no 'one right way' to grieve.
- Discussing the need of other siblings to know what has happened, which will mean talking about death (see Chapter 8 for resources for children). It can be useful to point out to parents that it is easy not to tell siblings because the loss is not visible. However, it can be a shock as an adult to find out that they had a brother or sister.
- Preparing women and families for events that may trigger their grief again (seeing babies, the expected date of delivery) and discussing how to deal with these, e.g. plan to meet a friend or decide to cuddle a baby.
- Valuing memories of the pregnancy and the baby.
- Valuing the individual's choices whether to have an abortion or plan a funeral.
- Discussing information about goodbyes, which the parents may not have done at the time and which they may do years later.
- Ensuring families have the contact number for a parents' group and offering our services to phone on their behalf to obtain the name of a person to see them or send information if they feel unable to make a 'cold' contact to an unknown person.

	TICK	SIGN	DATE
Mother's name			
Address			
Mother informed of death by			
Father informed of death by			
Home phone number			
Baby seen by mother			
Baby seen by father			
Father's name			
Baby held by mother			
Baby held by father			
Other children	Baby seen/held by other relatives		
name age			
	Photos taken of baby		
	Photos offered to parents		
	Photos put on file		
Baby's name			
	Mementos offered to parents		
	stills from scan		
	cot card		
LOSS NOW weeks gestation	name band		
	lock of hair		
miscarriage	foot/hand print		
stillbirth	other		
neonatal death			
PREVIOUS LOSS	Chaplain or parents' own religious adviser notified (if desired by parents)		
Date			
miscarriage	Baptism or other religious ceremony offered		
stillbirth			
neonatal death			

	TICK	SIGN	DATE
Consultant obstetrician informed			
Consultant paediatrician informed			
Appropriate worker informed-			
social worker			
maternity liaison sister			
bereavement counsellor			
Parents given opportunity to discuss their baby's death with -			
senior doctor			
midwife			
nursing sister			
GP informed by phone			
by letter			
Health visitor informed by phone			
by letter			
Community midwife informed			
by phone			
by letter			
Consent for post mortem requested			
Consent given / refused			
If refused, other investigations requested			
Consent given / refused			
Post mortem form completed and signed by both parents			
Preliminary post mortem results explained to mother and father			

	TICK	SIGN	DATE
Death or stillbirth certificate completed, explained and given to parents			
Certificate for baby born dead before the legal age of viability offered to parents			
Certificate accepted/put on file			
Information given on when and where to register stillbirth, birth and death			
Information on funeral arrangements given and discussed			
Parents' decision -			
Hospital: burial / cremation			
Private: burial / cremation			
Chapel service explained requested/not requested			
Parents told about book of remembrance			
Parents given -			
hospital/unit parents' book			
SANDS parents' booklet			
Mother given information about suppressing lactation			
Parents seen by consultant or senior staff prior to discharge			

Post natal follow-up appointment date

clinic sister notified [ ]

Genetic counselling appointment (if appropriate)

	TICK	SIGN	DATE
Local support groups telephone number given -			
SANDS			
MISCARRIAGE ASSOCIATION			
TAMBA			
SATFA			
Other			

Would parents like a group member to contact them?   YES / NO

Hospital contact:

Name

Telephone number

**COPIES OF THE CHECKLIST CAN
BE OBTAINED FROM SANDS**

Figure 2.4 Checklist for hospital staff to be used after miscarriage, stillbirth or neonatal death. (Reproduced by kind permission of The Stillbirth and Neonatal Death Society from *Miscarriage, stillbirth and neonatal death: guidelines for professionals*, London: SANDS, 1991.)

Plan for contact

Women and families need to have an identified health worker who provides ongoing contact and or counselling. In some areas this is in the remit of a social worker, communtiy midwife or health visitor. In many areas no care is offered after pregnancy loss, and it depends on an ad hoc approach from the GP. Whoever provides the care should consider offering a contract of care to the family (see Chapter 7).

It is impossible to have a routine plan for visiting; it will be based on assessment of the individual. Some may reject follow-up and others have cultural beliefs which mean that grieving is not a response to this event. Issues to consider are:

• Men and women at work – how do we contact them?
• Options of phone or visiting contact?
• Who provides follow-up after abortion? Do women accept it?

Details of how long a visit should be and what we might say are discussed in Chapter 7.

As a general plan, it is important to think of weekly contact with the family until at least 6 weeks and then as needed. Six weeks after the event is an important time point to make an appointment to see the family and discuss how they are. Especially after abortion it may be important to check that there are no physical complications and that the chosen contraception is acceptable to the woman (and her partner). If a postmortem was performed the results need to be discussed and a copy of the findings, preferably as a written letter in everyday language as opposed to medical jargon, given to the family.

How can family and friends help?

For a detailed discussion of the support they can offer, see Chapter 7. Points include:

• being there and not avoiding the family;
• showing that they care, whether a hug or asking how they feel;
• practical help such as the housework and shopping;
• finding out about bereavement and loss to appreciate what has happened; grandparents especially may need support or information, e.g. Appendix 8, to help them support their children.

Planning Future Pregnancies and Babies

Shall we have another baby?

The first question for most families is whether to have another baby. For families who have had a therapeutic termination for maternal illness in pregnancy, this is not an option, and permanent sterilisation may be considered. Particularly if the previous pregnancy ended in miscarriage or therapeutic termination, for which no 'cause' was found, the idea of having another pregnancy can be a frightening act of faith that all will go well. Some couples may feel unable to cope if it all 'goes wrong' and avoid pregnancy at any cost. Other couples may decide having a baby is what they want and pursue this until they succeed. In doing so they may become obsessive, or divided with one partner wanting a pregnancy more than another.

One mother wrote about her need to become pregnant again soon after the miscarriage:

> All I wanted to do was be pregnant, I was only interested in the fertile time of the month. How Ian coped I don't know – one minute he was in demand, the next – rejected.

For a woman who has had an abortion in the past, there may be fears raised by the media of damage to the cervix and risk of infertility. Honest discussion with a health worker can allay some of these fears. It may be necessary for families to talk with health workers about the risk of recurrence. Table 2.3 shows the risk for miscarriage; the risk of fetal abnormality depends on the type and needs to be discussed with an obstetrician or geneticist. Equally, individuals may need to review what has happened in the past and be given any practical preconceptual advice on balanced diet and exercise, avoiding smoking, irradiation and alcohol.

When to try for another pregnancy

Advice is often given freely to families after pregnancy loss. In a UK survey, 72% of women (who had had a total of 219 miscarriages) had been advised

Table 2.3 Risk of recurrence of miscarriage

Number of past miscarriages	Percentage of next pregnancies that miscarry
0	15–20
1	24
2	26
3	32
4 or more	32

From Oakley et al. (1990).

to wait for 3 months (Oakley et al. 1990). There is no physiological basis for this, apart from the expectation that this will allow ovulation and menstruation to recommence, which means that the expected date of delivery can be calculated. With the use of ultrasound scans to date the pregnancy accurately, this is not absolutely necessary. In terms of emotional adjustment there have been concerns that a pregnancy rapidly following a bereavement leads to delayed mourning (Lewis 1979). However, grieving is individual; it may happen quickly or take years. The information we need to give individuals is: (a) try for another baby when it feels 'right' to you; and (b) consider avoiding conception 3 months after the pregnancy which ended, otherwise delivery of the new pregnancy is around the same date as the pregnancy which ended.

Specific issues

After abortion some women may wish to deny the event and carry on with life. It may be at some later point, such as another pregnancy, when the woman needs to talk. It may be the midwife offering antenatal care who needs to listen to what has happened. It may be important to the woman that a new partner does not know that she has had an abortion. What are the arrangements we can offer her to guarantee this confidentiality? It may be a code in the notes, or a red line between new partners and pregnancies.

For some women, part of the antenatal care we need to offer may be about grieving and separating themselves from the previous pregnancy and baby. Suggestions we can make include: writing the story of their experience, writing a poem, drawing a picture, planting a tree or making a visit to somewhere special as a way of saying goodbye. For other women, the abortion is part of their lives and they feel comfortable with normal antenatal care. However, if anything happens during pregnancy, e.g. vaginal bleeding, they may have an unspoken question we need to address – is this is a consequence of the abortion?

After miscarriage or therapeutic termination, the care we need to offer reflects the concerns of families about the outcome of this pregnancy. This section is dealt with in Appendix 8. Points that need to be considered are the support antenatally, the care in labour and any specific postnatal support (Table 2.4). We also need to remember that care and attention is needed for all pregnancies. It is generally given to the first baby after a baby had died, but the anxieties and concerns can be as great with *each* pregnancy.

What About Ourselves?

Miscarriage, therapeutic termination and abortion raise personal, professional and ethical issues for all of us. It is about the beginning and ending

Table 2.4 Checklist of points for care in a subsequent pregnancy after a previous baby has died

---

Antenatally parents need:
- an opportunity to discuss with health workers any questions about the pregnancy that ended
- to have a clear contract (in written form) of the care and support that they can expect to receive
- to have access to health care for reassurance and time to talk
- to have the contact address of the local self-help group to talk with other parents who 'survive' having another child
- to have any available tests or treatment that may prevent recurrence of the previous loss

In labour parents need:
- to have the opportunity to state clearly what they want in their birth plan to make it different from their last baby
- to have staff who are aware of the previous loss and sensitive to the fears parents may have in labour

Postnatally parents should have:

- the opportunity to have their baby examined by a paediatrician and the findings discussed
- to be clear if there is the opportunity for 'extra' postnatal care from community staff to develop their self-confidence as parents

---

of life, in which we have a part to play. We need to be clear about our own feelings in the care of families. We need to know where we go for support, which should be formal, in the form of debriefing or supervision (a term we borrow from counselling) to give some space to our own feelings. Otherwise, over years of practice, caring for individuals and families, a layer of anger and sorrow may build up which clouds our ability to care effectively. This is discussed more fully in Chapter 10. Finally, we need to acknowledge that nothing in our professional practice is static; having sufficient support means that we have the energy to constantly review and challenge ourselves to improve our care and practice.

Key points
- Recognise that grief is individual and that some women and men will welcome the opportunity to talk and others will be silent.
- Be sensitive to cultural and social aspects of grieving.
- Recognise the need of individuals during these events for information and honesty from health workers.
- Appreciate the vulnerability of some individuals to difficulties resolving grief and the need for follow-up, e.g. teenagers and families after therapeutic terminations.

- Provide resources to women and families such as written information, contact with a self-help group.
- Appreciate the grief of fathers, siblings and grandparents.
- Keep an updated folder of information and practice in your unit, with names of local contacts of self-help groups, funeral directors, interpreters and community workers.
- Try writing information handouts for parents if you have none that are suitable.

References

Adler B, Kushnick T. Genetic counselling in prenatally diagnosed trisomy 18 and 21. Psychosocial aspects. *Pediatrics* 1982; 69: 94

Bansen S, Stevens HA. Women's experiences of miscarriage in early pregnancy. *J Nurs Midwif* 1992; 37(2): 84

Borg S, Lasker J. *When pregnancy fails*. London: Routledge & Kegan Paul, 1981

Broome A. Abortion counselling. *Nurs Mirror* 1984; 158(20): 19

David HP. Psychosocial studies of abortion in the United States. In: David HP, Friedman HL, van der Tak J, Sevilla MJ (Eds) *Abortion in psychosocial perspective: trends in transnational research*. New York: Springer, 1978: 77–115

Furlong RM, Black RB. Pregnancy termination for genetic indications: the impact on families. *Soc Work Health Care* 1984; 10(1): 17

Henshaw RC, Cooper K, El-Refaey H, Smith NC, Templeton AA. Medical management of miscarriage: non-surgical uterine evacuation of incomplete and inevitable spontaneous abortion. *Br Med J* 1993; 30: 894

Hill S. *Family*. London: Penguin Books, 1989

Hutti M. A quick reference table of interventions to assist families to cope with pregnancy loss or neonatal death. *Birth* 1988; 15(1): 33

Jones W. *Miscarriage*. London: Thorsons, 1990

Kaltrieder NB. Emotional patterns related to delay in decision to seek legal abortion. *Calif Med* 1973; 118(5): 23

Kohner N. *A dignified ending*. London. SANDS, 1992

Lewis E. Inhibition of mourning by pregnancy: psychopathology and management. *Br Med J* 1979; 2: 27

Lewis E, Bryan E. Management of perinatal loss of a twin. *Br Med J* 1988; 297: 1321

Lloyd J, Laurence KM. Sequelae and support after termination of pregnancy for fetal malformation. *Br Med J* 1985; 290: 907

Nilssen L. *A child is born*. London: Faber and Faber, 1977

Oakley A, McPherson, A, Roberts H. *Miscarriage*. London: Penguin Books, 1990

Pepper L, Knapp R. *Motherhood and Mourning*. New York: Praeger, 1980

Polkinghorne Report. *Review of the guidance on the research use of fetuses and fetal material*. London: HMSO, 1989

Raphael-Leff J. *Psychological processes of childbearing*. London: Chapman & Hall, 1991

SANDS *Miscarriage, stillbirth and neonatal death – guidelines for professionals*. London: SANDS, 1991

Swanson-Kauffman K. *The unborn one: a profile of the human experience of miscarriage*. University of Colorado: Unpublished doctoral dissertation, 1984

Townsend R, Perkins A. *Bitter fruit*. Alameda: Hunter House, 1991

Webb C. Barriers to sympathy. *Nurs Mirror* 1985; 160(1) (suppl): vi

Wells R. Managing miscarriage. *Postgrad Med* 1991; 89(2): 207

White-Van Mourik MCA, Connor JM, Ferguson-Smith MA. The psycho-social sequelae of second trimester termination of pregnancy for fetal abnormality. *Prenatal Diagn* 1992; 12(3): 189

Resources for Families and Health Workers after Miscarriage

Organisations

Miscarriage Association
PO Box 2, Ossett, W. Yorkshire WF5 9XG, UK
Tel: 0945–830515
Provide local groups, befriending and information resources.

Stillbirth and Neonatal Society
28 Portland Place, London W1N 4DE, UK
Tel: 071–436 5881
Provide local groups, befriending and information resources.

The Child Bereavement Trust
1 Hillside, Riversdale, Bourne End, Buckinghamshire, SL8 5EB, UK
Offers video and book resources for bereaved families and training for professionals.

Books

Hill S. *Family*. London: Penguin Books, 1989

Jones W. *Miscarriage*. London: Thorsons, 1990

Kohner N, Henley A. *When a baby dies*. London: Pandora, 1993

Kohner N. & Thomas J. *Grieving after the death of your baby*, Riversdale, Bucks: The Child Bereavement Trust

Moulder C. *Miscarriage – women's experiences and needs*. London: Pandora, 1990

Oakley A, McPherson A, Roberts H. *Miscarriage*. London: Penguin Books, 1984

Pizer H, O'Brien-Palinski C. *Coping with miscarriage*. London: Jill Norman, 1980

Leaflets

From *'An ache in their heart'* resource package, see p 50 for details.

Resources for Families and Health Workers after Therapeutic Terminations

Organisations

Support Around Termination for Fetal Abnormality (SATFA)
29–30 Soho Square, London NW1V 6JB, UK
Tel: 071–287 3752
Support group offering local contacts and some branches with befriending for couples. Organise a newsletter and have information resources. Have a new handbook in 1993 available for all parents making the decision to have a termination.

The Child Bereavement Trust
1 Hillside, Riversdale, Bourne End, Buckinghamshire, SL8 5EB, UK
Offers video and book resources for bereaved families and training for professionals.

Books

Books on abortion and information can be obtained from SATFA

Resources for Families and Health Workers after Abortion

Organisations

Brook Advisory Centres
Central Office, 153A East Street, London SE1 2SD, UK
Tel: 071–708 1234
Centres located in cities; advice and contraceptive supplies to young people aged less than 25 years.

CHOICE

PO Box 20, Oxford, UK
Tel: 0865–242333

Telephone counselling for women making a decision to have an abortion and afterwards.

LIFE

Head Office, 7 Parade, Leamington Spa, Warwickshire CV32 4DG, UK
Tel: 0926–21587
Organisation opposed to abortion; provides counselling and temporary accommodation for pregnant women.

Pregnancy Advisory Service

Central London Bureau, 11–13 Charlotte Street, London W1P 1HD, UK
Tel: 071–637 8962
Centres throughout the country; provide pre- and post-abortion counselling, access to termination less than 22 weeks.

Women's health and reproductive rights information centre

52–54 Feather Street, London EC1, UK
Tel: 071–251 6332
Provide a whole range of information on different aspects of women's experience, including abortion and miscarriage. Can put women in contact with support groups.

Books for individuals

Francke L. *The ambivalence of abortion.* London: Penguin, 1980
Personal account of feelings surrounding the decision to terminate a
 pregnancy.
Frater A, Wright C. *Coping with abortion.* London: Chambers, 1986
Choices of having an abortion, other options and feelings.
Gardner J. *Abortion: a personal approach* USA: Healing Yourself, 1985
Perspectives and information on abortion.
Townsend R, Perkins A. *Bitter fruit.* Alameda: Hunter House, 1991
Experiences of women having abortions and adoptions.

Resources for Health Workers when Pregnancy Ends before Birth

Books

Jolly J. *Missed beginnings.* London: Austen Cornish, 1987.
Kohner N. *A dignified ending.* London: SANDS, 1992
Kohner N. & Thomas J. *Grieving after the death of your baby,* Riversdale,
 Bucks: The Child Bereavement Trust

Raphael-Leff J. *Psychological processes of childbearing.* London: Chapman & Hall, 1991

SANDS. *Miscarriage, stillbirth and neonatal death – guidelines for professionals.* London: SANDS, 1991

Thomas J. *Supporting parents when a baby dies – before or soon after birth.* This written booklet is a guide for staff, antenatal, labour ward, postnatal, gynaecological and neonatal teams. Available from Mrs J Brown, The Child Bereavement Trust, 1 Millside, Riversdale, Bourne End, Bucks SL8 5EB, UK.

Ward B. *Healing grief.* London: Ebury Press, 1993

Leaflet

Guide to postmortem examination – brief notes for parents and families who have lost a baby in pregnancy or early infancy, by the Department of Health, produced in consultation with the National Advisory Body for the Confidential Enquiry into Stillbirths and Deaths in Infancy, SANDS and FSID. Use the leaflet with parents as an aid to discussion.

Videos and training packages

Death at birth: two part video. This aims to help professionals understand parents' needs after loss of a baby, deal with their own feelings and identify areas to improve practice.
Made by Jenni Thomas, The Director of the Child Bereavement Trust, 1 Hillside, Riversdale, Bourne End, Buckinghamshire, SL8 5EB, UK.

When our baby died: video, and accompanying book, *Grieving after the death of your baby.* Has been made for parents and familes and those who care for them. Made by Jenni Thomas.

An ache in their heart. For professionals and parents to equip them as companions for bereaved families. Resources include training sessions, handouts for families, children's books, a video, materials to form a memorial and medical information in layperson's language.
Cost: $A250. Yvonne Connelly Tel: 07 840 8154. The University of Queensland Department of Child Health, Clarence Court, Mater Children's Hospital, South Brisbane, Australia.

Chapter Three

Death Instead of Life: At the Time of Birth or Soon After

Oh tell her, brief is life but love is big.

(Tennyson, *The Princess* 4)

Within this chapter

1. Society's views of grieving after stillbirth or neonatal death
2. What are the feelings of parents after a baby is born dead or dies soon after?
3. What are the specific aspects of grief for fathers, siblings and grandparents?
4. A reflection of our own attitudes to death at the time of birth
5. How can health workers, families and friends help them at the time of death?
6. What long-term bereavement care, extending to future pregnancies, can be offered?

Introduction

In the Middle Ages, infant mortality was high and parents expected to have children who died at the time of birth. Death was part and parcel of life (Aries 1974). Paradoxically, in the twentieth century, when we can visit the moon, study viruses and know so much more about life, we are less able to grieve and mourn for a child. The viewpoint of society, giving no place to mourn miscarriages or babies who die at or soon after birth, was illustrated by Alice Lovell, who in 1982 wrote an article entitled 'Mothers and babies in limbo'. In religious terms limbo is the region bordering on hell where unbaptised babies go. It is also a place where unwanted or forgotten things collect.

In the 1990s our expectations in Western society are that pregnancy can be planned, guaranteed healthy with screening tests and can produce a squalling bundle of baby. The reality for parents whose baby dies at the time of birth, or soon after, is an event that is outside the 'normal' experience of family and friends. Young parents, who may never have known anyone die, have few skills to cope with the shock of the death of their baby. Even worse, family and friends may be able to offer little support by being frightened and fearful of the extremes of behaviour that can come from the pain of bereavement. Yet as Jones and Jones (1990) point out: 'Grief is a positive, healthy response to either personal or object loss'; a fact we can appreciate from exploring our own experiences of loss in Chapter 1.

With the current views on grieving for a dead baby, the support of health workers is crucial if parents are to be able to grieve and acknowledge their child.

Definitions

Before we look further into the feelings and needs of families we need to clarify some definitions. This is for ourselves and also for accuracy and explanation to parents.

Stillbirth

This includes any baby born after 24 completed weeks gestation, who shows no signs of life. This was amended in the The Stillbirth Definition Act (1992) from the previous limit of 28 weeks of pregnancy and acknowledges the consensus view that 24 weeks is the age at which a fetus can be assumed to be viable.

Perinatal death

This includes babies who are stillborn or who die in the first week of life. Therefore, it includes babies born at any gestational age, e.g. 22 weeks, who have shown signs of life, albeit briefly.

Neonatal death

This includes babies who have shown any signs of life and who die up to the age of 28 days.

If we look at the 1990 figures in England and Wales, we get an idea of the scale of grief after stillbirth and neonatal death. There were 3256 stillbirths and 3221 babies who died as neonatal deaths (aged less than 4 weeks) (OPCS 1990).

For families there are both similarities and differences between stillbirth and neonatal death. Having a stillborn baby, the parents have only the memory of their baby as dead; having a baby die days or weeks later, the parents have known their baby alive. Both these situations tend to arise in hospital.

We will start by looking at families' feelings in these two different situations, then look at some of the similarities in their grief, before we conclude by looking at the care we can offer. Some babies die in a Neonatal Intensive Care Unit (NICU) aged more than 28 days (which is the definition of neonatal death). The grief of families and the care we can offer is included in this chapter because the babies have generally been in hospital with illness since their birth. Babies who have lived and then die at home, at any age, will be considered in Chapter 4.

Stillbirth

How and when does stillbirth happen?

The poignancy of the word 'stillbirth' conveys the sadness, quietness and emptiness surrounding a baby born dead. A baby born still, unmoving and dead is a cruel contradiction to the anticipated birth of a baby. One father, after his son had been born dead, said that the whole labour and birth felt unreal and bizarre, because when he held his son and felt his damp, unmoving skin, it contrasted with all the pain and movement that had preceded his birth.

Stillbirth may be totally unexpected during labour (intrapartum), or it may have been anticipated and the baby identified as dead towards the end of pregnancy (intrauterine death). Either situation is devastating for the bereaved parents and in terms of grief there can be no best option, either starting in labour knowing that the baby is dead, or being excited at the beginning of labour only to have the baby die in the process.

Intrapartum death

For some parents the labour may begin with a live baby, at home or hospital. The contractions may progress normally for a period of hours and the baby appear active or quiet. Then at one of the 'routine' checks to listen to 'see how the baby is' the fetal heart cannot be heard. The situation can become uncertain and even fraught with panic as different midwives and doctors try to find a recording of the fetal heartbeat, increasing the volume of the cardiotocograph (CTG) or sonicaid and using different places on the mother's abdomen in case the baby has changed position. From the health worker's viewpoint there is the knowledge that the fetal heart is often hard to find, especially during the second stage of labour, when the woman is pushing and generally the situation ends with a live, squalling baby. However, there is always the fear and reality of stillbirth occurring in a late stage of labour. When stillbirth does happen suddenly it can mean that parents are lost in confusion and have lasting images of rapid movement, action, delivery, attempts at resuscitation or a sudden silence and someone telling them 'I'm sorry your baby is dead'.

Grieving begins at the point when the security that all is going well is lost. Most parents worry from the early weeks in pregnancy about all the things that could 'go wrong': miscarriage, fetal abnormality, preterm labour and so on. Starting in labour at term, when the baby is due, can bring a sensation of safely 'surviving the pregnancy'. The birth of their dead baby proves this is a false security, and a devastating one, when they so nearly had their live baby in their arms.

The medical words used at the time of stillbirth can have a profound effect on parents' grief. Misperceptions place a burden of guilt on the parents. For example the use of the term 'fetal distress', in layman terms, can appear to mean 'pain and agony' (Horowitze et al. 1980). In medical terms it means that the heart rate is rising or falling indicating possibly hypoxia. Parents who reflect back on the sudden death of their baby at delivery often comment on the emergency response of health workers, which removed 'control' or involvement of the parents from the situation. This response creates a sense of unreality, which has to be turned into a reality for parents to be able to mourn. Unfortunately, as Thearle and Gregory (1992) point out, there is a 'hospital factor' which makes parents' mourning harder, precisely because health workers do not want to discuss and debrief with the parents about what happened and what was said.

Intrauterine death

Other families may enter labour knowing that their baby is dead. They may have realised several days earlier that the baby was moving less and contacted their doctor. Alternatively, the mother may have attended a routine antenatal check to discover that the fetal heart cannot be found. In either instance, intrauterine death is generally confirmed after CTG and ultrasound scan fail to find a fetal heart. Again, having midwives, doctors and radiographers attempting to hear the heartbeat with rising tension at their inability to do so, can be torture for the parents. For professionals there is the dilemma of when and who will tell the parents that their baby is dead. Hospital policy may require that a senior professional 'tell' the parents. Delays in contacting the person can create unacceptable stress for the parents. Decisions then have to be made about whether to induce labour or wait for it to start naturally. In terms of mourning, some parents may start anticipatory grieving before the labour, adjusting to the death of their baby, hopes and future. For others it is not possible to face the shocking reality and they may withdraw into numbness, going through labour in a trance-like state or even denying the fact that they will not have a live baby at the end.

Families grieving at the time of stillbirth

As Thearle and Gregory (1992) point out: 'Stillbirth combines two of the most crucial life stresses: birth and death.' There is no division or separation between the two events; parents have to live through both at the same time. This requires being able both to *celebrate* the birth of their baby and to *mourn* the loss of their child. Often, the celebration of the beauty, the features, the size and shape of their child is lost in the enormity and confusion of how to mourn for their baby. We need to remember that the celebration of the baby born creates the memories for the baby dead.

Part of the process of grieving, whatever model we choose to use, is the need to perceive the loss, accept reality and eventually adjust to a life without the baby. The difficulty for families whose baby is stillborn is having someone to mourn. Stillbirth has been described as a traumatic 'non-event' and for parents to make the grief real means 'bringing the baby back from death' rather than having a 'black hole in the mind' (Lewis 1976). In practical terms it means having memories in order to be able to grieve. Schwiebert and Kirk (1981) sum this up when they say there is a real need for these parents to have time to 'say hello' before 'saying goodbye'. Part of this is valuing the life the parents knew with the baby before death – too frequently these months of pregnancy are discounted. Jones and Jones (1990) wrote:

> The bonding of mother, father and child is a process which begins from time of conception. This creates problems. The parents would already have internalised the image of their child or projected idealised aspects of the self onto the unborn baby and will grieve for a person who already exists in their mind. This is often in conflict with society's objective perception of the loss, i.e. that as the child had no separate identity, therefore there is nothing for which to grieve. (p. 32)

The bonding of mother to growing fetus may account, in part, for evidence suggesting that mothers appear to grieve more deeply and longer than fathers (Dyregrov and Matthiesen 1987; Helmrath and Steinitz 1978). Differences in grieving after a stillbirth may reflect the lack of support in our society for men to express their grief (Dunlop 1979) and this is discussed further in Chapter 7.

Apart from valuing antenatal memories, there can also be memories after birth of sitting, holding, dressing their baby and taking their baby home with them. This time together can be invaluable for grieving. In a study of 130 parents after perinatal death, those who had seen and spent time with their dead baby had less depression and higher self-esteem (Murray and Callon 1988). If we look to the work of Klaus and Kennell (1982) on parent–

infant bonding, *time together* is the basis of bonding and attachment to a baby. This appears equally true whether alive or dead and is explored in some of the theories of grieving in Chapter 1.

Finally, bereavement is about the loss of hope. Part of the unreality of stillbirth is letting go of hope. Even when their child is born and parents touch, retouch and are told that their child is dead, they hope against hope that it is all a dreadful mistake. Maria wrote after her first baby died as a stillbirth:

> I wanted to hold him. I wanted to avoid him, I didn't know what I wanted to do and all the time I kept looking at him and hoping that he would breathe. Then it would be alright, we would go home with him and we all knew that lots of babies don't always breathe immediately at birth. The time went on, the clock ticked loudly and after half an hour I knew that he would not breathe and then I knew that he was really dead.

Death Soon After Birth

Times when babies die

Death of a baby, shortly after birth, or several days or weeks later, can be devastating for the couple newly confirmed in the role of proud parents. The grief is surrounded by the excitement and poignancy of having a baby alive.

There are different situations in which a newborn baby may die. A baby born at a very early gestation (21–22 weeks) may die soon after delivery, and may not have been expected to live. It may have been agreed with the parents that no attempt to resuscitate the baby will be made even if the baby shows any signs of breathing. There may be minutes or hours whilst the parents sit and hold their baby. There can be agonising thoughts for parents and staff – if they did something, would the baby be 'saved'? Will the baby live despite . . . . Yet in the process there is also the chance for parents to hold and watch the living baby and to enjoy the chance to hold the warm body of their baby. Other parents may have their baby transferred to NICU at birth, or soon after, for treatment. Just having a baby in NICU means that parents have to adjust to the loss of their dreams of a 'normal, healthy baby', which involves mourning and is discussed further in Chapter 6. For parents whose baby dies at any age in NICU, there may have been elation when the baby appeared to be well and then despair when the baby rapidly deteriorated and then responded rapidly to treatment. It means that parents are on a roller-coaster of hope and despair, from which it is hard eventually to achieve a balance, if their baby dies.

In NICU the death may be anticipated if the baby has a condition that is incompatible with life or is deteriorating quickly. If the baby's death is planned with withdrawal of life support, then parents need careful support and counselling to avoid subsequent guilt and recriminations such as 'they chose to let their baby die' (Benfield et al. 1988).

Families' grief

Similar to parents whose baby is stillborn, parents who have a newborn baby die, are often met with the supposed reassurance, 'Never mind, you didn't really get to know your baby' or 'Well it's all for the best your baby would have been handicapped.' Particularly when their baby dies minutes after birth, or has been in NICU, surrounded and sustained by whirring machines, it is hard for parents to take a perspective, 'This was my baby.' This lack of support and opportunity to grieve can ultimately mean delayed or pathological grief. Aside from the denial of space to grieve, there is the difficulty of who to grieve for? A baby, a hope, a body on a ventilator? It is confusing having a baby die in NICU.

> After the birth, intensive care technology can have two contradictory effects on parents. There is the reassurance that everything possible is being done to treat the baby, but on the other hand the complexity of technology imposes a barrier between parents and baby. (Thearle and Gregory 1992)

Again, like stillbirth, to have a reality and not a 'black hole', parents need to have the chance to see, hold, know and say goodbye to their child. It may mean a chance to dress their child, change a nappy and put them to the breast – the things that parents want to do for their child.

It might be expected that parents of babies who have fought and struggled with a tenuous hold on life would have a sense of relief at the ending. Instead, there can be considerable guilt, regret and not acceptance. Susan Hill summed this up after her daughter Imogen's fight for life in NICU resulted in death:

> Watching someone die of a grave, long illness, someone who is old but who has had some good life, is hard, of course it is, but there is an element of acceptance in the onlookers as well, perhaps, as in the dying person themselves. My mother had known that she was dying and had given in to it. I had waited for it, been prepared, accepted that it was the right, best and only thing.
> But a child, a baby, whose time is not ripe, who has had no life yet to speak of, who has all hope, all potential, everything to come – it is impossible to accept, one's instinct is to hope against hope, to do battle, to fight for its survival no matter what. So in a sense, I did not ever 'accept' Imogen's dying. (Hill 1989, p. 222)

For some parents the fear or knowledge that their baby will die in NICU can lead them to try and avoid the feelings of distress and upset of grieving by denying their relationship or avoiding time with the child. By trying not to become attached to the baby there is the hope that it will prevent the pain of loss. In reality it often means that the loss is still there, with the guilt at not having spent time with their baby.

Guilt, Self-Esteem and Anger in Long-Term Grief after Stillbirth and Neonatal Death

The feelings and issues in loss and bereavement care are discussed in detail in Chapters 1 and 7. We need to think about the following issues where death is close to the time of birth.

After shock at the death of their baby, there may be a time of questioning and guilt interlinked with depression and sadness. For parents, families, friends and health workers, there can be a sense of futility, pointlessness and unreality with 'nothing' to show at the end of 9 months pregnancy. Parents are left with empty arms and a cot and clothes that are not needed, and family have ungiven presents. What cannot be taken away from them and needs to be acknowledged, shared and cried over is the fact that they became parents of their first, second or third child.

The question that goes round and round for bereaved parents is 'Why did my baby die?' For most deaths in NICU, the answer is clear in terms of a cause, e.g. the baby had immature lungs or had a congenital abnormality. The reasons for some stillbirths may be obvious, such as a cord prolapse, but for many there is no adequate explanation of why an apparently healthy developing baby died. The lack of an answer to 'Why did my baby die?' is one of the most difficult parts of parents' grief. It is outside the normal sequence of events for children to die before their parents. As Susan Hill wrote, she could accept the death of her mother, but the death of her baby, with so much potential for life which was unlived, has no pattern or justice in it. The need for explanation is part of grieving and with none provided, may be turned inwards to become self-recriminating guilt: 'My baby died because I smoked or ran for the bus.'

Especially for parents whose first child is stillborn or dies soon after birth, their whole view of themselves, their ability to be a parent and their self-esteem may be shattered. There is an assumption within our society that 'anyone' can have a baby. Parenthood is demeaned in comparison to professional training and employment. To find that pregnancy and parenthood are not automatically obtainable can be a demoralising shock. We can appreciate that this can be worsened for parents who have never taken their baby home and been seen by others to *have* a baby.

Special thought needs to be given to any parents whose baby is born stillborn at a home delivery. For them, the grief is compounded by being in the setting where their baby has died. It may be strengthening or devastating. The guilt and recriminations centre around, 'If we had been in hospital would it have been different?' There is still considerable resistance in the community and the medical profession to the idea of home birth being safe (Tew 1990).

Part of the range of emotions in grief is anger: 'Why me?' Anger can also be directed at health workers who 'allowed it to happen'. The need to talk repeatedly about what happened and to have a time of debriefing with carers is vital to reaching acceptance. For many parents the horrors of their imagination of what happened is far worse than the reality of the known (Bergman 1969).

On the basis of having some memories of a living child, it might be supposed that it would be easier to mourn for a baby who has lived than a baby who is stillborn. However, as Peppers and Knapp (1980) note, there is no clear hierarchy of grief. For each person, grief represents their loss and the type of support and care the individual has, and thus there are differences in couple's grieving (see Chapter 7). Grief goes on and on; it comes again at anniversaries of the expected date of delivery, of the birth day, of the death day, when they should have gone to school and so on. It can take a long time for parents to reach a balance in their lives after a baby dies at or soon after birth (Murray and Callan 1988).

Fathers after Stillbirth and Neonatal Death

As in all aspects of emotional care surrounding the death of a baby, there has been little emphasis on fathers; this is discussed in Chapter 7 in the section on differences between parents' grieving. As discussed previously, grieving without memories and reality is difficult, and certainly men do not have the same chance as the mother to bond to the baby physically during pregnancy. However, it is impossible to predict what opportunity they may have after birth. The father of a baby in NICU may be working and looking after the other children; this support role limits the contact and reality of their baby. Conversely, the father of a baby dying soon after going to NICU, whose mother had a Caesarean section, may have been more actively involved in visiting NICU than the mother, who may have spent the first few days with only limited visits (Peppers and Knapp 1980).

Siblings and Grandparents

Siblings

Industrialised countries in the past 30 years have seen death in young families become a rare event; consequently a decision is often made not to tell the children anything because it will upset them and they should be 'protected' (Stephenson 1985). It sets the pattern of how they respond to bereavement for the rest of their life. Siblings of any age know that something is different if their parents are distressed and it affects their behaviour. They will probably have been involved during pregnancy in knowing about the 'new baby'. To pretend that the baby has gone, and not to explain why, is an injustice and an underestimate of even young children's cognitive abilities. This is discussed in detail in Chapter 8.

Grandparents

For grandparents, theirs is the 'double grief' of the death of their grand-child and the pain that their child is experiencing. They may be involved in a supporting role in the everyday running of the house and looking after siblings, or they may be visiting the baby in NICU. Often stillbirth or the death of a baby can act as a trigger for long-gone griefs to re-emerge. Grandparents and bereaved feelings are discussed further in Chapter 7.

What About Twins?

Having twins is an exciting event and means being 'different' to most pregnancies. Having twins delivered where only one survives birth or dies later in NICU can be both painful and confusing for the parents. Modern technological advances have meant that where both twins born prematurely would have died 15–20 years ago, now one or both are surviving. Where only one survives, parents may direct all their attention to the surviving twin, they may transpose all their hopes onto that child and become overprotective. Conversely, they may ignore the surviving baby and concentrate their emotions and energy on the baby who died. Part of being able to mourn is seeing the twins as separate. Using photographs and names can help to see each as an individual who lives or dies (Lewis and Bryan 1988).

What can Health Workers do to Help?

This section is for anyone who cares for families at home or in hospital, whether midwife, GP, obstetrician, paediatrician, health visitor or social worker. I have referred to our care as 'we' because it is a team that supports the grieving family, both short term and long term. A detailed discussion of care, including what to say, when to go and how to plan care, is given in Chapter 7. The following points apply to bereavement situations of still-birth or perinatal/neonatal death. There is no expectation that any care we offer will involve in-depth counselling. The assumption is that grief is normal and that families only need assistance to work through their grief in their own way.

The aim of our care

The principles of our bereavement care are based on:

- *Honesty* – explaining and preparing parents for what happens.
- *Being there* – often not saying anything, just the physical comfort of someone being there. Long (1992) wrote about the care these families need: 'Cliches and platitudes are unhelpful. All carers need to realise that words are often not only unnecessary, but can be positively unhelpful; however listening is vital.'
- *Valuing individuals* – each has different needs and ways of grieving, which are based on cultural, social and personal beliefs.
- *Valuing ourselves* – we have something to offer, even if it is only the fact that we care about people.

We need to be clear at the outset that we can only do our best, we cannot make it 'right'; only having their baby would be right. Our concern is to try not to make it 'worse'; for a quick list of don'ts see Table 3.1 and read through the section in Chapter 7, 'What helps bereaved parents most/ least?'

The care we can give involves two interlinked roles of information-giving and support. We will consider it over two time periods: at the time of death and long term.

Self-awareness

As we explored what loss meant for us in Chapter 1, we need to review our practice, which is generally about striving against death. What effect does this have on us? It can mean that we have difficulty facing our patients

Table 3.1 Some don'ts when caring for families whose baby dies at birth or soon after

---

In trying to get it 'right', and in the rush:
- **Do not** be tempted to be protective and not give parents an honest answer about what happened in labour or in NICU – it is their baby
- **Do not** think that everyone is the same – grief varies according to self, culture, event
- **Do not** feel the need to fill all the silences by saying something
- **Do not** say, 'Well at least you didn't get too attached, your baby didn't live long'
- **Do not** assume that families know what is happening during delivery or in NICU
- **Do not** assume that families hear and understand what you say the first time – would you if you were in shock after labour?
- **Do not** try to rush families in making choices – there is time; and there needs to be time to sit and see their baby after delivery or in NICU

dying and acknowledging that life and death are not totally within our control. We need to be able to grieve gracefully, not to feel that a stillbirth or neonatal death is automatically a failure of our practice. Sometimes, it is a failure within the expectation of current practice in developed countries; generally it is unpreventable with current knowledge. If we do not accept this then our feelings can make it even harder for the parents to live with what has happened. Bourne (1968) pointed out that many doctors tried to forget about stillbirths and colluded in a 'conspiracy of silence', avoiding a real death situation by whisking the baby away immediately after delivery. You may be able to think of some hospitals today who continue with this practice. We need to be able to move away from feelings of failure, from revulsion at the sight of a macerated baby and fear at the uncontrolled pain of parents when we generally live in an emotionally plastic-wrapped world. We need to look at something much bigger and wider: how parents, and ultimately society, grieve for these babies.

Care at the Time of Death and Immediately Afterwards

Organisational issues

Firstly, we need to think about organisational details and policies that provide the resources to care. Increasingly, there has been an awareness in hospitals of the environment in which families spend time with their dead baby. In the delivery suite and NICU there needs to be a comfortable private room where parents can close the door and be quiet. Rooms should preferably have a double bed for parents to hug together – physical contact can be a comfort and that might be what they would do at home. Part of the setting is the staff, and it is important that we always introduce ourselves to families who may become bewildered by shift changes and staff changes. Most hospitals seek to minimise the numbers of staff families meet either in the delivery suite or NICU, so that there is a chance to establish relationships and families are not exposed to the constant pain of having to repeat information. It is always important, as with any guest in our own home, that we ask families if they would like time alone, or if they would like our company. We need to make families aware of the facilities for them during this time. During a stillbirth the mother may wish for strong analgesia to remove some of the discomfort of contractions, the family may need supplies of tea and coffee, and a toilet. We need to make the family as comfortable as possible and not forget the practicalities of life amidst the emotional pain.

If there are cultural or language differences we need to be able to contact community workers or interpreters to be able to share, discuss information and give parents choices. Some of the cultural aspects of grieving we need to be aware of are covered in Chapter 9.

Information at the time of death

What is happening?

Parents whose child is dead or dying need information to make choices. For example, do they want to see and hold their child? This information needs to be gentle and unassertive, not pushing the parents to do something they are uncomfortable with on personal, religious or cultural grounds. Choices need to be talked about in advance and parents given the option to think and choose what they would like to do. Many parents say that looking back they wished they had done . . . Part of the shock of bereavement is finding difficulty in making decisions, or making snap decisions that we might want to change later. Parents need *time* to think about their choices. These include whether to:

- sit and hold their baby alone or have someone with them;
- wash and dress their baby or have someone else do this;
- have their baby in the room in a cot and be able to look or leave;
- have siblings and grandparents visit in the hospital;
- have their baby baptised or not by a hospital or other religious worker;
- stay in hospital or go home with their baby (which depends on whether they have a postmortem or not);
- carry their baby symbolically out of the hospital, as they would have done if the baby was alive.

For families whose baby is removed from life-support in NICU, the choice is whether to be there at the time and to sit and hold the dying baby. They need to know what this will involve; it is generally a quiet death and not a gasping death as in the films. They need to know who will be there so that they are not alone. We need then to work with parents' choices such as providing a baby bath to wash their baby or contacting the requested person to organise a baptism before or after the baby dies.

What will my baby look like?

Parents need preparing for what their baby will look like in death. They have probably never seen anyone who is dead and rely on stories or films for their ideas. In the case of an intrauterine death the baby may be macerated, with white peeling skin or yellow staining from meconium. For a baby born intrapartum, often termed a 'fresh' stillbirth, their skin is often red. If there has been a placental abruption in labour then the baby may be pale. If the baby has been in NICU then the parents may never have seen their child without wires, tubes and general paraphernalia attached. They may be unprepared for how small and vulnerable their baby looks.

Support for parents at the time of death

How we respond, what we can say and how we might feel are explored in
Chapters 7 and 10. It means that we do some of the following:

Showing our feelings. We need to show we care, whether saying 'I'm sorry'
or hugging and crying with the parents. If we hold the baby cuddled to us,
as a baby, wrapped in a blanket, drawing attention to the small but perfect
parts of the baby, then we help parents to 'see' their baby.

Making memories. Being able to say goodbyes after hellos means that, as
part of our support for the family, we need to think of tangible suggestions
to contribute to the parents' memories. These points apply to all babies who
die and are discussed in more detail in Appendix 1 – *please read this*. A brief
outline of mementos for parents can include:

- photos – polaroid and a 35 mm roll of film (Appendix 2);
- foot and handprints (try having a pair) on a card;
- lock of hair – if the parents agree;
- wrapping or dressing the baby;
- keeping something (e.g. a blanket or bootees) that has been touched by
  the baby;
- having a copy of records of pregnancy and delivery.

Information immediately after the death

There is an immense vulnerability after bereavement, which brings fear and
insecurity about what will happen next in life. We need to make sure that
families going home or already at home know:

- where their baby is, if not at home with them, e.g. in the hospital
  mortuary;
- who to contact to arrange to see their baby e.g. specialist worker, senior
  nurse;
- when they can visit their baby (is this option available through the 24
  hours?);
- what their baby will be like if in the mortuary – their body may feel cold,
  stiff and solid to touch;
- what arrangements they can make for their baby to leave the hospital,
  e.g. would they like to carry their baby out of the hospital, to take their
  baby home before the funeral or to take them to the funeral parlour;
- who they can contact if they want to talk, e.g. social worker on call,
  counsellor, midwife
- what to expect both physically and emotionally (see below);
- who has shared the same event in their lives and can offer support –
  the contact number of the national/local self-help group (in the UK,
  such as SANDS, BLISSLINK, NIPPERS).

You will need to check the policy where you work to fill in the accurate information above.

Discussing with the parents what to expect in the next few days is part of returning some control and understanding to them amidst this tragic event.

Physically for a mother who has had a stillborn baby or has been expressing breast milk for her baby in NICU, her milk supply will be a painful reminder of her loss and she needs to know how to suppress this, e.g. with a firm breast support and Panadol. Shock and distress are exhausting and some parents find that sleeping tablets 'help' them to sleep, but they often bring confused dreams and are not a short-term or long-term escape from the pain.

Emotionally, families need to be prepared that they will be tired, that they may hallucinate and think that they can feel or hear their child. This is a normal part of the intensity of pain. When we talk with families in normalising grief we are not minimising it, we are seeking to give a reference point against which to hold themselves. Otherwise, to a young couple who have never experienced the depths of extreme emotions, the anger and the distress in themselves and each other can be very frightening. The feelings of bereaved parents and the factors that make grieving difficult are discussed in detail in Chapter 7. We also need to prepare the parents that many family and friends will be uncomfortable and even avoid contact. It is part of society's way of dealing with death, but it can be very hurtful to have friends cross to the other side of the street when they see you.

Saying all this information to families is too much for them to recall at the best of times – in shock little will be retained. Having a written handout, which is a resource suited to the hospital, with current phone numbers and contact information is invaluable for parents. Sometimes voluntary organisations supply these with spaces to append relevant numbers; other times it is easier to write or adapt one, such as Appendix 1, to suit your own needs.

Information on postmortems, funerals and registration

Postmortems

A postmortem may be suggested to the parents as a way to find out why the baby died. For many parents a postmortem is abhorrent – the idea of causing their baby to suffer any more and to what purpose? It is a legal requirement that parents consent to postmortems of babies after the legal age of viability (24 weeks), and that we respect their rights to refuse one. Some cultural and religious groups may refuse, unless it is performed quickly, because of requirements to bury the baby soon after death. Before parents decide they need to know:

- the benefits and risks of a postmortem (e.g. if the baby would not be repaired fully afterwards – generally face, arms and legs are untouched);

- what happens during a postmortem (see Appendix 4);
- when they will get the results of the postmortem (preliminary, final and written versions);
- other options such as partial postmortem (X-ray and only specific site investigated).

All parents should be given a copy of the new UK Department of Health leaflet *'Guide to the postmortem examination'* and this should be the basis for discussion. Any consent form needs to be signed and parents should be offered a copy of it.

Funerals

There is a legal requirement for any baby, who is stillborn or who subsequently dies, to be buried or cremated. The options for funerals need to follow the personal and religious preferences of the parents. In some instances, such as the Muslim and Jewish religions, there may be cultural requirements for the burial to be soon after the death. For other parents there is time to think about funeral options and the baby can remain in the hospital mortuary, at home or at the funeral parlour. We need to make sure that parents appreciate the importance of a funeral as a ritual of ending; it does not need to be a religious ceremony. SANDS (1991) points out that the issues the parents need to decide are:

- do they want their baby buried or cremated?
- do they want to organise the funeral themselves or have the hospital arrange it?
- what are the costs involved?

The information about these choices is discussed in Appendix 5.

If parents plan their own funeral, most funeral directors will talk about options with families. Some hospitals have a bereavement officer who can advise parents. A checklist of points for parents to consider is outlined in Table 2.2. Trying to remember all the information can be bewildering and frustrating for families. It can help if we are able to discuss and then give families written information, preferably in different languages. An example of a leaflet we gave families in Avon is shown in Appendix 6.

Certificates and registration

For all babies born after the legal age of viability (now 24 weeks) there is a legal requirement to register the birth and death. The midwife or doctor caring for the family needs to sign the relevant certificates, explain them to the parents, give the original to the family to take to the registrar's office and offer them a copy for their own use. We need to be sure that families

Table 3.2 Checklist of points to consider for siblings who are bereaved

- Give an explanation, at any age, that the baby has 'died'. Do not use words such as 'disappeared', 'lost', 'gone to hospital'; they can create fear and confusion for children who take what we say literally
- Should other children go to see the baby? Should they go to the funeral?
- Do other children wish to give anything to the baby, e.g. toy, picture?
- Would they enjoy a scrapbook of photos and a story to read about the baby?

Further details are given in Chapter 8.

understand the need for registration, because a certificate is required for the burial or cremation to take place. See Appendix 5 for details of this.

Support for families who want to see their baby again

We may be involved with families who want to see their baby and whose baby remains in the hospital mortuary prior to going home, having a postmortem or collection by the funeral director. We discuss in Chapter 7 the reality of death coming from being able to see and touch their dead baby, and an important part of helping parents to grieve is for them to have the opportunity to see their baby whenever they want. The issues we need to consider are outlined in Appendix 7.

Support for grandparents and siblings during and after the event

The feelings of, and care for, siblings is discussed in detail in Chapter 8, which includes a list of various books about death for children of different ages. The key points are honesty and the use of the word D-E-A-D, not 'lost' or 'gone away'. For a quick checklist of points, see Table 3.2. We may need to give grandparents time to talk and information about what has happened. In their own way they may be as shocked as the parents. Issues to consider are:

- information leaflets to leave with grandparents to read (see Appendix 8 or The Compassionate Friends leaflet for grandparents);
- referral contact with the GP of the grandparents to prepare them for the physical effects of grief in the context of the bereavement;
- discussing what a dead baby will look like, if their previous experience is of violent death in the World Wars.

Caring means administration and liaising

Finally, it is important that we support families by ensuring that they are not unnecessarily distressed. This includes:

- ensuring documentation is completed;
- labelling the baby with the mother's name and hospital number;

- liaising between hospital and community staff to make sure that all the health workers involved with the family are updated.

It is also important to contact health departments which operate computer printout reminders, e.g. outpatients and community health who send immunisation appointments, to make sure that an untimely reminder is not sent. These tasks are easily overlooked if there is not one person responsible. A checklist that acts as a useful reminder of what to do and who to contact has been proposed by SANDS (1991) (see Fig. 2.4). This could be amended to suit the locality of your practice.

Long-Term Information and Support

Chapter 7 deals in detail with long-term care, planning visits and recognising situations where grieving may be difficult. The following are points to consider in our care for these families.

Purpose of visiting

Listening and just being there are things that all health workers can offer. In doing this we are helping make the life, and therefore the death, of the baby a reality, not just a black hole. Some of the following information may need to be provided.

- Preparing parents for events that can act as triggers in their grief. One mother said that after 6 months she felt that on the occasional day the sun shone in her life and then she would see a baby, or find a toy or hear a piece of music and it would trigger a gulf of sadness and she would be back in the black clouds again. See Chapter 7 about anniversary events.
- Discussing questions about stillbirth or neonatal death.
- Discussing the needs of siblings who may be confused at the 'odd' ending to the pregnancy.
- Discussing how parents feel about their grief. Do they get angry? Can they focus it on to things or sports activities? Do they feel guilty? Can they rationalise it, express it, talk about it?
- Follow-up means recognising when grief becomes 'stuck' and seeking help for the individual (see Chapter 10).
- Suggesting keeping a journal as a safe outlet for thoughts is especially good for fathers, who receive little social support when a newborn baby dies (Schatz 1984).
- Advising mothers that they are eligible for free prescriptions and dental care, maternity allowance and either statutory maternity pay or payments from the Social Fund in the year after the baby's birth.

Plan for contact

We cannot expect that one explanation or discussion is sufficient; it takes time to assimilate all the events. Generally it is important that there is a discussion and debriefing at the time the baby dies. As we discuss in Chapter 7, there needs to be a plan of visiting with an *identified key worker* who then liaises with the other workers and ensures that there is follow-up of the family. This contact may be at the family home or as phone calls. As a rule of thumb there needs to be the offer of contact in the week after the funeral and at least once in the following weeks. It is a valuable practice to fix an appointment for the woman and her partner with a GP or paediatrician/obstetrician at 6 weeks. It is an opportunity to review:

- how the family feel physically and emotionally;
- any questions that have arisen;
- the postmortem findings (and give a written copy in everyday language);
- care in future pregnancies.

How can family and friends help?

For a detailed discussion, see Chapter 7, which includes some of the following points:

- being aware of what it means for the couple – not trivialising the death: 'Well the baby never really lived';
- being practical and offering help when needed, e.g. housework;
- being able to show that they care and letting families cry or kick the wall.

We can help by giving them information such as the leaflet by the Compassionate Friends, who support bereaved families (see Appendix 11).

Future Pregnancies and Babies

Shall we have another baby?

The decision to try for another baby varies according to the feelings of each parent, their decision as a couple, their previous experience and the reason why the baby died. For either parent, having another child can be an important part of re-establishing self-esteem and confidence in their ability to parent. It can be an all-consuming urge or a prospect to be avoided. Inevitably the reason, if any, the baby died is an important factor in any decision to have another baby. If it was due to an inherited genetic condition then parents need careful counselling on the risks of recurrence and possible prenatal diagnosis. Conversely, many parents have to accept the fact that there was no obvious cause for why their baby was stillborn or extremely preterm. This makes having another baby like stepping out into thin air, not having any control to do or avoid doing something that would protect the new baby from dying.

When to have another baby

Research suggests that a time space of at least 6 months between the death of the baby and the next pregnancy can be important for parents who have no support or counselling after perinatal death (Forrest et al. 1981). Some mothers have difficulty with mothering the next child, by being over-protective of the 'replacement child' (Bourne and Lewis 1984). So what should we say? Parents need time to say goodbye and the time for another baby is when they feel ready. Practical advice is to avoid conceiving exactly 3 months after the baby died, because this means the next baby would be born around the same day that their other baby died.

Support and care we can offer

For all parents, the support they receive from the GP, community midwife, health visitor and hospital staff can be vital. It can be the difference between having a nerve-wracking pregnancy and sinking into depression. Linked to this is the question for parents of whether to return to the same maternity care providers or to make a clean sweep and start afresh. Their decision, in part, reflects the care and support we have offered since their baby died. This section is dealt with in detail in Appendix 9, because it applies to all families who have had a baby die or a pregnancy end. A brief outline of points to consider includes antenatal access to support, labour care, postnatal examination and ongoing care (see Table 2.4).

Remember care and attention is often given to families having their first baby, after a baby has died. However, the anxieties and concerns can be as great with *each* pregnancy, despite having children who have lived. Time does not erase the experience, it merely gives grace and tools to cope.

What About Ourselves?

We need to recognise the emotional cost of caring for families who have been bereaved. It takes time, energy and adrenaline. In doing so, we need to know where our boundaries of practice are. Do we take our work home with us? Is it important for our grieving to support the family and go to the funeral? We need to recognise the signs of burn-out and know where to go for debriefing. Read through Chapter 10 and recognise that the quality of care we offer begins and ends with ourselves. In trying to do our best, nothing is status quo; we need to accept the challenge to change our practice to make the experience as positive as possible. Spend some time questioning your practice, the provisions and policies of the place where you work. Is it satisfactory for families and staff? What can you change?

Key points

- Recognise attitudes in our society and within the health professions that may make it hard for families to grieve after stillbirth and neonatal death.
- Be aware of the individual's response to bereavement, which is based on cultural, social and personal beliefs.
- Recognise the different aspects of grief for mothers, fathers, siblings and grandparents.
- Identify events that assist parents to have a reality in grieving for their baby, such as time with their baby and debriefing with health workers.
- Identify resources that may help provide parents with information and support, including leaflets, books and contacts with self-help groups.
- Accept the challenge to review your practice and to know the boundaries of your care.
- Make a resource folder for your work area, which has current information about caring for bereaved families and local contacts for support groups, funeral directors and interpreters.

References

Aries P. *Western attitudes towards death: from the Middle Ages to the present.* Baltimore: Johns Hopkins University Press, 1974

Benfield DG, Wadsworth J, Taylor B. Family recovery after the death of a child. *Arch Dis Child* 1988; 63(8): 942

Bergman AB. Crib deaths exact needless toll of grief in infants families. *Hosp Top* 1969; 47: 69

Bourne S. The psychological effects of stillbirths on women and their doctors. *J R Coll Gen Pract* 1968; 16: 103

Bourne S, Lewis E. Delayed psychological effects of perinatal death: the next pregnancy and the next generation. *Br Med J* 1984; 289: 147

Dunlop J. Bereavement reaction following stillbirth. *The Practitioner* 1979; 222: 115

Dyregrov A, Matthiesen S. Similarities and differences in mother's and father's grief following the death of an infant. *Scand J Psychol* 1987; 28: 1

Forrest G, Claridge RS, Baum JD. Practical management of perinatal death. *Br Med J* 1981; 282: 31

Helmrath TA, Steinitz EM. Death of an infant: parental grieving and failure of social support. *J Fam Pract* 1978; 6: 785

Hill S. *Family.* London: Penguin Books, 1989

Horowitze MJ, Wilner N, Marmer C, et al. Pathological grief and the activation of latent self images. *Am J Psychiatr* 1980; 137: 1157

Jones A, Jones K. Support for parents after a child's death. *Nurs Standard* 1990; 4(46): 32

Klaus M, Kennell J. *Parent–infant bonding.* St Louis: Mosby, 1982

Lewis E. The management of stillbirth: coping with an unreality. *Lancet* 1976; 2: 619

Lewis E, Bryan EM. Management of perinatal loss of a twin. *Br Med J* 1988; 297: 1321

Long J. Grief and loss in childbirth. *Midwives Chronicle and Nursing Notes* 1992; March: 51

Lovell A. Mothers and babies in limbo. *Nurs Mirror* 1982; Nov 3: 53

Murray J, Callan V. Predicting adjustment to perinatal death. *Br J Med Psychol* 1988; 61: 237

OPCS (Office of Population Censuses and Surveys) DH3 91/2. *Infant and perinatal mortality.* London: HMSO, 1990

Peppers L, Knapp R. *Motherhood and mourning.* New York, Praeger, 1980

SANDS (Stillbirth and Neonatal Death Society). *Miscarriage, stillbirth and neonatal death. Guidelines for professionals.* London: SANDS, 1991

Schatz W. *Healing a father's grief.* Redmond: Medical Publishing Company, 1984

Schwiebert P, Kirk P. *When hello means goodbye.* Portland, Oregon: Department of Obstetrics, University of Oregon Health Sciences Center, 1981

Stephenson JS. *Death, grief and mourning.* New York: Free Press, 1985

Tew M. *Safer childbirth.* London: Chapman & Hall, 1990

Thearle J, Gregory H. Evolution of bereavement counselling in sudden infant syndrome, neonatal death and stillbirth. *J Paediatr Child Health* 1992; 28: 204

Resources for Parents

Self-help groups

BLISSLINK
17–21 Emerald Street, London WC1N 2QL, UK
Tel: 071–831 9393
For parents of babies in NICU who live or die.

Compassionate Friends
53 North Street, Bristol BS3
Tel: 0272–292778
Support for parents; groups, leaflets

The Miscarriage Association (MA)
PO Box 24, Ossett, West Yorks WF5 9XG, UK
Tel: 0945–830515
Local groups and newsletter.

NIPPERS Bereavement Group
c/o Sam Segal Perinatal Unit, St Mary's Hospital, Praed Street, London W2
1NY, UK
Tel: 071–725 1487
Support for bereaved parents of preterm infants and parents in NICU.

The Stillbirth and Neonatal Death Society (SANDS)
28 Portland Place, London W1N 4DE, UK
Tel: 071–436 5881
Support for parents whose babies are born dead or die soon after birth.
Local groups, newsletter.

The Twins and Multiple Births Association (TAMBA) Bereavement Support
Group
PO Box 30, Little Sutton, South Wirral L66 1TH, UK
Tel: 051–348 0020
May have local contact, remembrance service, newsletter.

Books

Hill S. *Family.* London: Penguin, 1990
Kohner N, Henley A. *When a baby dies.* London: Pandora, 1992
Kohner N, & Thomas J. *Grieving after the death of your baby,* Riversdale,
    Bucks: The Child Bereavement Trust
Ward B. *Healing grief.* London: Ebury Press, 1993

Leaflets

See *'Ache in their heart'* resource package below.

Resources for Health Workers

As for parents, plus:

Books

Rando T. (ed). *Parental loss of a child.* Illinois: Research Press, 1986
Thomas J. *Supporting parents when a baby dies – before or soon after birth.* This
    written booklet is a guide for staff, antenatal, labour ward, postnatal,
    gynaecological and neonatal teams. Available from Jenni Thomas, The
    Director of The Child Bereavement Trust, 1 Millside, Riversdale, Bourne
    End, Bucks SL8 5EB, UK.

Leaflet

'Guide to postmortem examination – brief notes for parents and families who have lost a baby in pregnancy or early infancy' by the Department of Health, produced in consultation with the National Advisory Body for the Confidential Enquiry into Stillbirths and Deaths in Infancy, SANDS and FSID. Use the leaflet with parents as an aid to discussion.

Videos and training packages

Death at birth: two part video. This aims to help professionals understand parents' needs after loss of a baby, deal with their own feelings and identify areas to improve practice. Made by Jenni Thomas, The Director of The Child Bereavement Trust, 1 Hillside, Riversdale, Bourne End, Bucks: SL8 5EB, UK.

When our baby died: video, and accompanying book, *Grieving after the death of your baby.* Has been made for parents and familes and those who care for them. Made by Jenni Thomas.

An ache in their heart. For professionals and parents to equip them as companions for bereaved families. Resources include training sessions, handouts for families, children's books, a video, materials to form a memorial and medical information in a layperson's language.
Cost: $A250. Yvonne Connelly Tel: 07 840 8154. The University of Queensland Department of Child Health, Clarence Court, Mater Children's Hospital, South Brisbane, Australia.

Chapter Four

Death in Infancy

Life is what happens to you while you're busy making other plans.

(John Lennon, *Beautiful Boy*)

Within this chapter

1. Situations where an infant dies – suddenly or anticipated
2. What is the impact on the different family members when an infant dies?
3. What care can health workers offer at the time?
4. What ongoing care for families can be offered, extending to any future pregnancies?
5. How can family and friends help?

Introduction

Impact of infant death

Emotionally, the death of a baby is a crisis, which can bring chaos and destruction. Perception of the loss varies between cultures. For example, in Western society we have an expectation that all babies will live, therefore the loss is an unexpected 'theft', whereas families from developing countries may see infant mortality as part of everyday life.

The crisis is not confined to the family; the ripple effect extends much further. It affects parents, siblings now and in the future, grandparents, parents' siblings, friends and family, the community such as shops and schools, and health workers who have been involved with the family, e.g. the GP and health visitor (Fig. 4.1).

Infants die at home and in hospital, and can generally be divided into two groups. The first group comprises infants with a known life-threatening condition such as AIDS, malignancy or a genetic disorder. The second

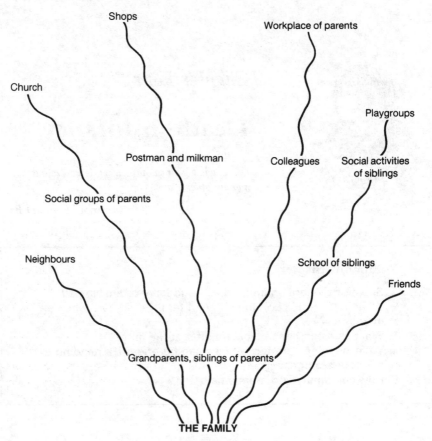

Figure 4.1 The ripple effect of grief after the sudden, unexpected death of a baby.

group comprises apparently healthy infants who die suddenly as a result of infection, accident or for no reason at all – cot death. In this chapter we will look at the two situations separately, starting with sudden deaths, which are the most common in infants aged less than 1 year.

SUDDEN DEATHS IN INFANCY

Definitions

Infants do die suddenly in accidents such as house fires, road accidents and drowning. By far the largest group are sudden unexpected deaths in infancy (SUDI) where infants (less than 12 months of age) die with no prior warning of life-threatening illness or abnormalities. A detailed history and postmortem examination can subdivide this group into sudden infant death syndrome (SIDS), where no cause of death is found (a diag-

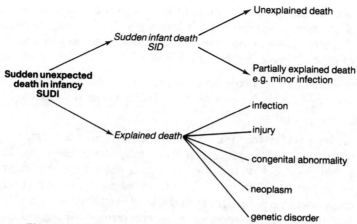

Figure 4.2 The causes of sudden unexpected death in infancy.

nosis by default), and 'explained' deaths, e.g. where death is due to an unknown abnormality or infection (Fig. 4.2). The lay term 'cot death', first used by Barratt in 1954, denotes the fact that most SIDS are found in their cots. The full definition of SIDS was formulated by Beckwith in 1970 as: 'The sudden death of any infant or young child which is unexpected by history and in which a thorough postmortem examination fails to demonstrate an adequate cause of death.' In this book we will use the term SID rather than SIDS, because it appears likely that there are multiple factors that create a situation where a baby dies suddenly and unexpectedly, therefore it is not a *syndrome* as such.

Parents' feelings

The feelings of bereavement following the death of a loved person are discussed in detail in Chapters 1 and 7. Sudden unexpected death brings particular issues, which are discussed below.

The suddenness of death can feel like a bolt out of the blue; totally unexpected and unwarranted. Cot death, stillbirth and accidents bring similar difficulties for parents who mourn: guilt, lack of memories and low self-value as a parent (Benfield et al. 1978; Lewis 1979). One recent study has found that the cot death of an apparently healthy child can result in higher levels of anxiety and depression than in families who have had a neonatal death or stillbirth (Vance et al. 1991). This is possibly the result of the judiciary system response to sudden death (see below). Denial, shock and disbelief tend to follow all sudden deaths. Parents often say that they do not believe their baby is really dead. As they hold their dead baby they still have the hope that, if they wish hard enough, their baby might start breathing again. The intensity of shock and disbelief can lead to parents hallucinating that they hear their baby cry, or having panic attacks and nightmares of trying to resuscitate their baby again and again. Anger can be directed at oneself or others. With hindsight it can focus on failing to provide adequate safety or not going to check on the baby sooner. Maria, whose baby died as a cot death, said:

> I was overwhelmed and so mad with myself, Daniel had slept longer than usual and I had enjoyed a lie in, if I had gone in at the usual time he might still be alive.

Guilt can be part of the anger, and especially SID parents, with no medical cause of death such as infection, may desperately try to find something that they did or did not do which caused the death. Infants who die in accidents are commonly in house fires, motor vehicles or drown in baths or swimming pools. In a study in Australia, Pearn and Nixon (1977) found that factors associated with children of all ages drowning were lack of supervision, tiredness of parents, large families, unrealistic expectations of children and children supervising other siblings. In retrospect this leaves plenty of room for guilt afterwards, even though we know that many other families will have done the same things and an accident will not have occurred.

Kalish (1977) points out that death of a child results in more stress than any other cause of death, regardless of whether it is 'explained' or not. This is partly because the parenting role is linked to the well-being of the child – death of the apparently well child can be perceived as the ultimate parenting failure. We explored the effects of loss of self-esteem and confidence in Chapter 1 and can appreciate that death of one's child can shatter a belief in one's ability to be a parent. Mothers can be particularly vulnerable to infant death as they adjust from the pregnant to the parent role. Wright (1991) refers to situations where a developmental crisis, which is a normal life milestone (in this case pregnancy), is compounded with a coincidental crisis (death of the baby).

As we discuss in Chapter 7, men and women respond and grieve in different ways. After the sudden death of a baby, mothers often become sad; fathers are more action-based and focus on decisions and work (Williams and Nikolaisen 1982). In North European cultures this in part represents the gender roles and opportunities to release grief. Wendy Harman, who shared her experience of cot death in the *British Medical Journal*, summed this up when she wrote:

> My husband was able to return to his work routine shortly after the death . . . It was more difficult for me, as that dead baby was my routine; both actively and intellectually I was thrown into a vacuum. The all-consuming emotion is that of experiencing what feels like first-degree robbery, the ultimate theft. (Harman 1981)

The impact of the sudden unexpected death of their baby on the relationship of the parents can strengthen it or lead to stress and breakdown

(Mandell et al. 1980). Lord and a co-worker in counselling families noted that there is no predictable outcome to patterns of coping (Lord 1987). There were relationships where:

- some live on a surface level and separate;
- some live on a surface level and stay together;
- some struggle honestly and openly and stay together;
- some struggle honestly and openly and separate;
- some battle it out and separate;
- some battle it out and stay together.

Impact of the legal response to sudden death

Sudden deaths generally come under the jurisdiction of the Coroner. In the case of accident this is to ensure that there were no 'suspicious circumstances'. In the case of cot death, when the doctor is called and sees no obvious cause of death, he is required by law to notify the Coroner. Under the Coroner's Act of 1882 (amended) the Coroner is required to inquire into the death, to establish the cause and circumstances of the death and issue a certificate of registrable cause of death. The duty of the Coroner's officer (generally a seconded policeman), or in rural areas the police acting on the Coroner's behalf, is to:

- obtain information on the circumstances of the death;
- have the body identified;
- supply a report to the Coroner.

In the case of cot deaths and most accidents the Coroner pays for a funeral director to take the body to a mortuary and for a pathologist to carry out a postmortem examination to ascertain the cause of death. The results of the postmortem are given to the Coroner, who either completes the death certificate, which is used to register the death, or calls a public inquest prior to completing the Certificate of Inquest (Fig. 4.3). The impact of these legal requirements is for parents to feel that not only has the bottom fallen out of their world and their baby has died, but now they are under judicial scrutiny. The next leap is to feel that they are on trial for killing their child.

Feelings of siblings, grandparents and other caregivers

Siblings

Contrary to the popular view that 'children don't really know what is going on', there is plenty of evidence that siblings are affected by the sudden and unexpected death of a brother or sister as an accident or cot death (De Frain et al. 1982; Raphael 1984; Golding et al. 1985). Many siblings will have been present when their parents found the baby dead,

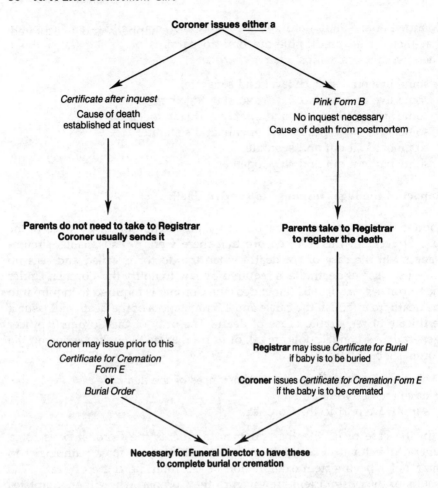

Figure 4.3 Certification and registration of a baby who dies suddenly and unexpectedly in the UK.

perhaps sitting in the corner during attempts at resuscitation and surrounded by feelings of panic and fear. One father talked about his remaining son, who used to hide under the bed when he heard the wail of emergency sirens. As the child grew older and had the words to express what he felt, he said that he thought they were coming to 'take him away'. Wendy Harman (1981), writing about the death of her son Charles, made the comment about her $3\frac{1}{2}$-year-old son:

> He developed a morbid fascination with death and a jarring habit of making remarks like 'You looked after me when I was a baby, so I didn't die, why did you kill Charles?

This illustrates children's appreciation of what happens and is explored further in Chapter 8.

Grandparents

Grandparents can be very distressed and upset. We discussed in previous chapters about their 'double grief': the loss of their own grandchild and the loss of happiness for their own child. After accident or cot death, I have known grandparents go home to cry, sit feeling empty and wonder why they have been left alive when their grandchild has died. 'Survivor guilt' includes feelings of injustice and illogicality of living at the end of lives when their grandchild, who they had seen growing healthily, died at the beginning of life. Death can precipitate other griefs and this is discussed further in Chapter 7.

Other caregivers

In the current social climate where many families have both parents working, infants may have an accident or die as a cot death whilst in the care of another person. This may be the grandparents or a childminder. The impact on the carer can be tremendous, with a weight of guilt and self-recrimination at failing in their care of a baby who was not their own. In the panic and confusion of the situation, questions and comments from the parents who are trying to find out what has happened can compound this sense of failure. It is a crisis situation for all concerned.

Friends

Support from family and friends can be vital. As John Lennon wrote: 'I get along with a little help from my friends.' For many families after their baby dies, support may be lacking. Many family and friends have either fears about grief, or misperceptions about sudden deaths as 'killing your baby', so they avoid seeing the parents. Sara, whose baby died aged 3 months, lived on a housing estate with many other young families around her, and said:

> I can remember going to the shops for the first time without the pram, it felt naked. I walked along, trying not to see babies. I saw some of the mothers we had visited and children we had played with. They looked the other way, they didn't come up and say anything and two must have seen me coming because they dodged the traffic and crossed the road.

How can Health Workers Help?

Who are the health workers involved?

Both hospital and community staff are likely to be involved, with the family having contact with the GP, health visitor, midwife, staff in the Accident and Emergency Department or Paediatric Intensive Care Unit, if a child is admitted after resuscitation and then dies. For a detailed view of bereavement care, see Chapter 7. The following section outlines some of the issues in caring for families after sudden unexpected death of their baby, and these need to be adapted to your work area. For detailed guidelines for the role of different health workers involved in cot death, contact the Foundation for the Study of Infant Deaths (FSID). This section is not intended to provide specialist care in a situation of complicated mourning, such as when parents are known to have killed their child.

The aim of our care

The aim of our care is to support families in their own journey through grieving. As we have stated before, we cannot make the situation 'better' by bringing their child to life; we can only ensure that our practice does not make it 'worse'. Some of the things we do not want to do are outlined in Table 4.1 and are discussed in Chapter 7 in the section on 'What helps bereaved parents most/least?'.

The principles of care, which we have referred to in previous chapters, are important:

- *Honesty* in giving information and in our responses;
- *Accessibility* – to be there at the times when information and support is needed, not just on a 9am–5pm basis;
- *Valuing individuals'* grieving, which is based on personal, cultural and social beliefs (see Chapter 9 for more discussion on cultural aspects);
- *Valuing ourselves* – we have something to offer even if it is only that we care.

Table 4.1 Some don'ts when caring for families after the sudden, unexpected death of their baby

---

- **Do not** forget to warn parents about the involvement of the police or Coroner's officer
- **Do not** hide the truth that their baby will have a postmortem
- **Do not** assume parents will not want to see their baby before or after the postmortem
- **Do not** think that all people will react in the same way when their baby dies
- **Do not** ignore what has happened and try not to talk about it
- **Do not** treat the baby like a body
- **Do not** say, 'You'll get over it'
- **Do not** tell parents not to feel guilty
- **Do not** forget about the ripple effect of grief when a baby dies

---

Self-awareness

Guilt

It is important to be aware that the involvement of the police and Coroner can create a sense of guilt in both parents and ourselves. In our wish to try to 'help', we can clumsily try to wipe out this sense of guilt by telling parents not to feel guilty, thus implying that they should be. Wendy Harman illustrated this with her experience after cot death:

If the bereaved mother does not initially feel guilty she certainly will shortly thereafter by dint of the many 'professionals' who repeatedly tell her not to feel guilty'. (Harman 1981)

The Irish Sudden Infant Death Association (ISIDA) guide for professionals, contact with a cot death family recommends that everyone state that cot death is *unpredictable and unpreventable*. This is more accurate than telling parents not to feel guilty. In the light of some of the research in the 1990s, we need to expand this to point out that no study has identified factors that can be guaranteed to *predict* all babies who will die as SID, nor a cure to *prevent* SID, although we do know of risk factors for SID. The same principle should apply after accidents. We can honestly say 'I'm sorry', but without knowing the facts we cannot say 'It is not your fault' without compounding a sense of automatic guilt.

Support at the Time a Baby Dies Suddenly and Unexpectedly

Where the baby dies

The particular support and information parents will need depends in part on the situation where the baby dies. For the family of a baby who is found dead at home, whose parents call the ambulance and the baby is *transferred to hospital* for resuscitation which is then discontinued, there is a need for time and support in the Accident and Emergency Department. This means allocating one member of staff to be with the parents whilst there are any attempts at resuscitation. There needs to be a private room with nearby facilities for toilets and tea or coffee. Other support and information that is needed is outlined below.

For a baby who is found *dead at home* and is obviously dead, the parents phone either the GP or the emergency services. They should be given time, by whoever responds to their call for help, to cuddle their baby and say goodbye before their baby goes to the hospital or city mortuary for a postmortem. Details of the support and information needed are outlined below.

Supporting and debriefing

It is important that we recognise the cultural variations in response to death and contact an interpreter, as necessary, to offer support and information and to find out what happened to their baby.

- Part of the immediate care of any family, at home or in hospital, may be dealing with shock, hysteria or silence. Most importantly we need to acknowledge their loss by saying 'I'm sorry'. It may not be heard at the time but they may remember it afterwards.
- We can help to provide parents with familiar supporters by finding out where the other members of the family are and organise to contact them, e.g. the father at work, the grandparents to come for support, or someone to care for siblings.
- We need to listen to the parent(s) who found the baby dead and from this record the following.
  Name and address of the family.
  Details of how they found the baby, and what they did.
  Any previous history of illness or unusual behaviour in the last 24 hours. A copy of this information should be given to the pathologist (as background to the postmortem) and to the person who will follow-up the family (as the basis for answering questions and offering counselling).
- By talking about what has happened we are offering parents an acknowledgement of their actions and their child's death; it is an opportunity for them to debrief. This might include comments on the appearance of the baby. For example, in cot death a blotchy blue-red discolouration of the face can occur if the baby has been lying prone. It is caused by pooling of the blood after death, not by bruising. Frothy, white or blood-stained bubbles, seen around the mouth and nose, are a feature of cot death.
- Supporting parents to see their baby. Even after a fire, when an infant is severely burned, the reality of seeing their child is a step to believing their death. If there are puncture marks from intravenous sites, during resuscitation attempts, these need to be covered with sticking plaster and explained to the parents. In hospital, parents may wish for a Chaplain to baptise their baby, or other religious ceremony, before they leave their child.
- When families are ready to go home, it is our responsibility to ensure that they have some safe means of going home. Parents should not be reliant on a bus as a consequence of arriving in an ambulance and coming without any money. It may require emergency access to hospital social funds to pay for a taxi to ensure this does not happen.

Similarly, as a parent of a family goes home, we need to make sure that some-one will stay with them and that they will not be left bereaved and alone.

Information

As we discuss in Chapter 7, parents need to have accurate information about the situation, this includes the following points:

- what is happening to their baby;
- who is the person looking after them and their baby (especially important if they are in hospital with unknown staff);
- the opportunity to see their baby.

Explaining their baby's death as far as possible is very important, e.g. smoke inhalation probably happened in a fire, or in the case of SUDI there may be a reason we do not know yet. This leads on to outlining clearly the involvement of the Coroner (see below). As part of this explanation to SUDI families, give a copy of 'Information for parents following the unexpected death of their baby' (leaflet available from FSID). Consider writing your own information leaflet for families whose child dies in an accident. We also need to explain what will happen to their baby:

- where their baby will be, e.g. hospital or city mortuary;
- when the postmortem is expected to be (should be in the next 24–72 hours);
- who to contact if they want to see their baby;
- who will contact them about their baby and the postmortem report.

What about twins in cot death?

If a baby dies suddenly and unexpectedly for no apparent reason, then the twin seems to have an increased risk of cot death, possibly by being exposed to the same environmental or genetic factors. Generally the medical response is to admit the other twin to hospital for observation. If this is done, we need to be aware that parents are being exposed to an unknown environment at the time of maximum vulnerability and will need support and care from hospital staff, with their own space to be private on the paediatric ward.

The Coroner and the postmortem

Coroner's role

Families need to understand and know the extent of, and reasons for, the involvement of the police or Coroner's officer. We used to explain to families that it is a legal requirement for the Coroner's officer (or police) to be involved in any sudden death. This does not presuppose thoughts of foul play; it is the law of the land. A point that some parents have found comforting is that it is for the parents' own protection to have an independent person collect information, if anyone ever asks questions afterwards. It can help to note the human aspect – that police do not like visiting, and they often have young children themselves. Depending on the local area, the police or Coroner's officer will ask the family to: (a) identify their baby, although this is being waived in some instances nowadays; and (b) give a brief history of when and where they found their baby and what happened in the previous 24 hours.

Postmortem

Parents need to know why a postmortem is necessary and what it involves. We can give them a copy of the UK Department of Health leaflet *'Guide to the postmortem examination'* and use this as a basis for discussion.

Why have a postmortem? It should be made clear to parents that all sudden deaths without an obvious cause, of any age, are legally Coroner's cases. This generally involves a postmortem. The key point is that they are not being treated differently. However, the upsetting part is that they do not have a choice to consent to the postmortem. For cot death parents, whilst it is upsetting to think of their baby having a postmortem, it can provide useful information as to why their baby died. The question nearly all parents want answered is 'Why?'.

What does a postmortem involve? It is important that we rapidly and briefly allay any misperceptions that families have about postmortems. If we take too long in a ponderous explanation of the whys and wherefores of postmortems, they will not hear us when we explain what actually happens. The key point is that their imagined postmortem, based on knowledge from films and books, is generally far worse than any reality. An outline of the explanation we give to families is shown in Appendix 3. It will need to be checked and adapted to any particular practices of the pathologist in your locality.

When will it happen? There should be an expectation that it will happen within 24 hours of death; the *'Guide to the postmortem examination'* by the Department of Health recommends within 72 hours. During this time the parents remain in limbo, not knowing if they did something to cause their baby's death and unable to finalise the funeral without the death certificate. The idea of a postmortem may be incomprehensible and unacceptable to some cultures and will need to be explained carefully either through an interpreter or with community leaders. See Chapter 9 for further discussion of these issues.

Care on the Day of Death

It can be very useful to visit the family's home when the family have had a chance to come together. The visit should preferably include community health workers such as the GP, health visitor or midwife (depending on the age of the baby) and any staff in the locality with experience of infant death, e.g. a paediatrician. The purpose of the visit is to provide information and support.

Support

Listening. We need to listen to the family talk about what has happened and how they feel. Coming to grips with the belief that their baby has died needs time to repeat what has happened and to ask questions.

Checking for support. Families need to have the contact number of the local and national parents' groups such as FSID or Cot Death Research in England and Wales, ISIDA in Ireland and the Scottish Cot Death Trust. Whilst predominantly for cot death families, there are an increasing number of families whose child has died for other reasons. These groups firmly espouse the idea of befriending and having support from other parents.

Information

After a crisis, an event which is outside the experience of an individual, there is a tremendous need for information to make sense of it and retain control of what is happening.

About the death. Information may be needed on what SUDI is, post-mortems, when a funeral is likely to be organised (subject to the Coroner completing the certificate) or registering the death, which generally needs to be done before the funeral (please read Appendix 4 for details).

Planning a funeral. This is a concern for many young families who have had no previous experience of funerals. The importance of goodbyes cannot be overestimated and we need to be able to give them information on finding a funeral director, the choices available and the costs involved (see Table 2.2 and Appendix 4). It can help to leave the family with some written information (Appendix 5).

Practical advice. If a mother has been breastfeeding then all too soon her breasts are painful reminders of what she has lost. She needs information about suppressing lactation, which, depending on current practice, may include using firm breast support and taking Panadol. Families who have fears about sleeping need to know that sleeping tablets may have a short-term value. Many families find that they result in confusion and make it worse. They are an aid, not an escape.

Preparation for consequences of the death. The parents should be prepared for the response of some family and friends who may avoid them; for possible media response, as local papers seek to 'cover' the event; for the reactions of siblings and the need to be honest with them (see below).

About normal grieving. This is discussed in much more detail in Chapter 7. Feelings can include feelings of shock, anger and frustration and strong positive or negative feelings about lovemaking. Most importantly, parents need to be reminded that they may grieve differently in their own way. We can say to parents: 'You need to give each other understanding and a big hug when words are difficult. There is no right or wrong way to react.'

Administration and liaison

Wherever the death occurs, at home or hospital, there needs to be one person who takes responsibility to inform appropriate health workers, to change hospital and community records thus preventing appointment reminders being sent and to update any research studies of which the baby may have been part. Designing a checklist for your locality may be useful (Table 4.2).

In the Days Before the Funeral

As discussed in Chapter 7, there needs to be a key worker who will provide the family with support and information, and when a postmortem is performed, discuss the findings.

Information and support for parents

Preliminary findings of the postmortem

Either the pathologist or someone with experience needs to explain the findings. In the FSID survey of parents in 1974–81 only 12% heard the findings from their GP. The majority heard it from the Coroner or police (Golding et al. 1985). The postmortem may provide information about the manner of death, e.g. smoke inhalation in a fire; or sudden death due to undetected heart anomaly or a genetic disorder such as enzyme deficiency medium chain Acyl CoA dehydrogenase (MCAD); or no cause of death is found (SID) in which case it needs to be turned round to explain what was found: 'Your baby is a perfectly formed, well developed, well nourished baby . . .' Parents or the GP can obtain a copy of the postmortem from the Coroner for a small fee. It is very important that if parents have a copy of the postmortem that it is explained to them by a health worker otherwise the medical terminology may increase distress.

Table 4.2 Checklist of information and health workers and agencies to contact after a baby dies suddenly and unexpectedly

---

Information
Name and address of baby
Sex of the baby
Baby's hospital number
Mother's name, address, phone number
Father's name, address, phone number

People contacted

Police or Coroner informed of death (name of person contacted)	Informed
GP's name, address, phone number	Informed
Health visitor's name, address, phone number	Informed
Midwife's name, address, phone number	Informed
Social worker's (if involved with family) name, address, phone number	Informed
Community Health Records	Informed
Any specific person who follows-up SUDI, e.g. paediatrician	Informed
Medical records in hospital where the baby was born	Informed
Grandparents' name and address:	
maternal	
paternal	
Grandparents' GPs	Informed
Research studies in which the baby may participate	Informed
Pathologist contacted with notes of history and details of any puncture wounds during resuscitation	Informed
Name of any hospital workers involved in care of family	
Name and phone number of *key worker* for follow-up of family	

Mementos and property if the baby is in hospital care
Baby has name bands (×2)
Photos of baby taken (photos given to parents/in medical notes)
Hand/footprint of baby taken (prints given to parents/in medical notes)
List of clothing and property with the baby in the mortuary

Memories

Support is also about helping parents to make memories. There will be some families whose baby is only a few weeks old and they may have few photos or mementos. Others will have accumulated lots of memorabilia over 10 months of life. Both families need to have mementos (tangible items) of their baby. These include photos, footprints or notes of pregnancy, and labour or ultrasound scan photos may now be doubly precious (see Appendix 1).

Seeing their child

Some families will not want to see their child again before the funeral. Others may have concerns about what their baby will look like after an accident or a postmortem. You will need to check the policy of the pathologist in your area to prepare the parents for the type of scars the baby will have after the postmortem (face, legs and arms should be untouched). If families want to see their child who is in the hospital mortuary, we need to organise where they will see their baby, who will be there and what access there is for visiting; these are discussed in Appendix 7. If their child is at a funeral parlour, we can help find out for parents when they can go to see their child and decide whether it is appropriate for us to accompany them. We cannot overestimate the importance of parents feeling able to see their child at any time. Ariane said, after her 3-month-old baby Joseph died:

> I woke up in the middle of the night and I knew I had to see him and to wrap him up. So we got some clothes and a blanket and we went to see him at 2 am in the morning, then I went home and slept.

One further issue about parents seeing their baby concerns the policy of the Corner or pathologist prior to the postmortem or certification of death. Some may be unhappy for the parents to see their baby alone, before the postmortem findings are established. This may reflect a fear that parents might remove the baby, and in the case of non-accidental injury resulting in death, the baby's body is the evidence. You need to clarify with your work area what the policy is. If it appears restrictive, then find out the rationale on which it is based. In reality, parents generally want to be accompanied by a health worker to see their baby.

Information and support for grandparents and siblings

Siblings

The feelings of siblings and how we support parents to tell siblings about death are discussed in detail in Chapter 8. Key points are: telling children that the baby is dead (not using words such as 'lost' or 'gone away' which children may take literally); involving siblings in family mourning and being prepared for changes in their behaviour. Resources such as *'Helping younger bereaved brothers and sisters'* by the Compassionate Friends can help parents. Books for children include *Where's Jess?*, the story of a baby who is a cot death, and *Am I still a sister?*, the feelings of 11-year-old Alicia when her brother Austin dies. For older children, of school age, it can be helpful if we, or the parents, contact the school and teacher to prepare them. It can also be a chance to talk in a classroom setting about death in life, as part of children's lifeskills.

Grandparents

Grandparents need information about what is happening. They may be bewildered or express concerns about how an accident occurred. We need to listen to their grief. They may make the comment that 'we didn't have cot death in our day'. We can point out that early this century more babies died of polio and gastroenteritis; now they are living and dying for other reasons. Grandparents may find it useful to have a leaflet such as those produced by FSID and the Compassionate Friends (see also Appendix 7). We need to assess whether they have particular concerns about seeing their dead grandchild based on previous experience of grief. It may be necessary to talk about what a dead baby looks like, if parents decide to have their baby home before the funeral.

Ongoing after the funeral

Plan for contact

A plan for bereavement care is discussed fully in Chapter 7. As a general rule of thumb, contact needs to be at least weekly until 6 weeks. At this point it can be useful to have a *reviewing* appointment, preferably with someone experienced in infant death. This appointment needs to review:

- physical and emotional status of the family;
- any postmortem findings (the final report should now be available) and provide a written record of this in lay terms;
- questions parents may have about the numerous causes of SID (Table 4.3);
- the support available if the family decide to have another child;
- that the family have a contact name with a self-help group;
- the resurgence of anguish SID families may feel at media stories about 'new causes' and suggest that they contact us or the FSID for accurate information.

Purpose of visiting

The purpose of ongoing visiting is to provide support and information on the grieving journey, which may be needed intermittently over the years. This is discussed in Chapter 7 with sections on what to say, how to assess need, etc. Issues after sudden death include the following.

Providing support and space to talk. One mother said that after the death of her child, there was a need to go over and over what had happened. Her life felt like a needle in a record that had got stuck. Only when it had been talked about enough, and the groove worn out, could the record carry on playing. Keeping a journal, making a scrapbook of the baby's life or drawing pictures can be another way of looking back before going forward. Talking to someone else who has experienced in their own way the same event of a baby dying suddenly is often the most valuable form of

Table 4.3 Some of the many proposed causes of SID

Allergy to cow's milk
Apnoea
Botulism
Breathing abnormalities
Cardiac abnormalities
Electromagnetic fields
Fungal infection of the mattress
Hyperthermia
Hypernatraemia
Hypoglycaemia
Infection: viral, bacterial
Infanticide
Mineral deficiencies
Rebreathing of carbon dioxide
Stress
Vitamin deficiencies

support. Having the contact number of a parents group does not mean that families feel able to ring an unknown person and talk about their own pain. With their permission we can access this support for them by acting as an intermediary and phoning on their behalf to arrange contact with another parent.

Anger is good and healthy and frightening. We need to share ideas on expressing it outwardly through action, exercise or writing. Anger can be focused on health workers. Following the campaigns on reducing the risk (RTR) of cot death, there is now a small group of families with anger that they followed the health message and put their baby to sleep supine, did not smoke, and breastfed, etc. Why did their baby die? Who got it wrong? We need to respond to their anger by exploring the health message which is one of *risk reduction not prevention*.

Guilt is so much a part of sudden death; what Miles and Demi (1986) term 'death causation guilt'. They suggest:

> . . . related method for reducing guilt is having bereaved parents focus on the positives in their relationship and experience with the child who died. Each time the parent begins to focus on guilt, he should be instructed to change that focus to a positive thought about something good he did during the child's lifetime. (Miles and Demi 1986, p. 115)

Following the RTR campaigns there are now families who are able to focus their guilt on not having implemented the RTR advice, either through choice or ignorance. Again exploring the idea of *reduction not prevention* is central to facing their guilt.

Emptiness. Wendy Harman wrote that there may be a tremendous lack of pattern and routine for a mother whose 24 hours has centred around the baby and family. Suggestions can include taking up new activities, returning to work, or becoming part of the local parents group. We also need to mention the effects of anniversaries on grief (see Chapter 7).

Practical information needs to be given on:

- Maternity benefits. The mother is still eligible for free prescriptions, dental care and statutory maternity pay or allowance in the year after the pregnancy as if the baby was alive.
- The Child Benefit book needs to be returned to a Social Security office.
- If there are savings schemes in the child's name, these need to be closed within a year of their baby's death.

Assessing grief. We may meet parents who say 'I murdered my child'. We need to be able to listen and to refer for expert help; it may be the truth or it may be that their grief is 'stuck' (see Chapter 10).

How can family and friends help?

This is discussed in detail in Chapter 7 and includes the following key issues.

- Being there and spending time with the family.
- Realistic knowledge about the death. This is important, because there are many misperceptions about accidents and cot deaths. In Melbourne, counsellors from the Sudden Infant Death Research Foundation go to coffee mornings with family and friends to talk about what cot death is, what has happened to the baby who died, what the family may be feeling and what supporters can do to help.
- Practicalities such as offering to help out with the shopping when the family are emotionally exhausted.

We can help by giving information to family and friends, such as the leaflet from the Compassionate Friends about how to support parents (Appendix 11).

Future Pregnancies

Can we have another baby?

There will be some families who had felt that their family was complete and had sterilisation only to find that their last baby died. If they wish to have another baby to complete their family, they will need to see an obstetrician to discuss the possible success of reversal of the operation.

Shall we have another baby:

For families this question may be unspoken, but is thought of even in the hours and days after their baby died. It is not a denial of their baby who died; it is partly an expression of their wish to have a baby in their arms. For them, having a baby is probably the only way to eventually move forward. For other families there is a fear of having another baby and 'risking' all that pain again. Families whose previous baby died of an inherited disorder need to be clear about the opportunities for screening tests, treatment available and choices for termination.

Specific to cot death – risk of another?

There are varying expert estimates that differ on the likelihood of cot death recurring. It is generally accepted that there is an increased risk compared with a family who have not experienced a cot death. This is likely to reflect the fact that risk factors in the family reappear, e.g. young maternal age or antenatal smoking. Whatever the current risk of cot death in your area, present the information positively. During the late 1980s in the UK, three to four siblings out of 500 died, which means we can tell parents that 496–497 of 500 siblings live.

When to have one – replacement babies?

The need to fill the gap with a baby means that some families go on to become pregnant at any cost. Advice is freely given by friends and family as to when to have one. Health workers need to be more sensitive and advice needs to be honest:

- Have another one when it feels right to you and you have made your goodbyes to the previous baby.
- Consider not getting pregnant 3 months after your baby died, because it means the next baby's birthday would be around the anniversary of the death of the previous baby.

If goodbyes are not said with an acceptance of what has happened, it can be very hard to view the next baby with equanimity. There can be issues of anxiety and overprotection for siblings (Bluglass 1992).

Having another baby

All families need support and recognition of their fears and anxieties in entering into the role of parents again. What can we offer newly bereaved families? The issues we need to consider are outlined in Appendix 9 and summarised in Table 2.4.

Specific to cot deaths, in over 146 UK health trusts, Care of the Next

Infant (CONI) schemes were set up in the late 1980s and 1990s, supported by FSID. The scheme involves close liaison between hospital and community staff with parents given structured support and various aids such as an apnoea monitor, scales and a symptom sheet. The value of this scheme is to provide a formalised structure of support, which acknowledges fears that families have.

All parents whose infant dies need practical information and skills as part of ongoing bereavement care. In acknowledging what has happened in the past and offering practical tools we can help to restore parents' shattered confidence in their ability to be a parent. This can include the following.

- Cardiopulmonary resuscitation training, either by paediatric staff or St Johns Ambulance.
- Risk reduction advice about cot death from the UK 'Back to Sleep' campaign (Table 4.4).
- Recognising and responding to illness in young babies, e.g. using Baby Check (Fig. 4.4).
- Information on home safety measures to prevent accidents (leaflets are available from the Royal Society for the Prevention of Accidents (ROSPA) and the Department of Health).
- Advice on the value of breastfeeding with regard to promoting infant health.

Key points
- Appreciate the crisis impact that sudden death of a baby has on the family
- Appreciate the effect of individual, social and cultural beliefs on grieving
- Appreciate the features of sudden death that make grieving particularly hard
- Appreciate the need families have for memories, mementos and times to say goodbye to their baby who has died suddenly
- Locate resources for families, such as the contact number of local groups, leaflets, books and videos
- Make a resource book of current information about infants who die suddenly

HOW BABY CHECK WORKS

Baby Check contains 19 simple checks which test for different symptoms or signs of illness. Each check has a score. Go through all the checks, then add up the scores. The higher the score the sicker the baby is likely to be.

Do not use Baby Check if your baby:—

- **stops breathing or goes blue**
- **has a fit**
- **cannot be woken**
- **is unresponsive and not aware of what is going on**
- **has glazed eyes and is not focusing on anything**
- **has been badly or seriously injured**

These conditions require urgent medical help

See page 14 if you think your baby is seriously ill.

HOW TO USE BABY CHECK

Read the booklet and try the checks when your baby is well. You will then find it easier to use if you are worried about your baby. If there are any checks you don't understand talk to your health visitor, midwife or doctor.

When you want to check your baby:

- **Undress your baby in a warm place.**
- **Carefully follow the instructions for each check.**
- **Write down the score.**
- **Only score if a check is obvious. If in doubt, don't score.**
- **After doing all 19 checks, add up the scores.**
- **Page 13 tells you what the total score means.**

Figure 4.4 Excerpts from Baby Check: a scoring system using 19 signs and symptoms of acute systemic illness in young babies less than 6 months of age. (Reproduced with kind permission of Dr Colin Morley. Addenbrookes Hospital, Cambridge. Full copies of Baby Check can be obtained from Lurista House, Stalham Road, Wroxham, Norwich NR12 8DV, UK.)

UNUSUAL CRY

You will know your baby's usual cries from hunger or tiredness. An unusual cry could be: weak, high-pitched, moaning, or painful.

If your baby has an unusual cry
Score 2

FLUIDS TAKEN

Think about the amount of fluid your baby usually takes in 24 hours (do not include solids). Then think about the amount of fluid he or she has actually taken in the last 24 hours.

If you are breast feeding you will know for how long your baby usually feeds, and whether your baby is sucking normally. Judge how much your baby is taking.

If your baby has taken a little less fluid than usual
Score 3

or

If your baby has taken about half as much fluid as usual
Score 4

or

If your baby has taken very little fluid
Score 9

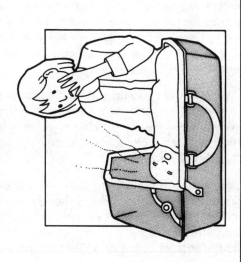

Table 4.4 Reducing the risk of cot death: The UK 'Back to Sleep' campaign (1991)

- **Sleeping position**
  Babies should be laid to sleep:
  (a) on their backs or
  (b) on their sides, with the lower arm forward to stop them rolling over
- **Temperature**
  Babies should be kept warm, but they must not be allowed to get too warm
- **Smoke-free**
  Create a smoke-free zone for your baby
- **Other recommended measures**
  If your baby seems unwell seek medical advice early and quickly

ANTICIPATED INFANT DEATH

Families' feelings

Having an infant die after prolonged or short illness, or knowing since birth that the baby is terminally ill, is an emotionally draining and physically testing situation. Death either at home or in hospital has its own benefits and costs. In hospital the family is living on 'foreign ground', at home there are nursing demands and fears of being alone with a dying child. Bozeman et al. (1955) studied the feelings of families whose children had leukaemia. The journey of bereavement reflects other situations where the child is known to be dying. Parents may start out with disbelief that their infant may die, especially if they appear to be only mildly ill. Then they may accept the diagnosis but deny the possibility of death (the baby only appears to be mildly ill), then accept the diagnosis and look for a cure by fighting for access to treatment. This may have a major impact on the family. The mother of 11-year-old Alicia Sims, who wrote a book, *Am I still a sister?* (1986), after Alicia's brother Austin died at the age of 13 months, wrote in the preface:

> We fought for Austin's life with a nationwide search for answers that forced us to send Alicia to live with my sister and brother-in-law. When we were finally able to reassemble the family we were faced with the destructive forces of cancer. We took our son home and tried to rebuild a family.

For some infants, there may be periods of readmission to hospital, aggressive treatment and a roller-coaster of hope and despair until the decision to accept palliative care, the chance to say goodbyes and to start anticipatory grieving.

The needs of the sick child can divide the family, with the mother involved in intensive nursing and the father being the provider at work and at home. After the infant dies there is another change in family dynamics. Raphael (1984) wrote, 'Not only is the child mourned as a person, but his role and meaning for each family member are mourned too.' There can be the emptiness for the mother, the father isolated having coped on his own, the siblings who now expect to have their parents' attention. Grandparents may experience the helplessness of being able to do nothing and seeing their grandchild going through the process of dying, which is normally associated with their own generation. For all the family there may be anger at 'Why us? Why our baby?'

How can Health Workers Help?

There are likely to be both community and hospital staff involved with families. There is no expectation that this section will cover issues that are dealt with by specialists in the area; it looks at some aspects of care and Chapter 7 provides a detailed view of 'Caring for the bereaved'. As discussed earlier in the chapter, our support is based on principles of: honesty, accessibility, valuing individuals and valuing ourselves. The aim of our care is to provide the resources to enable parents to survive the demands and strains of knowing for a brief or long time that their child is going to die.

What about ourselves?

We need to be aware of the coping mechansims that we may develop in a situation where we are not going to 'win' against death, which can be destructive to the family. This includes becoming distant and not involved as a 'professional', or being overprotective of the child and removing the parents' caring role.

Information and support during and after death

Families need to be part of whatever happens to their child and to look back and feel that they were part of the child' death. This means knowing:

- what the diagnosis and prognosis is;
- what to expect physically in terms of how their child will deteriorate or die (will it be quick, sudden, slow?);
- what the options are for support from hospital, community and settings such as Helen House, UK (specifically for dying children);
- what skills they need to care for their child, e.g. how to change the wound dressing of a baby with spina bifida;
- what to be prepared for in terms of sibling jealousy towards the attention that the dying child receives.

It means decision-making between parents and health workers. For example:

- looking at the benefits and harm of treatment;
- when to stop and take the time to say goodbyes;
- the provision of adequate analgesia and not an assumption that infants do not feel pain;
- planning goodbyes (where the infant will die, who will be there and what they would like to do).

There needs to be effective liason between hospital and community staff if families decide to go home with their child, so that they receive continuing support. In some areas this is provided by specialists from neonatal or paediatric areas; it also needs to include the community health workers who will be involved with the family long term.

After the Death

Immediately after the death families need an identified health worker to guide families through some of the choices and processes after death. This includes whether it is appropriate to have a postmortem, and if so, consenting after knowing the risks and benefits. We can use *'Guide to the Postmortem Examination'* by the Department of Health for discussion. Parents then need to know about collecting the Medical Certificate of Cause of Death (having a copy of it), registering the death, choosing burial or cremation and planning a funeral (Appendices 4 and 5). After the intensive input before the infant's death it is important that we do not allow the care to lapse after the death, so that it remains family-centred.

Longer term, families need the care that is discussed in Chapter 7. This includes planning visits, what to say and when to stop visiting. The care outlined earlier in this chapter, in general, applies to this situation; amendments necessary are with regard to the involvement of the Coroner and the sudden death, which are not features of this situation.

- Care in the days to the funeral (postmortem findings, memories, seeing their child);
- needs of siblings and grandparents;
- long-term care (plan for contact, purpose of visiting, practical information, e.g. benefits);
- how can families and friends help)
- future pregnancies (support and recognition of worries).

Finally, support through contact with other parents whose child has died, e.g. The Compassionate Friends, or other families with an infant with the same condition can be invaluable. We need to help families find the resources that they need and organisations such as Compassionate Friends can help to make contact with resource groups for rare medical conditions.

Key points
- Appreciate that even knowing that your infant is dying does not remove the impact of loss
- Recognise the effect a dying infant has on family dynamics
- Recognise the importance of parents owning and planning the death of their child

What About Ourselves?

Facing infant death, as health workers, raises a wealth of feelings. When we asked community health workers in Avon, UK about their experience of caring for families after a sudden unexpected death of their baby, the repeating themes were of vulnerability, inadequacy and awe at the pain the families felt. We need to acknowledge our humanness when we care for these families. We cannot remain behind a professional image; as we agreed in Chapter 1, we are 'real' people. Death shakes us to our core, and we question the whole purpose and meaning of life when an apparently healthy and well baby dies for 'no detectable reason'. It affects our practice, which is centred on saving life. It affects us personally, because many health workers have their own young children. These fears, sorrows and weaknesses should be acknowledged. We need to decide where our own support networks are and we would urge that this is not reliant on family and friends or a quick sentence over coffee with a colleague. Have a read through Chapter 10 and think about where you go at the end of your working day.

References

Barrett AM. Sudden death in infancy. In: Gardner D (ed) *Recent advances in paediatrics*. London: Churchill, 1954

Beckwith JB. *Observations of the pathological anatomy of the sudden infant death syndrome*. In: Bergman A, Beckwith JB, Ray CG (eds). *Sudden infant death syndrome*. Proceedings of the Second International Conference n Causes of Sudden Death in Infants. Seattle: University of Washington Press, 1970

Benfield DG, Leib SA, Volman JH. Grief response of parents to neonatal death and parent participation in deciding care. *Pediatrics* 1978; 62: 171

Bluglass K. The sudden infant death – psychological consequences and role of the medical team. *Annales Nestlé* 1992; 50: 81

Bozeman M, Orbach CE, Sutherland MM. Psychological impact of cancer and its treatment: the adaptation of mothers to threatened loss of their children through leukaemia. *Cancer* 1955; 8: 1

De Frain J, Taylor J, Ernst L. *Coping with sudden infant death*. Canada: DC Heath and Co., 1982

Golding J, Limerick S, Macfarlane A. *SID: patterns, puzzles and problems*. Shepton Mallett: Open Books Publishing, 1985

Harman WV. Death of my baby. *Br Med J* 1981; 282: 35

ISIDA. *The professional, the family and cot death*. Dublin: ISIDA, 4 North Brunswick Street, Dublin 7

Kalish RA. Dying and preparing for death: a view of families. In: Feifel H (ed) *New meanings of death*. New York: McGraw-Hill, 1977

Lewis E. Mourning by the family after a stillbirth or neonatal death. *Arch Dis Child* 1979; 54: 303

Lord JD. *When a baby suddenly dies*. Melbourne: Hill of Content, 1987

Mandell F, McAnulty E, Reece KM. Observations of paternal responses to sudden unanticipated infant death. *Pediatrics*; 1980, 65: 221

Miles M, Demi A. Guilt in bereaved parents. In: Rando T (ed) *Parental loss of a child*. Illinois: Research Press, 1986

Pearn J, Nixon J. Prevention of childhood drowning accidents. *Med J Aust* 1977; 1: 616

Raphael B. *The anatomy of bereavement*. London: Unwin Hyman, 1984

Sims A. *Am I still a sister?* Louisiana: Big A and C, 1986. Personal comments and letter with pictures of a sister whose baby brother died.

Vance JC, Foster WJ, Najman JM et al. Early parental response to sudden infant death, stillbirth or neonatal death. *Med J Aust* 1991; 155: 292

Williams RA, Nikolaisen SM. Sudden infant death syndrome: parents' perceptions and response to the loss of their infant. *Res Nurs Health* 1982; 5: 55

Wright B. *Sudden death*. London: Churchill Livingstone, 1991

Resources for Parents and Health Workers

Organisations

Compassionate Friends
6 Denmark Street, Clifton, Bristol BS1 5DQ, UK
Tel: 0272-292778
An international organisation of bereaved parents for other bereaved parents. Has information, leaflets, meetings and a postal library. Booklets that may be useful include: A father's grief; On inquests; To bereaved grandparents; Bereaved parents and the police; Helping younger brothers and sisters

Cot Death Research
8a Alexandra Parade, Weston-super-Mare, Avon, UK
Tel: 0934-613333
Provides befriending, information and leaflets and fundraises for research.

CRUSE
126 Sheen Road, Richmond, Surrey TW9 1UR, UK
Tel: 081-940-4818
Provides support to the bereaved by trained counsellors.

Foundation for the Study of Infant Deaths
35 Belgrave Square, London SW1X 8PS, UK
Tel: 071-235-0965
Provides befriending, local groups, information and leaflets and supports research.

ISIDA
4 North Brunswick Street, Dublin 7, Ireland
Tel: 01747007 (Dublin)
Organisation for the support of families after cot death.

Videos

I'm sorry your baby is dead but I can't tell you why. Made for professionals to understand the needs of bereaved parents.*You are not alone* and *After our baby died.* Two films on one video. The first gives the reactions of couples after SID and the second one is designed to provoke discussion on provision of counselling for families.

Both of these are for purchase or hire from FSID

Books for parents and health workers

Baby check – booklet for parents Obtained from PO Box 324, Wroxham, Norwich NR12 8EQ, UK. Scoring system to recognise illness in babies under 6 months of age.
Baum D, Dominica F, Woodward B. *Listen my child has a lot of living to do.* Oxford: Oxford University Press, 1990. Perspectives of caring for dying children.
Golding J, Limerick S, Macfarlane A. *SID: patterns, puzzles and problems.* Shepton Mallet: Open Books Publishing, 1985. A comprehensive book about research, theories and ideas about cot death and the support for families.
Lord J. *When a baby suddenly dies.* Melbourne: Hill of Content, 1987. Written by a counsellor whose baby died. A comprehensive view of the family's feelings and needs after cot death.
Murphy S. *Coping with cot death.* London: Sheldon Press, 1990. Personal perspective which is a comprehensive overview of theories, grieving and support for families.
Parker M. *Coping with cot death.* Auckland: Reed Methuen, 1986. Personal perspective of cot death and surviving
Ward B. *Healing grief.* London: Ebury Press, 1993

Leaflet

Guide to the postmortem examination – brief notes for parents and families who have lost a baby in pregnancy or early infancy, by the Department of Health, produced in consultation with the National Advisory Body for the Confidential Enquiry into Stillbirths and Deaths in Infancy, SANDS and FSID. Use the leaflet with parents as an aid to discussion.

Books for siblings

Johnson J, Johnson M. *Where's Jess?* Nebraska: Centring Corp. Picture book about a baby who died and his family.
Sims A. *Am I still a sister?* Louisiana: Big A and C, 1986. Personal comments and letter with pictures of a sister whose baby brother died.

Books for health workers

Rando T (ed). *Parental loss of a child*. Illinois: Research Press, 1986. Review of situations of parental loss.
Wright B. *Sudden death*. London: Churchill Livingstone, 1991. Discusses crisis management in situations of sudden death with reference to SUDI.

Training package

An ache in their hearts. A training package for professionals and parents to equip themselves as companions for bereaved families. Resources include training sessions, handouts for families, children's books and a video. Cost: A$250. Yvonne Connelly Tel: 07 840 8154. The University of Queensland, Department of Child Health, Clarence Court, Mater Children's Hospital, South Brisbane, Australia.

Chapter Five

Real Grieving? – Infertility and Adoption

Give me children or I shall die.

(Rachel said to Jacob, *Genesis 30:1*)

Within this chapter

1. Infertility as bereavement
2. What are the feelings and events on the journey of infertility?
3. What does infertility mean to families and friends?
4. How can health workers, families and friends help?
5. Who is in the adoption triangle?
6. What does it feel like in the adoption triangle?
7. How can health workers, families and friends help?

Introduction

The biblical story of Rachel's wish for sons, her response to give Jacob her maid Bilhah to have sons by, who were then raised by Rachel, illustrates the strength of desire to have children. It is also a story that demonstrates the interlinking of infertility, surrogacy and adoption which exists today. Couples who experience infertility or adoption share the loss of having a child of their own body, but they differ in their journey of adoption and infertility. This chapter considers infertility and adoption separately.

INFERTILITY

Infertility as bereavement

Bereavement is commonly associated with the death of a person, which is a visible endpoint. It also applies to developmental loss, where an individual's expected sequence of life events, such as finding a partner, becoming a parent and being a grandparent do not occur (Erikson 1977).

One of the major painful events an individual or couple may face in life is the invisible bereavement of infertility, which brings the loss of choice and a chance to have their own baby. Especially in industrialised societies, we have an expectation that fertility can be controlled with contraception and then organised to reappear at the time when it feels 'right' or 'convenient' to have a baby. To repeatedly not conceive, and to see the evidence at each menstrual period, is to face the fact that fertility is not an absolute right and that possibly years of contraception may have been unnecessary.

Infertility is generally defined as a situation where conception does not occur after a year (or two) of normal, unprotected intercourse (WHO 1975; New Zealand Infertility Society 1990). According to varying estimates, this situation confronts 1:7 to 1:15 couples in the Western world. It may be either primary, where a couple have never conceived, or secondary, where a couple have previously conceived and then do not subsequently conceive. Both situations bring particular questions and issues for couples.

For many men and women who experience *primary infertility*, never having had a pregnancy raises feelings of incompleteness, lack of fulfilment and questions about sexuality. Many cultures closely link perceptions of sexuality, body-image and gender, to the ability to be a parent. Centuries of societal and cultural definitions of success and fulfilment for women have centred on the mother role, whilst the fathering of children is valued as evidence of a man's virility and potency. We can realise that these values are questioned and violated for a couple who do not become pregnant. They are bereaved of fitting into the 'normal' pattern where this happens. The questions are, 'Why? What did I do wrong? Isn't it unfair when all we wanted was to have a child?'

For couples with *secondary infertility*, having a previous child or children and not conceiving again, there is the shock and loss of expectation that they will become pregnant as they did previously. The questions are, 'Why? What has changed?' We can also appreciate that this may be an issue in new relationships where one or other partner has a previous child and the expectation, based on existing evidence, is that a pregnancy and baby will be quickly achieved within this new partnership.

Feelings and events for couples on the journey of infertility

Initial bereavement for couples is the loss of hope, over a period of months, that pregnancy will occur quickly and easily. With this comes the shock at the delay, the sense of frustration and uncertainty of when and how pregnancy will occur. As time goes on couples may question the need to seek advice or treatment from an outsider in a private area of their life. Anxiety can precipitate or delay a visit to the general practitioner (GP) where discussion may reveal no obvious cause and reassuring advice is given: 'relax and go on practising'. Bland reassurances can add to couples' frustration and increasing sense of losing out; with feelings of using their sexuality to 'baby make' not 'love make.'

Edith talked about her experience of infertility and stressed that at the beginning, when she still hoped for a pregnancy, all she could think about was her fertile period, and how often they could make love during that time:

It became mechanical. Rushing home from work, doing it, not spontaneous, not fun; it was serious.

During the period of waiting, for a year or more, for investigations or referral to a specialist, couples may become increasingly uncertain, angry, bewildered or sad. They may even start a process of anticipatory grieving, not allowing themselves to appear hopeful for a pregnancy in the fear that they will be disappointed: 'Perhaps, we will never have a child.'

The option and decision to have 'tests' can be an opportunity to confront the uncertainty. There are some couples where one or both partners will reject investigations for fear of tests, doctors or negative findings that might shatter their sense of sexuality. It is a way of coping by avoiding confirmation of infertility, which brings with it a label and a bereavement of self, identity and the future. For many couples, having laparoscopies, keeping temperature charts and producing sperm specimens can feel impossibly invasive and humiliating, with a loss of dignity, privacy and intimacy in a sexual relationship which is opened up to public view. Uncertainty as to what to do and a continuing sense of time passing by can cause anger and resentment. There may appear to be no place to take these feelings; not to a partner who will get upset, or to an infertility specialist who is offering 'help'. We have probably all experienced situations that prevent anger being released or acknowledged. When it is turned inwards, it can become a fermenting volcano for later eruption. For others, any investigation is seen as positive and worthwhile as a means to accurately establish levels of fertility. One couple said:

All we want is to have a baby, the home is ready, we are ready. If we can't get a baby on our own – then we'll do anything that they tell us to do – if it will help.

Depending on the findings of investigations, there may be either a diagnosis of infertility or no explanation for the lack of a pregnancy. Having infertility confirmed may be the end of uncertainty, but it is the beginning of the bereavement of hope that a pregnancy will occur either easily or possibly ever. It creates a psychological crisis of values and identity (Kraft et al. 1980), with questions of 'Who am I, if I'm not going to be a parent? Where am I going in life?'

We may see couples where the infertility is conjugal – 'owned' by the couple – or it may be assigned to one or other partner. Infertility has traditionally been viewed as a female 'problem' (Christie 1980), irrespective of whether the physiological cause of the infertility lies with the woman. It is generally assumed that women, who receive reminders of non-pregnancy in the form of periods, experience more distress than their partners at the diagnosis of infertility. Some studies indicate that the distress caused by infertility is not gender-related. What differs is the coping response, with women seeking social support and men seeking distraction in their work (Berg et al. 1991). We see this pattern of grieving in other areas of reproductive loss, such as stillbirth and cot death. It may reflect genetic differences in coping styles, but in Western society it also represents cultural expectations that men are 'emotionally strong'. There are different gender meanings and responses to infertility in different cultures, depending on the link between self-identity and proven parental role.

The diagnosis of infertility can result in a bereavement that is *incomplete* or *complete*, depending on whether there are options for treatment to become pregnant. *Incomplete* bereavement refers to couples who need to mourn the loss of achieving a pregnancy unaided, but for whom options of treatment remain.

Feelings of couples having infertility treatment – incomplete bereavement

Their bereavement is often placed 'on hold' because they do not know whether any of the treatments will give them the baby they want. Couples having treatment may enter what feels like a 'roller-coaster' of hope and despair as conception does not follow treatment(s). In can be the peaks and troughs that highlight the loss of having a child in their lives, causing anxiety and depression (Newton et al. 1990). The desperate need to have a child means that families are willing to pay almost any price. This was demonstrated in a survey of 40 women in Australia, who responded to a request to share their experience of in vitro fertilisations (IVF). One woman shared her feelings of desperation regardless of the personal risks. She noted:

> I was worried about the lack of information. I knew we were guinea-pigs but I could not find any literature. Also, I desperately wanted IVF to work . . . and to believe the doctors who told me not to worry. (Klein 1989, p. 21–22)

Individuals and couples may find it difficult to know at what point to put a final end on hopes of treatment. Some may never lose the hope that one day they will have their own baby. Anna, who I met after she eventually adopted two children, said:

I always hope, even though the fertility drugs and the surgery and the treatment for endometriosis failed and then IVF failed – there's always the hope. Now I'm drinking herbal teas . . . you never know.

There has been a rapid expansion in treatment to assist reproduction, ranging from drugs to treat endometriosis, drugs for non-ovulation, artificial insemination by husband (AIH) or donor (AID) to IVF and surrogacy (see the glossary for detailed definitions). With these treatments has come a huge range of social, legal, ethical and emotional issues. In this chapter, we will only focus on the bereavement aspects; for a more detailed discussion of these issues we would refer the reader to texts such as *Baby Making* (Downie 1988). For example, AID can result in the husband bereaved of his own biological child, having a social parenting role in contrast to his partner who has both roles. The reverse happens in surrogacy where the father may have biological and social roles. What effect does it have on the couple's relationship if surrogacy involves the father having sexual intercourse to create the pregnancy with another woman, as opposed to providing a semen sample for transfer to the uterus of the surrogate mother by mechanical means? In the former situation the wife may be left to mourn the loss of a monogamous sexual relationship as the price for the child.

In this section we will look at the common themes of loss for couples who face the label of 'infertility' permanently, or who have the experience of treatment (an umbrella term that covers a variety of methods).

Feelings about having no treatment or unsuccessful treatment

Specialists providing treatment may set an endpoint on the treatment but point out that the possibility of pregnancy always remains. For many couples, treatment such as IVF is the height of their hopes, and this is supported by media stories such as 'Fifty-nine-year-old woman delivers twins by IVF in 1993'. Current pregnancy rates per IVF cycle range widely and may be as high as 30% (Hull et al. 1992), but that still leaves many couples with no baby. Oke (1990) points out that infertility is a journey to an acceptance of childlessness with 'acknowledgement that your hopes weren't to be and that you have to make some readjustments. It is not something you suddenly do, but rather gradually'. That gradual process may be through the ups and downs of treatment.

For some couples there may be no option for treatment to secure their own biological child. For example, a woman without a uterus faces a complete bereavement of biological childbearing, or the couple may jointly decide not to pursue treatment. Coming to terms with permanent childlessness involves mourning lost hopes and a changed identity, which still needs to be a valued identity. 'Coping with your infertility means coming to accept yourself as a childless person . . . without children, no more, no less' (Pfeffer and Woolett 1983). This means valuing aspects of life and self, and the opportunity to develop relationships, work and leisure activities (Goodyer 1988). Acceptance may be tangled in the difficulties of valuing self without children. Some couples may cope by withdrawing, feeling stigmatised as a failure and having anger directed at themselves, health workers or the world (Raphael-Leff 1991). Others find strength and pleasure in other aspects of their lives. For some individuals it may be impossible to reach this acceptance. For example, access to reproductive technology in many countries is barred to couples in terms of treatment costs or impossible travel distances to centres of expertise. For these couples the question that may gnaw away, preventing acceptance of their childlessness, is: 'What if we had had treatment . . .?'

The difficulty for all individuals is the lack of an identifiable 'rites of passage' ceremony, which so many cultures use to mark life changes such as marriage, christening or funeral. Infertility and childlessness have no visible markers to focus on and to grieve the loss of; there are no memories to internalise or to cry over; there is only the invisible, uncertain state of 'If . . .'. Feelings and behavioural responses follow a similar pattern to those mourning death, including: *shock and disbelief* ('It can't be true'); *denial* ('We will get pregnant soon'); *anger and guilt* at trying to locate a cause or understanding of the situation; and *despair* at the loss of the creating, nurturing elements of the parental role. Acknowledgement of the bereavement depends on the individual having a good support network and a strong sense of self-worth as a person, who is not solely defined in a parenting role (Raphael 1984).

The relationship where infertility/childlessness is located can be a source of strength and solace, or tension and division (Cook et al. 1989). Survival of the relationship depends on the ability to understand that each are different, to take turns at being strong or weak, to share activities and to have time alone. For some individuals with pre-existing stressors such as unemployment, infertility can precipitate a more complicated grief (discussed further in Chapters 7 and 10). This means that for some people, psychotherapy is a helpful option to centre their new sense of identity (Raphael-Leff 1989).

We need to make brief reference to those families who do become pregnant. It can be a time of joy and rejoicing, equally it can be a time of nervous tension and hope. Getting a balance between the two states is a necessary part of coming to terms with infertility.

> The long awaited conception. . . . The hallmark of overvalued pregnancy is a heightened emotional investment in the process which takes on the quality of a Supreme Court Trial. The woman feels her ability to produce a live, healthy 'special baby' is being tested from moment to moment. (Raphael-Leff 1991)

This is a dramatic quote about pregnancies after infertility or previous death of a child. It conveys the sense of desperation and urgency for

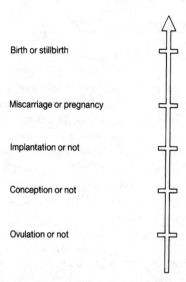

Birth or stillbirth

Miscarriage or pregnancy

Implantation or not

Conception or not

Ovulation or not

Figure 5.1 Early steps on the ladder of parenthood

parents to protect the pregnancy and the child. Unless there is a perspective of valuing themselves with or without a child, then the consequence can be an unbalanced parent–child relationship.

What does infertility mean to the family and friends?

Couples have to face a decision of whether to acknowledge their infertility to family, friends and work colleagues and how to cope with their reactions. Family may be supportive, embarrassed, silent, recriminating about lifestyles causing infertility or sad at the loss of grandchildren. Friends may be caring, sharing, honest or silent on the subject. These reactions can act as powerful pressure to make the couple feel either supported or isolated. A couple's decision not to share news of infertility or treatment can deny their access to support, leaving them open to constant teasing or jibing comments of 'When are you going to get pregnant – need some help?' or 'Getting the best of two incomes are you?' These comments reflect views that will exist in our society until there is acknowledgement of the many couples who are childless through no choice of their own. For many families and friends, evidence of fertility is holding a child in their arms. It may be difficult for them to appreciate that for these couples there are numerous steps on the ladder of parenthood accompanied by bereavements such as non-ovulation, failure to implant and miscarriage (Fig. 5.1).

What can Health Workers do to Help?

Who are the health workers involved?

It may be the infertility team (consultant, nurse and counsellor) providing specialist care, or it may be the GP, health visitor and midwife who provide general, long-term care in the community. The purpose of this section is to review what the latter can offer; there is no intention to detail the specialised counselling offered by an infertility team. The latter is now a developing practice in the UK; since the Human Fertilisation and Embryology Act became law in 1991, there has been a requirement for every licensed fertility clinic to provide all clients with the opportunity for counselling.

The aim of our care

Our care is based on similar principles to other bereavement situations.

- *Honesty* – of explanation and information to individuals about what is happening.
- *Accessibility* – for individuals to contact us when they wish to.
- *Valuing individuals* – that the same events represent a different experience for each person on the basis of personal, cultural and social beliefs.
- *Valuing ourselves* – that we have something to offer, even if it is only the fact that we care about people.

We need to be clear about the aims of care. We cannot solve the problem or get it 'right' – only having their own child would do that. Our aims are to help make the bereavement more bearable, and for individuals to reach, in their own way, a point of acceptance in their lives. Chapter 7 explores 'Care for the bereaved' generally with reference to parents whose child dies, but many of the issues apply to infertile couples. I have outlined some of the specific points of our care in both *information* and *support* roles.

Self-awareness

In Chapter 1 we explored some of our own feelings and appreciated that, as health workers, we need to be 'real' people, with real feelings, to care for people. To listen and share with individuals we do not have to undergo the same experience, but we do need to reflect on our own feelings and attitudes. What is the language about infertility that we use? Does it convey stigma of failure (phrases such as 'Trying to get pregnant, failing to conceive, being barren'). Terms such as 'Hoping to get pregnant, wanting a child' reflect the more positive side. What are our own views on reproductive technology? Can we appreciate the all-consuming need for some people to try anything to become a parent? Equally, we should not feel embarrassed at an infertile couple's knowledge of our own pregnancies or children. If we feel uncomfortable in being honest about who we are, then we are seeking to avoid pain and protect the couple. In doing so we are making the loss invisible and giving no place for their pain to be talked about.

Information During the Time of Questions, Tests, Answers and Treatments

Planning care

Any health worker who is the initial contact for a couple who are worried about not conceiving, needs to take time to do the following.

- Listen to fears of their infertility and any special concerns about their private lives.
- Provide practical information for questions as 'Is it my job? Is it what I eat? How quickly should we expect to get pregnant?'
- Make a plan of action to give clients a sense of control, because many couples feel that they are dismissed with the reassurance 'practise, keep trying', which increases stress, itself a potential cause of infertility (Wright et al. 1990).

The timing of referral to a gynaecologist for investigations varies, but it is generally advocated after 1 year of unprotected intercourse that has not resulted in pregnancy. We need to remember that a year is a long, long time in a relationship that is waiting for a child. The referral offers the couple the opportunity for detailed information, tests, answers, treatments and counselling support. Many centres now employ an infertility nurse who provides specialist counselling to prepare couples for the multiple mini-bereavements of the ups and downs of undergoing tests and treatment, or refer clients to a counsellor with specialist knowledge.

Providing information about infertility

Information is a powerful tool, which we should not underestimate, during bereavement. It enables individuals to understand and feel in control of what is happening to them. Otherwise, there can be the sensation of being in a canoe, shooting white water rapids with no ability to plan or steer to a destination. One couple who shared their experience said:

We always felt lost, not knowing what was going to be offered next, we knew what was happening now, but not what was round the corner.

Often in response to listening we may see a need for information, either at a basic or detailed level, according to the individual. Initially it may

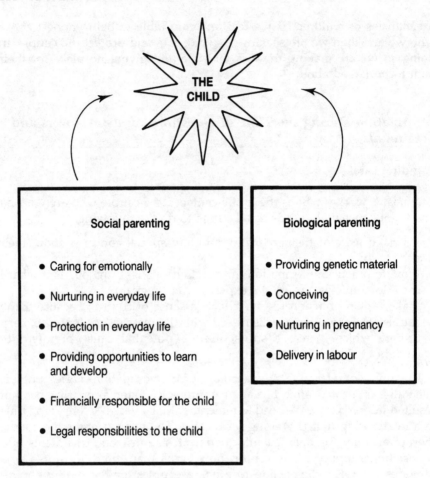

Figure 5.2 Different aspects of parenting.

answer questions of confusion and disbelief such as 'Why, who else has this? What caused it?' Then it may respond to the *guilt* and *anger*, placing in proportion overriding concerns such as whether previous sexually transmitted diseases, irradiation or age at first intercourse caused the infertility. Reaffirming known information about investigations or options for treatment is important at the point when individuals may want to *deny* what is happening.

Locating other sources of information and support

We need to ensure individuals have access to other sources of information and support specific to their own experience. This might be information in books and leaflets, or meeting other individuals with infertility through established self-help groups such as CHILD or the National Association for the Childless (see resources at the end of the chapter). Sharing others' perceptions of the same experience may have a value and strength that nothing else can.

Exploring other options

For some couples, having a child by any means is an all-consuming desire. It may mean adoption or even surrogacy. It is vital that neither is presented as another treatment option for infertility. These situations require clear and balanced consideration, because the couple need to recognise their loss of biological parenthood and accept the option of social parenthood (Fig. 5.2). Whereas adoption is a more established social institution, surrogacy remains a contentious issue because of the ethical and legal dilemmas. Currently, under the UK Human Fertilisation and Embryology Act (1991), a court can legalise the adoption of a child from a surrogate mother to a couple, where the gametes of either the husband or wife are used to create the embryo. Other avenues that need to be discussed with the couples include fostering, change of employment or environment as a response to the opportunities which exist because they are childless.

Supporting Couples During the Experience of Infertility

Listening not doing

We need to be able to listen to feelings, questions and confusions. Infertility represents a whole series of questions, choices and decisions of 'What to do? Why? Who to tell?'

- Listening to feelings and accounts of their experience is tangible acknowledgement of the individual's loss, which, whilst invisible, is none the less painful.
- Part of caring is asking simply 'How are you feeling?' and 'How can I help?' In the survey of women in Australia undergoing IVF, one woman shared how depressing she felt it could be.

  I felt like a baby machine, no one was interested in me as a person. I was just a chook with growing eggs inside and if they didn't grow properly it was my own fault. (Klein 1989, p. 26)

- It means ensuring that each person has *social support* for their bereavement: 'Do family and friends know and if not will you tell them? What might their response be?' 'If they know, can you talk to them about what is happening and do they have enough accurate information to understand what infertility means?'

- Helping to develop a sense of self-worth and perspective to infertility might include suggesting:

  couples having identified times to share activities together;

  valuing times with family and friends;

  recognising that individuals grieve differently – one partner will not be the same as the other;

  developing leisure activities to balance their lives against the consuming uncertainties of infertility.

Support in pregnancy

It is very important that we listen when couples do become pregnant. They may need considerable time and support from maternity care providers to address fears of 'something going wrong'. Again, care is largely not about action and 'doing' but offering time. It may take extra antenatal visits and explanations, teaching parents to be aware of fetal movements, or photos of the baby on ultrasound scan. Appendix 9 outlines aspects of care for families who are pregnant after a baby has died; some of the issues about extra Tender Loving Care (TLC) apply. Couples' fears need to be valued as part of a very precious pregnancy. Equally, there needs to be a valuing of themselves and the child as normal, real people to prevent the baby being overprotected and for them to be able to enjoy *being* parents.

Take a proactive, long-term role

As health workers we need to develop society's awareness of infertility issues. Having a low sperm count, a delay in conceiving, or using fertility drugs are not things that just happen to people in the newspaper, they are part of our everyday community. Accepting this fact can remove the stress of 'failure' and help provide a safe place for individuals to acknowledge their worries or their infertility. Finally, we need to change the values in societies that place such a premium on the success of producing a baby.

How can Family and Friends Help?

The care that family and friends can offer after bereavement resulting from death is discussed in Chapter 7. Many of the points discussed there apply to infertility. The key points are:

- Showing that they care and being sensitive to the possibility of infertility – not always asking 'When is my nephew or grandchild coming?'

- Finding out about infertility to have some insight into it and not confused perceptions and stigmas.
- Being honest, not avoiding couples or not telling them about their own children and pregnancies.
- Practical help may be offering a lift to the hospital at odd times of the day or week for treatment to coincide with hormone levels or ovulation.

Key points
- Appreciate the high rates of infertility in Western society – it touches the lives of many couples.
- Appreciate the unique grief each individual has who experiences infertility – their feelings are based on personal, social and cultural beliefs.
- Recognise the bereavement effects that infertility or childlessness can have on self-esteem, sexuality and identity.
- Reflect on your own attitudes to infertility, e.g. phrases such as 'trying to get pregnant', and our own feelings of possible embarrassment that we have been 'fortunate' to have children.
- Appreciate the value of listening and acknowledging feelings to make the loss visible.
- Assist family and friends to take a support role.
- Appreciate and locate resources for individuals, both written information and contact with local and national self-help organisations.

ADOPTION

Who is in the 'triangle of adoption'?

Adoption is a social institution which exists across cultures and over centuries. It has only been legalised in the UK since 1926. With regard to children, it is the transfer of rights and responsibilities for the child's welfare from birth parents to adoptive parents. However, a transfer on paper does not transfer, begin or end feelings in relationships. Adoption involves three parties (adopters, adoptees and birth parents) interlinked in what has been called the 'adoption triangle' (Sorosky et al. 1978), which can be a triangle of support or tension. For the three main parties there are obvious bereavements including loss of proof of fertility, loss of knowledge of one's origins and loss of a child. Less visible are the bereavements of other people such as grandparents, foster parents and existing or future siblings (Fig. 5.3).

Who is adopted? Babies have traditionally been at a premium for adop-

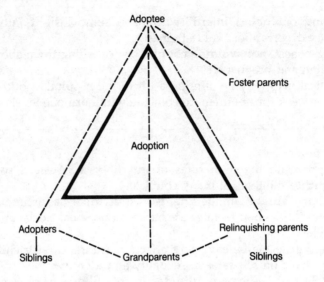

Figure 5.3 Relationships in the triangle of adoption (adapted from Sorosky *et al.*, 1978)

tion, allowing adopters to begin parenting almost at the point of birth. However, changes in social attitudes to solo parenting and access to contraceptives have meant that the number of babies for adoption, in most industrialised countries, has fallen dramatically. There has been a shift to adoption of children who are older, handicapped or from overseas.

Who adopts? Adopters have a wide range of reasons for adopting, including: couples with infertility; couples who have a hereditary disease; birth relations of the adoptee, e.g. grandparents, step relations after remarriage; foster parents; existing families wanting to offer a child a home; and situations of surrogacy.

Who places for adoption? There are equally a wide range of reasons why birth parents place a child for adoption: teenage mother; solo mothers; and families who feel unable to care for more children.

The process of non-familial adoption, in most western societies, is regulated by adoption agencies registered with the Government. In the UK this may be either a social services department or a voluntary group such as the Catholic Children's Society. The last 10 years have seen a radical change in the philosophy surrounding adoption, moving from the assumption that all ties with the relinquishing birth parents can be severed, to a child-centred 'open' approach that retains ongoing contact between parents who are relinquishing their child, the adopters and the adoptee. Whilst adoption has traditionally been seen as the province of social workers, we can appreciate that numerous other health workers (GPs, midwives and health visitors) are involved at different stages, in the bereavement process.

What does it feel like in the adoption triangle?

The feelings and reactions to loss are explored in more depth in Chapters 1 and 7. Some of the specific issues arising in adoption are discussed below.

Birth parents

Generally, it is the birth mother who places the child for adoption, and unless she is married to the father, she is the only one to sign the agreement to the adoption. We know little about fathers' feelings or choices, and realistically they probably do not receive the time and attention that they should have. We stress the need to reconsider the roles and needs of fathers, but in this section we focus on the birth mother and what is known of her feelings. The scale of birth mothers' grief has probably never been fully recognised by health workers. Howe (1988) estimates that currently in the UK there are 600 000 relinquishing mothers.

A mother may have anticipated, during pregnancy, relinquishing the baby for adoption; or she may have had a child in care who was then placed for adoption; or she may have placed her body in a contractual relationship as a surrogate mother. In all situations, the adoption order formalises the relinquishment, as a marker of the changing relationship with loss of legal, moral and nurturing rights of parenthood. Similar to the situation of divorce, grieving may be particularly difficult because of the inability to reach a 'closure' of the relationship. On paper the separation is completed, but the heart and mind know that the child is not 'dead' and has a life elsewhere with other people. Another aspect that makes grieving difficult is the lack of sympathy. When a person dies, community sympathy and support is generally offered to the family, because the death is perceived as a major loss outside the control of surviving family members. However, the perceptions of adoption are similar to those of abortion; the birth parent is seen to have made a voluntary choice to be bereaved, which denies them the 'right' to grieve (Howe 1988). The experiences of Donna illustrate the pain of adoption:

> When I look at my relinquishment paper now, I see my little childish teenage signature all rounded. And that was that, that was the absolute end, over, it was done. It was never discussed in my family ever again, never, not once, until I brought it up in recent times. My mom went back to work, I went back to bed and the women in the blue suits went back to the welfare office and that was the absolute end as far as they were concerned. Of course, it wasn't the end of it for me by any means; it was the beginning. But I didn't know it at the time. What I do know now is that within about six weeks I started taking drugs and I didn't stop for ten years. ('I was officially and formally declared immoral' in Townsend and Perkins 1991, pp. 186–7)

We can all appreciate that the denial or secrecy surrounding adoption can create confusion of self-identity. The birth mother's role is an anomaly as both a 'mother' and a 'non-mother' (Roll et al. 1986). How does she introduce herself and answer questions such as 'Do you have any children? Are you a mother?' Workshops with birth mothers reveal that the effects of the loss may be felt deeply over a period exceeding 40 years after the adoption (Post Adoption Centre (PAC) 1990). For many there is no acceptance of the bereavement, nor any professional help to do so, because contact with the adoption agency generally ceases after the adoption order is passed. An Australian survey found that women who had long-term support and counselling had lower rates of anxiety, depression, physical ailments and substance abuse, which illustrates the need for bereavement care (Winkler and Van Keppell 1984).

Opponents of open adoption argue that ongoing contact with the adoptive family, whether in writing or face to face, can hinder the process of accepting loss. Certainly, without sufficient support, it can be very difficult and painful. Sara, a woman in her thirties, looked back on her experience of having her child adopted 15 years ago by family friends. At the time, it was an unorthodox arrangement, and it meant that she stayed in contact with the family. She had feelings of gladness for her child in the home he had, of frustration when the adopters did not parent as she would have, and of sadness at missing out on his childhood. Whilst she had ongoing counselling, she felt that for her the contact was a 'bittersweet pill'. Open adoption can have benefits when we consider that completing the tasks of grieving (discussed in Chapter 1) often needs tangible memories. Birth parents often need memorabilia of their baby (e.g. cot card or name bands at birth) to be able to mourn them (Ritchie 1989). The value of open adoption can be for the memories to develop and strengthen to give a reality to the grieving of total parenting as well as celebrating being the biological parent. Given the lack of opportunity or support to grieve, we can appreciate that for some women, a transition point in the future, such as a new partner or a pregnancy, may precipitate a flood of memories that have previously been denied.

Adopters

In accepting another person's child, adopters experience the loss of normal expectations of parenthood where biological and social parenting are synonymous (Fig. 5.2). Brebner et al. (1985) note that a successful adopter has 'special tasks' of bereavement, which may include acknowledging one's own infertility, telling a child they are adopted and becoming attached to a child who is not of one's body. Unresolved bereavement of not having their own biological child can have confused feelings of rivalry and competition with the birth parents (Smith 1984). One of the strengths of open adoption is that continuing contact can help to understand and acknowledge where the child has come from and to live with reality. Especially important for adopters is coming to terms with the loss of their own 'ideal' child. Otherwise, the 'nature versus nurture' question arises meaning that unexpected or unwanted behaviour in the adopted child may not be accepted as part of the child but attributed to the genetic origins of the child (Kornitzer 1968).

Increasingly, we are seeing in remarriages a situation where one partner in a couple is the birth parent and the other is the adopting parent. This creates complex family dynamics, because one partner may be experiencing a sense of loss or isolation outside a blood relationship, and the other may have a sense of joy or relief at integrating different members into the 'family unit'. Equally the other birth parent, now divorced from the partner who has remarried, may contest the adoption, feeling angry and bereaved at having their position usurped. If parents are unable to recognise and respond to their own feelings of loss, the children may suffer.

An extra dimension of grieving for adopters occurs when they adopt a child with special needs. There are a range of definitions for this term, but in general it means a child other than a healthy infant who has needs that relate to physical or mental disability, emotional problems or other factors such as abuse. In these instances, adopters may be involved in grieving for the loss of potential for the child *and* grieving for themselves *and* starting a parent–child relationship, all at the same time. A parent who wrote about their experience in the Parent to Parent Information on Adoption Services (PPIAS) book *Adoption* said:

> Our son Peter, now 13 years old, arrived in our family when he was nearly seven, with a history of rejection and lack of care. I can remember being very hurt initially, as the slightest physical contact with me would cause him to shrug me off, although he was prepared to accept affection from my husband. (Austin 1987, p. 67)

For many adoption agencies, there is a rigorous screening process before couples are approved, followed by the waiting period for placement, and then the statutory supervisory period during which the birth mother may contest the placement. All of this may combine to make the adopter feel that they are in a 'no-win' situation. They may experience the loss of their self-esteem by constantly feeling insecure and 'judged', bereaved of the chance to be everyday parents who are not constantly scrutinised. Questions such as 'Why did we do this?' 'Will the child ever settle?' may feel impossible to voice, because of perceived expectations that adopters will be superhuman, approved parents and that any doubts could jeopardise their application for an adoption order (Fraser and Howe 1989).

Adoptees

The knowledge of being adopted brings a wealth of questions, ideas, losses and few answers. One of the hardest ideas for any of us is that of being given away or rejected. Most cultures place a value and premium on family relationships, with adages such as 'blood is thicker than water'. Adoption goes against the sense of family commitment. Misperceptions are easy: as one child said, 'I must have been really bad to have been sent away.' People who know that they are adopted face the loss of their birth parents, which either involves grieving or denying the implicit sense of rejection: 'Why didn't they want me?' (Triseliotis 1973). In Chapter 1, we explored the importance of self-esteem in our hierarchy of needs to be a whole person.

The answer prior to 'open adoption' was to deny the adoption and therefore 'spare' the child the loss. The consequences on adoptive family relationships can be devastating at the point the secret is discovered, causing the adoptee to lose faith and trust in the adopters (Chennells 1987). The idea we have seen repeatedly in relation to bereavement and children is the idea that they should be 'protected' from anything painful. In reality it does not teach them to face life, but it does protect parents from the discomfort of having to answer questions.

Adoption can bring an unresolved loss of identity for some adoptees – the feeling of 'Where do I belong?' They can feel the pain, confusion and anger of bereavement, directed towards everyone who put them in this position.

> Whenever my parents told me off or wanted me to do something I didn't want to do, I'd say 'My real mum would have let me' or 'She'd have understood.' I didn't mean it – I'd no idea whether she would or not – but it was a way of getting back at them. Somehow they put up with me even when I was trying to be so awkward like this. I even ran away twice but I went back. Later, when I met my first mother, I felt I had much more in common with them than with her after all. I didn't realise till years later how much this must have hurt them. (The experience of one adoptee cited in Chennells 1987, p. 23)

Events such as teenage years, partnership and pregnancy are tradition-ally a time of adjustment and changing identity (Caplan 1965; Erikson 1977), which may precipitate the need to confront or deny aspects of their bereavement. Similar to birth parents, the unresolved nature of the loss, with the knowledge that birth parents are alive, may lead the adoptee to fantasise about their lives in fairy-tale style or have an urge to make contact with them. For adoptees who have not been part of an open adoption, acceptance of being adopted and having four parents may only be possible after making contact with birth parents and seeing the reality of their biological origins (Walby and Symons 1990). One adoptee who shared their experience wrote:

> I had been warned by the social worker not to expect too much from this meeting and I did not expect an instant wonderful family to rush forward to embrace me, because I knew we had spent 36 years leading our own lives and growing apart. (Austin 1987, p. 95)

Equally it can be a very painful step to take, because meeting one's birth parents removes the hopes and dreams and gives the opportunity to ask 'Why did you give me away?'

Bereavements of other members in the adoption process

Foster parents who have undertaken physical and emotional care of the child, whilst knowing it was for a limited duration, still have a bereavement and a sadness at saying goodbye.

We can appreciate that *grandparents* in adopters' and birth parents' families may have feelings of sadness, anger and frustration at not having their own grandchild. For both sets of grandparents it may be difficult or impossible to express their real feelings at the choice of their own child to relinquish or to adopt a child. Sometimes things are said in anger and shock that cannot be easily unsaid, resulting in division of parents and grandparents. For the grandparents, whose grandchild is placed for adoption, it may take time before they are ready to assume the role of grandparents. For grandparents of an adopted child, there may be fierce anger at not having their own bloodline continued. Conversely, facing the situation and acknowledging it may make grandparents a source of strength and joy in the family. We always need to be aware of the different meanings placed on adoption by people of different generations and appreciate that this may be part of their responses. It will reflect social and cultural beliefs. For example, for the current generation of European grandparents, Victorian views of illegitimacy and immorality preceding the necessity for adoption still exist.

Siblings in the adopting family may lose their position in the family hierarchy creating excitement, enjoyment, anger or behaviour disturbances. Future children in the birth family may be oblivious for decades to the existence of a sibling who was adopted and the unexpected revelation can be a gain and a loss.

What can Health Workers do to Help?

Who are the health workers involved?

Health workers based in the community and in hospital such as the GP, health visitor and midwife are the focus of this section. No expectation is placed in this chapter that they will provide in-depth counselling of losses experienced, only support and information. We recognise that social workers employed in this area will receive training on issues and management.

The aim of our care

The clear role of health workers mentioned above is to:

- provide continuing contact and information where appropriate;
- identify those participants who are having difficulty grieving and refer for specialist help as needed;
- provide space and opportunity for individuals to express and explore their feelings.

We need to be clear that we cannot provide a solution to each individual and we can only help them on their journey to reach an acceptance of the place adoption has in their lives. It depends on the individual, their resources and perspective, as illustrated in Fig. 7.1. In particular, there will be cultural issues in response to adoption and bereavement (see Chapter 9), particularly arising in transcultural adoptions. In a broader context of bereavement, Chapter 7 explores issues that are relevant to this situation, such as easing grief, assessing needs of families and contracts of care.

Similar to the outline in the infertility section, in our care we need:

- *Honesty*, in terms of self-awareness and giving information.
- *Being there*, to listen when needed.
- *Valuing individuals*, having different responses to adoption.
- *Valuing ourselves*, as having something to offer.

Self-awareness

As we established in Chapter 1, in all aspects of bereavement care it is important that we reflect on our own knowledge and attitudes. We are often unaware that our choice of words and actions betrays our views of, and attitudes towards, individuals and events. Brebner et al. (1985) note that carers need to be 'free of prejudice concerning illegitimacy, heredity, adoption'. This includes having an awareness and sensitivity to the use of words such as 'real', 'natural', 'first', 'birth' or 'relinquishing' mother/ parent. It often feels that there are no comfortable options. The words 'real' or 'first' may imply that adoptive parents are substandard or substitutes, which has led to the current usage of 'relinquishing parents'.

We need to be aware of the traditional view of adoption, based on the 'rescue motive', where a child is adopted into a new family who can provide material and emotional advantages that exceed those of the birth parents, who may then bear a stigma of failure, incompetency or inadequacy. Kirk (1964) points out that negative attitudes to adoption from individuals and society can prevent any of the participants resolving their grief and sharing their secrets. Appreciating this, we can recognise the importance of giving participants open acknowledgement of what has happened and to be comfortable with ourselves as being part of this. In addition, we need to be aware that, traditionally, adoption has meant adoption of a child by a married couple; it represented success and a stable society. We are now seeing changes with single people, lesbian and homosexual couples seeking to adopt.

Information Before, During and After Adoption

A practical component of listening may be responding to hearing the need for specific information to help individuals resolve either their uncertainties or adjust to change. Information can be a tool to do this, because it can help answer some of the questions 'Why?', which are part of bereavement in phases of denial, disbelief and guilt.

Information as potential adopters

Couples contemplating adoption may come for advice. Discussion and resources (books, self-help groups and adoption agencies) are needed to help couples explore the unique elements of bereavement involved in adoptive parenthood, which include:

- the elements of biological versus social parenting (Fig. 5.2);
- the process of adoption from assessment, approval and placement to the adoption order being passed (Fig. 5.4);
- imagining feelings of accepting a child who is not one's own;
- how to tell a child they are adopted;
- imagining how to cope at times when the child asks about their birth parents;
- what would be involved in open adoption;
- their views on their ability to cope with children with special needs.

Useful introductory reading is the British Agencies for Adoption and Fostering (BAAF) booklet, written by Chennells and Hammond (1987) *Adopting a child* and Jane Rowe's book *Yours by choice* (1982). At the beginning she writes:

> Successful adoptions grow from happiness and security and a mature desire for parenthood on the part of both husband and wife. Sometimes deep humanitarian concern leads to the adoption of unwanted, disturbed or handicapped children who so greatly need the security of loving parents. If you find that, on balance, you are more concerned with what you can do for a child than with what the child can do for you then you can feel pretty sure you are starting out with the right approach . . .'. (Rowe 1982, p. 17)

Practical choices as relinquishing parents

Initially the choice has to be whether the mother (or parents) feel certain that they want to place the child for adoption, or the choice may be out of

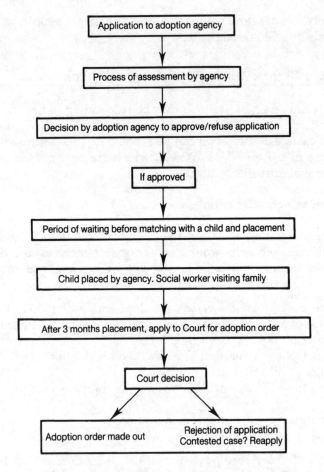

Figure 5.4 The process of adoption in the UK.

their hands. In the situation where the mother chooses the adoption, we need to remember that, like any bereavement, a key factor is having someone or something to mourn; this requires forming memories rather than fantasies. This means asking the question 'What memories would you like to *give* to your child and to *retain* of your child?' One suggestion is that the mother gives the adopters and child an *origins box* (the adoption agency may help to compile this), which gives tangible roots to the adoptee as they grow up. In open adoption this might be added to, or explored, during contacts between birth parent and adoptee. Items could include:

- a written life-history of the family (appearance, medical details, interests, education, jobs, place of birth);
- photos, videos and audiotapes of the family members (possibly with photos of them holding the child);

- items of clothing or jewellery;
- a lock of hair from the mother/father;
- a hand/footprint of the mother/father;
- a book or object of interest to the mother/father;
- a written letter to the child;
- copies of health notes relating to the child, e.g. antenatal or labour notes, cot card completed at birth, if the mother gives permission.

Then we can suggest that the parents keep similar items such as photos, a lock of hair, a handprint of the child, a piece of clothing and health records for their own *memory box*.

We may also be involved with parents, adopters and adoption agency social workers in planning *how* the birth parents say goodbye to the child. Choices include: where to do it, who is there and whether the child is given by the birth parents to the adopters. We need to remember the importance of goodbyes; they are the pictures, smells and sounds that the relinquishing parents will remember over the years as the point of handing over their child.

Information for adopters and telling the child they are adopted

We can help teach and share with adopters about caring for, enjoying and learning about their child. This may be offering parentcraft classes for approved adopters prior to placement (Stewart and Ring 1991); or teaching them how to put nappies on, while they room-in with the baby on a postnatal ward; or practical advice about caring for a child with developmental disabilities, or ideas of using boundaries of acceptable behaviour and familiar routines to help children to adjust to a new environment. The value of this information is to give parents confidence, offsetting feelings of loss at not being the parent who conceived and delivered the child.

An integral part of adoption nowadays is honesty. This means adopters telling their children from day one that they are adopted. It can be painful to 'tell', until there is a comfortable acceptance of one's role as an adopter. We can help support adopters in doing this, by supplementing the information that may be supplied by the adoption agency. Suggestions for acknowledging the child is not their own include the following.

- Saying to children 'you did not come from mummy's tummy but you were chosen and I am your adopted mummy and you are my special child'.
- Using children's books with stories of adoption (see list at end of chapter).
- Celebrating adoption day.
- Being prepared for questions from the child such as 'Why, when, how was I adopted? What do I say to my friends?'.
- Making a scrap book or life history book of the child before and after

adoption (see resource section). The comment of a parent explaining adoption to a child with special needs highlights how this can be done:

I wrote down a little story for my daughter which I called 'Emma is adopted'. It's very easy, with a sentence or two on each page, and photographs of her and us. It tells the story of how she came to us in a very simple way, with lots of repeated bits. She's always loved it – at one time we used to have to read it to her half a dozen times a day. Now she's taken it all in, but she still goes back to it sometimes and we build on it and add pages. I can't think of a better way. (cited in Chennells 1987, p. 19)

Other adopters can be a fund of support and advice and we need to make sure families have the addresses of agencies such as PPIAS and National Organisation for Counselling Adoptees and their Parents (NORCAP) (see end of the chapter).

Information for adoptees

The adoptee does not choose to become part of the adoption process, which then forces them into a situation where they have to grieve for one set of parents and be able to value another set of parents, a task many adults would find hard. If we ensure parents have information about groups such as PPIAS, there is the opportunity for children to meet other children at events such as picnics. It is a chance to feel that adoption is only one part of their lives.

We may meet clients in the course of other health care who wish to trace their birth parents and do not know how to do this. For many, it may be one way of resolving the question of 'Who am I?' Recent changes in the law in Britain have meant that children at the age of 18 years have the right to see their original birth certificates with the mother's name and address. It means that they can then choose to try to trace their birth parents. For some, this has a positive outcome of finding parents who welcome them; for others, it is a blank passage with no information to trace parents, or parents who reject them. The process of tracing birth parents is outlined in Appendix 10. The emotional consequences of this contact need to be considered carefully and we should advise that they take the chance to talk with an agency such as NORCAP.

As siblings of adoptees

Honesty is the only way to ensure that hidden secrets do not get disclosed at a later date. We need to support birth parents and adopters in their decision to tell siblings about adoptees. It clearly needs to be their decision, because they have to live with it. One of the most practical ways is using the children's books produced as resources for adoptees (see end of chapter).

Supporting During and After Adoption

Space to grieve

Follow-up by the adoption agency social worker often ceases after the adoption order. An identified health worker who provides long-term care, e.g. GP or health visitor, who phones or visits and asks 'How are you?' may be part of the grieving journey. Particularly if family and friends deny, ignore or do not know of the adoption, this may be the only emotional space for relinquishing women to be known as a mother, or for adopters to share the normal fears and frustrations of being a parent.

We need to stress the existence of an *open door* for contact at any time months or years later; many participants will reject contact initially and wish to 'get on with life' or set boundaries of contact that only concern the child or health issues, not their own feelings. Over months or years, this perspective may change and there may be a need to talk about what has happened and what they have felt.

Anticipating situations of unresolved grief

We need to recognise that if grief remains unresolved or denied, it may be precipitated by other events or become pathological. Chapter 7 outlines some of the factors that make grieving difficult and Chapter 10 looks at when grief becomes stuck, who to refer to and when to stop visiting. Particular situations to be aware of are the following.

- Future pregnancies for relinquishing mothers may precipitate a grieving reaction. Questions that may be valuable include:
  'How do you feel about the adoption now?'
  'How do you feel about this child?'
  'What would you like your partner to know?'
  'Would you like this baby to know about their brother or sister?'
- Adoptees, who have denied the pain or their adoptive identity, may find that starting to use contraceptives, being pregnant or having a parent die raises feelings about their adoption. Questions that may be valuable include:
  'How do you feel being adopted?'
  'What do you know about your birth family?'
  'Have you had contact with them?'
  'How do you think they might have felt?'
  'How do your adoptive parents feel?'

In the situations mentioned above, it may be helpful to refer individuals for specialist counselling (e.g. NORCAP or PAC).

How can Family and Friends Help?

Again Chapter 7 covers some of the issues in relation to support after bereavement by death. Many of the points apply here.

- Showing that they care with a hug or a smile and time to listen.
- Being able to share some of the pain:
  not denying relinquishing parents the right to grieve over their child
  appreciating that adopters, whilst 'fortunate' to have a child, still have losses and frustrations to share
  recognising that as adoptees grow up there are hurts and questions.
- Learning about adoption to appreciate what is involved for those in the adoption triangle – the insecurities and losses.

What About Ourselves?

We can recognise that, as with all situations of bereavement, infertility and adoption involve a series of losses and changes in a complex network of feelings, self-perceptions and relationships. Numerous questions arise about 'why' and 'how'. Truth is the basis of grieving, to acknowledge and accept loss and change in those relations. Resources, self-awareness, time and support are needed to come to terms with the bereavement and to achieve emotional and physical well-being. To do this we need to be clear about our own sources of training and support (see Chapter 10). As health workers we cannot resolve the pain for others, but we can share moments with these families and offer care, listening and practical advice to help make the situation more manageable.

Key points
- Identify the shared and unique bereavements in the adoption triangle.
- Recognise that the experience of adoption will be interpreted by the individual and we need to be sensitive to cultural, social and personal beliefs.
- Appreciate the importance of listening to and supporting those involved in adoption – it is a real grief.
- Recognise the importance of resources for birth parents, adopters and adoptees, both written information and self-help organisations.
- Develop your own resource file with information on agencies, groups, books and a list of interpreters or local community health workers.

References

Austin J (ed). *Adoption: the inside story.* Barn Owl Books: Parents to Parents Information Adoption Service Supplies, 1987

Berg BJ, Wilson JF, Weingartner PJ. Psychological sequelae of infertility treatment: the role of gender and sex-role identification. *Soc Sci Med* 1991; 33(9): 1071

Brebner C, Sharp J, Stone F. *The role of infertility and adoption.* London: BAAF, 1985

Caplan C. *Concept of mental health and consultation.* United States Department of Health, Education and Welfare, 1965; 183: 206

Caplan C. *Principles of preventive psychiatry.* London: Tavistock, 1969

Chennells P. *Explaining adoption to your child.* London: BAAF, 1987

Chennells P, Hammond C. *Adopting a child.* London: BAAF, 1987

Christie G. The psychological and social management of the Infertile couples. In: Peperell R, Hudson B, Wood C (eds) *The infertile couple.* London: Churchill Livingstone, 1980

Cook R, Parsons J, Mason B, Golombok S. Emotional, marital and sexual functioning in patients embarking on IVF and AID treatment for infertility. *Reprod Infant Psychol* 1989; 7: 87

Downie S. *Baby making.* London: Bodley Head, 1988

Erikson EH. *Childhood and society.* London: Palladin, 1977

Fraser J, Howe D. Approval versus preparation – adoptive parents' views of the adoption process. *Adoption and Fostering* 1989; 12(4): 31

Goodyer P. Life without children. In: Wannan S (ed) *The baby chase.* Australian Womans Weekly 107. Sydney: Aust Cons Press, 1989

Howe D. The loss of a baby. *Midwife, Health Visitor and Community Nurse* 1990; 21(1&2): 25

Hull MG, Eddowes HA, Fahy U et al. Expectations of assisted conception for infertility. *Br Med J* 1992; 304: 1465

Kirk D. *Shared Fate.* London: Collier McMillan, 1964

Klein R. *The exploitation of a desire.* Geelong: Deakin University, 1989

Kornitzer M. *Adoption and family life.* London: Putnam, 1968

Kraft A, Palombo M, Mitchell D, Dean M, Meyers M, Schmidt A. The psychological dimensions of infertility. *Am J Orthopsychiatr* 1980; 50(4): 618

New Zealand Infertility Society Inc. *Newsletters* 1990; 1(1): 2

Newton CR, Hearn MT, Yuzpe AA. Psychological assessment and follow-up after in vitro fertilisation: assessing the impact of failure. *Fertil Steril* 1990; 54: 879

Oke K. *Life without children – coping with childlessness.* Infertility Federation of Australasia Inc. Fact Sheet. Australia: PO Box 426, Erindale Centre, Wanniassa, 1990

Pfeffer N, Woolett A. *The experience of infertility.* London: Virago, 1983

Post Adoption Centre. *Groups of women parted with a child for adoption.* Discussion papers. London: PAC, 1990

Raphael B. *The anatomy of bereavement.* London: Unwin Hyman, 1984

Raphael-Leff J. *Psychological processes of childbearing.* London: Chapman & Hall, 1991

Ritchie SW. Adoption: an option often overlooked. *Am J Nurs* 1989; 89(9): 1156

Roll S, Millen L, Backlund B. Solomon's mothers. In: Rando TA (ed) *Parental loss of a child.* Illinois: Research Press, 1986: 257–68

Rowe J. *Yours by choice.* London: Routledge and Kegan Paul, 1982

Sorosky A, Baran A, Pannor R. *The adoption triangle.* New York: Doubleday, 1978

Smith C. *Adoption and fostering – why and how?* London: Macmillan, 1984

Stewart A, Ring W. What about adopters. *Health Visitor* 1991; 64(9): 297

Townsend R, Perkins A. *Bitter Fruit.* Alameda: Hunter House, 1992

Triseliotis J. *In search of origins.* London: Routledge and Kegan Paul, 1973

Walby C, Symons B. *Who am I?* London: BAAF, 1990

Winkler R, Van Keppel M. *Relinquishing mothers in adoption – their long-term adjustment.* Melbourne: Institute of Family Studies, 1984

World Health Organisation. *The epidemiology of infertility.* Report of a WHO Scientific Group Technical Report Series 582. Geneva: WHO, 1975

Resources for Couples and Health Workers on Infertility

Organisations

CHILD
PO Box 154, Hounslow TW3 0E2, UK
Tel: 081-571 4376
Provide support and information on infertility problems.

Foresight
The Old Vicarage, Church Lane, Witley, Godalming, Surrey GU8 SP7, UK
Tel: 0428-684500
Provide information and aim to improve health before pregnancy.

National Association for the Childless/National Fertility Association
318 Summer Lane, Birmingham B19 3RL, UK
Tel: 021-359 4887
Provide helpline, fact sheets and newsletter.

Women's Health
52 Featherstone Street, London EC1Y 8RT, UK
Provide a newsletter and an enquiry line.

Books for individuals and health workers

Downie S. *Babymaking.* London: Bodley Head, 1988. This is a book about reproductive technology.

Harkness C. *The infertility book.* California: Celestial Arts, 1992. Written by a mother who has experience of treatment, with views from specialist and women.

Houghton P, Houghton D. *Coping with childlessness.* London: Allen and Unwin, 1984. This is a book for consumers about infertility and other options for parenting.

Lasker S, Borg S. *In search of parenthood: coping with infertility and high-technology conception.* Boston: Beacon Press, 1987. About infertility and treatments.

Lee K. *Fertility: why can't I have a baby?* Aust: Core and Osment, 1992. Humorous look at the facts, treatment and findings of infertility.

Pfeffer N, Woolett A. *The experience of infertility.* London: Virago, 1983. A study of perspectives of infertility.

Stanway A. *Why us?* London: Granada, 1980. For individuals wanting to find out about infertility.

Resources for Families and Health Workers About Adoption

Organisations

British Agencies for Adoption and Fostering (BAAF)
11 Southwark Street, London SE1 1RQ, UK
Tel: 071-407 8800
Registered charity which acts as an adoption agency, trains workers and provides resources for adoption participants and professionals.

National Organisation for Counselling Adoptees and their Parents (NORCAP)
3 New High Street, Headington, Oxford OX3 7AJ, UK
Tel: 0865-750554
Support and counselling for anyone who is in adoption; particularly assists adoptees seeking to trace parents. Newsletter and local area groups.

Post-Adoption Centre (PAC)
Gregory House, 48 Mecklenburgh Square, London WC1N 2NU, UK
Tel: 071-833 2314/5
Provides a service of counselling, workshops and correspondence using professionals and members for birth parents, adoptees and adopters.

Parent to Parent Information on Adoption Services (PPIAS)
Lower Boddington, Daventry, Northants NN11 6YB, UK
Tel: 0327-60295
A self-help group which provides meetings, newsletters and support from adopters to adopters.

Books for adopters and health workers

Austin J (ed). *Adoption: the inside story.* Barn Owl Books: PPIAS Supply, 1987. Stories of adoptive parents' experiences.

Chennells P. *Explaining adoption to your adopted child.* London: BAAF, 1987. Detailed and practical outline to all the situations where adopters may need to explain adoption, e.g. adoption of baby, child, relation, disabled child, transracial adoption.

Chennells P, Hammond C. *Adopting a child.* London: BAAF, 1987. Includes all the addresses of adoption agencies in the UK.

Harkness L. *Looking for Lisa.* Australia: Random House, 1991. Six stories of mothers finding their children.

Howe D, Sawbridge P, Hinings D. Half a million women. Harmondsworth: Penguin, 1992

Jones M. *Everything you need to know about adoption.* London: Sheldon Press, 1987. Good, basic information.

Kremetz J. *How it feels to be adopted.* London: Victor Gollancz, 1982. Stories of adolescent adoptees.

Melina LR, Roszia SK. *The open adoption experience.* New York: Harper Collins, 1993

Rowe J. *Yours by choice.* London: Routledge and Kegan Paul, 1982. Discusses infertility and adoption for couples and parents.

Ryan T, Walker R. *Making life story books.* London: BAAF, 1985. Gives pictorial ideas of making a story book explaining adoption to the child.

Books for children

Althea. *Jane is adopted.* UK: Souvenir Press, 1990. Practical story for children aged up to 7 or 8 years about being adopted.

Bond M. *Here comes Thursday.* London: Puffin, 1966. Story about Thursday, who is brought up in a home for mice and then adopted into a family. (Also the Paddington series outline the story of Paddington Bear who is 'adopted' into a new home in England after leaving Peru.)

Holm A. *I am David.* London: Penguin, 1961. Story of a boy who escapes a prison camp and goes in search of his mother. Raises questions of identity for teenagers.

Garfield L. *The sound of coaches.* London: Penguin, 1966. Story of an adopted boy who seeks the truth about his birth parents. Particularly suited to teenagers who hope to trace their parents.

Livinstone C. *Why was I adopted?* Angus Robertson, 1981. Humorous look at adoption for the child aged 5–9 years.

Chapter Six

Lost Dreams

Dreams are true while they last and do we not live in dreams?

Tennyson, *The Higher Pantheism*

Within this chapter

1. Reducing the incidence and impact of preterm birth
2. Parents' initial reactions to, and feelings about, a preterm birth
3. Admission to a Neonatal Intensive Care Unit (NICU)
4. Visual and emotional impact of NICU on families
5. Separation of parents and their baby
6. Congenital abnormalities and handicap: role of health workers in prevention and detection
7. Reactions at birth and emotional effects for families
8. Handicaps not found at birth
9. What health workers can do to help families in these situations

---

Introduction

Pregnancy and childbirth are generally considered to be positive experiences, with the expectation that they will culminate in the birth of a perfect, healthy baby on, or near, the due date. The birth of a baby who is preterm (before 37 completed weeks of gestation), has a congenital abnormality (a syndrome or defect present at birth) or handicap (a developmental disability) shatters the dreams and expectations of the parents, resulting in bereavement. These situations are considered separately in the following text. This chapter is aimed at all health workers, both in hospital and the community, who care for these families, such as the midwife, obstetric and paediatric teams, neonatal nurses, GP, health visitor and social worker.

e pregnancy, great emphasis is placed on the importance of
ıg the expected date of delivery. This date is quoted ritualistic-
aı., that moment on, by parents and carers alike, with practical and
emotioьal preparations revolving around it.

Childbirth has, for a long time, been recognised as a major life event
(Holmes and Rahe 1967). Numerous psychological and emotional changes
accompany the transition into parenthood. The period towards the end of
pregnancy often acts as a time during which, as the parents finalise the
physical preparations for their new baby, they also begin to accept their
impending role change.

The preterm delivery of a baby throws all these psychological and
physical plans into disarray. Very few parents consider it a real possibility
that their baby might be born early, and are far from prepared for the
overwhelming range of emotions that they subsequently experience if
this does happen.

How can health workers reduce the incidence and impact of preterm delivery?

Preconceptual education, ideally started in schools, could do much to
eliminate some of the more common factors associated with preterm
delivery. By advising potential parents of possible risks and helping them
to avoid these, fewer parents would face the daunting prospect of a
preterm baby. These include advice about smoking, drug abuse, alcohol
abuse and poor diet among other topics. Contraceptive advice to young
people could reduce the subsequent number of terminations for unwanted
pregnancies. Several terminations have been shown to be associated with
an increased risk of a preterm delivery.

Antenatal education in the form of parentcraft classes aims to prepare
future parents for the pregnancy, birth and basic practical skills of impending parenthood. Discussion should take place around the possibility of
preterm labour and what to expect in this event.

Initial reactions

What will the baby look like?

Most parents have never seen a preterm baby and assume that it will look
like a miniature version of a term baby, with a rounded stomach and
smooth, pink skin. The reality is very different; the earlier the gestation
the more distant this image becomes. Very preterm babies may be cyanosed
at birth, with veins clearly visible through thin, loose, wrinkly skin. They
are bony, skinny and often much smaller than imagined, making them

seem even more frail than anticipated. Some parents have likened their baby to a 'wizened old man', a 'skinned rat' or 'ET', and many are shocked and even disgusted by the look of their baby. This natural reaction is in itself upsetting to the parents, who may have expected to love their child immediately.

What do parents feel at this time?

Fear is a feeling experienced when we are in a situation that is unfamiliar, threatening, not understood or over which we have little or no control. All of these apply to parents during a preterm labour and delivery.

Parents are encouraged to draw up birth plans with their midwife early in the pregnancy, to plan in detail how they wish their labour and delivery to be conducted. Suddenly all of these choices and decisions are removed from them, as the situation becomes 'abnormal', as defined by the doctors and midwives caring for them. Feelings of helplessness, inadequacy and lack of control are common. An emergency Caesarean section, forceps or ventouse extraction delivery compound the mother's feelings that she has no control over what is happening to her, and increase the sense of disappointment and failure at childbirth.

In trying to put the situation into a tangible light, parents try to reason why the baby should be born early. In doing so they express guilt over factors which they feel they may have contributed to, such as smoking. They may also lay blame on others, commonly the professionals involved, for not anticipating or preventing these events. Substance-abusing mothers who see their baby undergo withdrawal, exhibit these reactions very strongly. Guilt may also manifest itself if there were thoughts of terminating the pregnancy at any stage, if it is an unwanted pregnancy, or if the mother has previously had a termination of pregnancy. In these circumstances the blame is often placed on the mother herself, as events are interpreted by her as a form of punishment.

Many mothers feel cheated at having missed the end of pregnancy. These feelings usually occur as life is beginning to settle down again, often once the baby is home. This may be several months after the birth, which can be difficult to rationalise to family and friends.

Anticipatory grief

The anticipated baby and real baby are two different people, and the family need to grieve the loss of the normal, healthy, term baby they expected, before being able to focus on their actual baby. In mourning the imagined baby, the parents may initially reject their real infant. This process is compounded when the parents do not expect their baby to survive; as they refrain from developing too close a relationship in preparation for death, whilst continuing to hope that it will survive. This is termed *anticipatory grief* and may persist for many weeks or months, until such time as the parents really believe there is a chance of survival for their baby. The term 'anticipatory' grief was first used by Lindemann (1944) to describe the reactions of people who appeared to experience grief prior to a death, and subsequently were calmer if it actually occurred.

Anticipatory grief is frequently shown by parents who delay naming the baby whilst it is very ill, thus not giving the child its own separate identity, thereby acknowledging its independent existence. Religious ceremonies, such as the christening of a very ill baby in a neonatal intensive care unit (NICU), can push the parents into doing this sooner than they planned, and if not handled with care and understanding may cause abnormal or protracted grief reactions.

How can health workers help?

Information should be given regarding the viability of the baby according to its gestation and estimated size, if known. We should endeavour to prepare the parents for the infant's appearance, and wherever possible taking the parents to see the NICU before delivery.

Parents need a great deal of support and understanding from the staff caring for them during a preterm labour and delivery. Much can be done to alleviate some of their fears by explaining events honestly, sensitively and simply. We should give plenty of opportunity to ask questions, be prepared to just listen, and encourage the parents to share their fears and emotions. Reassurance over the normality of their feelings must be given, particularly when they are expressing rejection or disappointment, as many parents are shocked by their own reactions.

Parents should retain as much choice as possible in their labour, and many aspects of the original birth plan may still be able to be adhered to. This is important because it gives them some form of control over events, and some positive points to draw on from their experience of childbirth.

Separation of the parents and baby at birth

The process by which parent–baby relationships are developed is often referred to as 'attachment' or 'bonding' (Klaus and Kennell 1982; Sluckin et al. 1983). It begins early in pregnancy, becomes stronger when the fetus is seen on ultrasound scanning and movements are felt, strengthening even further when the newborn baby is seen and touched by the parents. There is a very sensitive period following delivery, when these relationships are nurtured, during which the baby is quiet, alert, makes eye contact with its parents and roots for the breast to feed. Parents respond by gently examining their baby whilst talking softly, in high pitched voices, maintaining eye contact and offering a feed.

The parents of a preterm baby are denied this opportunity if the baby needs resuscitation or urgent transfer to a neonatal unit. Most parents are shown their baby in the incubator or cot before transfer even if they cannot have a cuddle, but this first sighting of their baby, amongst blankets, tubes and wires, often shocks and frightens them. If the mother has had a general anaesthetic, she may not have the opportunity to see her child for several hours, and disbelief that she is actually a mother is not uncommon. In these instances many mothers say that the first time they see their baby, it is like meeting a total stranger.

> I was engulfed in the feeling that I'd dreadfully failed my poor little baby, who ought still to have been in my body; instead she was out in the world, and fighting for her life. I was overwhelmed with tears. My emotions were in a state of wreckage. I thought Anna might die in the night and they wouldn't tell me; I was awash with inadequacy . . . . (Harris 1983)

How can health workers help?

The unknown aspects of a preterm delivery are what cause most fears for parents. If we can provide them with information regarding realistic expectations of the labour and birth, it will help to alleviate some of their fears. The number of staff who will be present should be discussed, and their roles. Ideally these staff should meet the parents before delivery and allow them time to ask any questions.

Events following the birth should also be discussed – for example, a very immature baby would not be expected to cry at birth, would immediately be taken to the resuscitaire and electively intubated. This process must be explained to the parents sensitively so that they do not panic when this occurs. If the baby's condition is stable once resuscitated, the parents should be able to see, touch or cuddle their baby, even if it is only briefly, before transfer to NICU.

Admission to NICU

The admission of a baby to NICU causes a great deal of psychological trauma to the family involved, as it is a major crisis in their lives and if possible admission should be avoided. Transitional care wards in maternity units reduce the number of admissions necessary to NICU, and allow babies who need a little more help or observation than normal to still be cared for with their mothers. It is recommended that all maternity hospitals have these facilities.

In the case of smaller district hospitals, admission to NICU may involve transfer to another area or hospital. This adds physical distance to the emotional and practical barriers separating the mother and baby, and cause problems for the family with visiting. Fathers often feel torn ...en the needs of the mother and baby.

...lear photographs of the baby, taken as soon as possible and before too many monitors are attached, will help the family realise that they do have a baby, and give them a chance to begin to recognise their child despite being separated.

Term babies on NICU

NICUs are generally perceived as providing care solely for preterm and small babies. However, some term babies also require admission following delivery, for example for an infection screen, assessment of transient tachypnoea following a Caesarean section, or due to birth asphyxia or being very low birth weight.

The parents of a term baby are often even more shocked than those of a preterm infant, as the latter group expect their baby to need extra help because of its size or gestation. These parents experience a type of grief reaction similar to those of parents of preterm babies, in that they mourn the loss of the healthy child they anticipated, then gradually come to terms with the existence and needs of their sick baby.

With preconceived ideas of NICUs, parents of term babies frequently feel out of place and fraudulent, with a strong sense of failure. Their perception of priority of needs places the smaller and earlier babies' needs before theirs. They often refrain from asking staff too many questions for fear of wasting their time or distracting them (Swan Parente 1982). This initiates a circle of increasing anxiety, as the less parents know and understand, the more they worry. Anticipatory grief is often evident.

Most term babies do not need to stay very long on a neonatal unit, but if the parents have not fully understood the reasons for admission and treatments, their long-term perception of their baby may be distorted, and fears as to its future health may persist, interfering with the relationships between them.

The following sections apply to families with a baby in NICU for any reason.

How can health workers help?

During parentcraft classes, and chats with the parents antenatally, the midwife should explain the role of NICU in relation to services available – just as the possibility of a Caesarean section is considered, so should admission to NICU. The parentcraft tours of the local hospital should include NICU, and parents should be encouraged to ask questions. Parents who have some knowledge of NICU are generally less anxious, if their baby is admitted, than those who have little or no concept of its role.

The visual impact of NICU

The first impression a visitor to NICU has is of a hot, hectic, clinical, brightly-lit place, where complex, technical-looking machinery surrounding each cot or incubator bleeps or buzzes importantly, and the babies are lost amidst a mass of tubes and wires. The staff often appear very busy 'doing things', which does not make them appear particularly approachable. For the parents of a sick baby, this impression is overwhelming, threatening and extremely frightening.

How can health workers soften the impact?

Parents feel superfluous and out of place on NICU, especially during the first few visits. A midwife who knows the family should accompany them the first few times, taking time to explain the machinery and equipment, answer their questions and introduce them to the NICU staff. Once the purpose of a piece of equipment is known, it is not so frightening. We should also supply a clearly written leaflet with information about NICU for all parents. Some suggestions for inclusions in such a leaflet are listed in Table 6.1.

There are several cosmetic factors that can make NICU less clinical; these include having bright-coloured pictures and paintings of cartoon characters on the walls, pretty curtains in the nurseries, naming individual rooms after places in children's books, the provision of a play room and toys for siblings, staff wearing less formal clothing and clear name badges displaying first names as well as surnames. A quiet room for parents, away from the main unit, is of great value. It should be a homely place where the parents can relax and take 'time-out' from the stresses of the unit. Identifying one or two particular nurses as being primarily responsible for specific parents and their baby personalises the care, and makes the atmosphere much friendlier.

The emotional impact of NICU

The parents already have to cope with a wealth of emotions following the birth of a sick or preterm baby – shock, fear, guilt, disappointment and disbelief. For the mother there are also the physical effects of the labour and delivery to cope with.

When a baby is admitted to NICU the role of the parents is nothing like they envisaged throughout the pregnancy. If the baby is very ill or its condition is unstable, the helplessness that parents feel can be devastating. The complexity of the machinery and competence of the nursing and medical staff serve to intensify their feelings of being incapable of fulfilling the needs of their baby. The importance of involving families from very

Table 6.1 Possible topics for NICU parents' leaflet

- What to expect in NICU – heat, noise and light levels
- Brief explanations of commonly used equipment
- Who is who? – explain roles of different staff and the uniforms they wear
- Contact name of a key nurse, and telephone numbers for NICU
- Encouragement to ask questions and become involved in their baby's care
- Visiting policies for parents, family and friends
- Facilities for parents whilst on NICU, including rooms or hostel facilities where they can stay
- Information on hire or loan of breast pumps
- Details of local and national support groups
- Contact number for social worker
- Map or transport advice may be relevant for regional referral centres

early on is now well recognised and widely practised, yet parents still describe feeling 'in the way', 'useless' and 'superfluous'.

With very ill or preterm infants, progress is often slow and difficult. It is not unusual for them to have rapid changes of condition, and even when warned of this, parents find these swings hard to accept. Anticipatory grief is clearly exhibited in these families' reactions, which can be therapeutic as a coping mechanism or buffer against the instability of the situation. These feelings may continue for several weeks or months, and even when the baby survives to be discharged home, they are often not fully resolved.

How can health workers help?

Most units now have a family-centred approach to neonatal care, which is to be recommended. Open visiting policies give the family more freedom to play a major part in their baby's care, including siblings and extended family members. From the very first visit, parents should be made aware that their part in the care of their baby is unique, and every bit as vital as the nursing and medical care. In particular, the benefits of providing breast milk for their baby cannot be overemphasised, and is a role only the mother can fulfil. We should encourage parents to touch and talk to their child, when they feel able; even small, sick infants benefit tremendously from non-stress touch such as skin-to-skin contact in kangaroo care. The whole situation may overwhelm the parents initially. Any reluctance that they show in becoming physically involved with their baby at this stage is normal and should be acknowledged as such (Townshend 1987). Cuddly toys, pictures of the family or tape recordings of their voices may also be left on NICU for the baby.

There is a tendency for parents to focus on the machines rather than the baby, and we must help them see their baby as an individual character. Comments such as 'he held my finger this morning while I fed him', or 'she's been looking at the toy you brought her', can help to do this.

Dressing these tiny babies in bright-coloured clothes makes them appear more normal, and can be a great boost to parents.

When chatting to the parents it is important not to use negative phrases to describe the baby or its behaviour. For example, if a baby's condition has been unstable, explaining it as 'he's been really naughty this morning', or 'she's been playing up again', makes it sound as if it is a conscious decision of the baby to do this. This evokes parental reactions of anger and dis-appointment, and begins to develop the idea that their baby is difficult or naughty.

The wealth of information given to parents may be difficult for them to assimilate during such a stressful period. We need to remember that when we are bereaved, shock and disbelief make it hard to concentrate on information. It will need to be repeated several times over the following days and weeks (Kenner 1990). 'Being emotionally troubled does not make parents unintelligent, nor prevent them from using the intelligence they have' (Taylor 1986) – they need information. We need to support the family and spend time listening to them. Identifying a key nurse for the baby, and encouraging contact with the unit's parents' group and national self-help groups such as NIPPERS, help to increase the confidence and competence of parents (Minde et al. 1980).

Effects on other family members

We often forget and fail to meet the needs of the extended family. Siblings are welcomed on NICU, but little emotional support is available specific-ally for them. Parents express anxieties about how the child will react to the wealth of machinery and equipment. In practice, children often have a much simpler approach than adults, and are more fascinated than frightened. The emotional upset of their parents and upheaval of their routines often causes the most distress to them.

How can health workers help?

Grandparents are very much the 'forgotten grievers' (Gyulay 1975). As well as their own grief, they experience grief for the parents and their grand-child. They need the opportunity to express their fears and have their questions answered too. This in turn enables them to give the parents more empathy, strengthening the family network of support. As profes-sionals we tend to concentrate on the emotions of the parents, often leaving the extended family feeling frustrated and isolated, which in turn puts more pressure on the parents (Blackburn and Lowen 1986).

Siblings can help in many aspects of the baby's care, from getting nappies to helping to choose what clothes their brother or sister should wear. To help them understand and become involved with events, they could be encouraged to write a daily journal or draw pictures to put in the incubator or cot. It may be useful to use dolls to re-enact what is happening to their baby through play. Equipment such as intravenous infusion sets, with all dirty or sharp bits removed, might be used before being discarded. The parents should be encouraged to put aside some special time for siblings, who often feel pushed out when the new baby demands so much time and energy from the parents (Troy et al. 1988).

Separation

The issues of separation of the parents and their baby on NICU have been well researched. They may be physical and psychological (Valentin 1981). As early as 1907, Budin, a French obstetrician, recognised the impact of separation in a publication called *The Nursling*. He stated that 'Unfortunately, a certain number of mothers abandon their babies whose needs they have not had to meet, and in whom they have lost all interest. The life of the little one has been saved, it is true, but at the cost of the mother.' A great many parents express the feeling that the baby does not really belong to them until they take it home and have sole responsibility. Until that time their regimes are dictated by the staff, and they have to ask permission or help to do even the most basic of tasks, such as change a nappy or feed their baby. The physical separation also contributes to undermining the self-esteem of the parents, over their ability to care for their own baby (Swan Parente 1982).

The first few days are especially difficult for the family in terms of separation. While the mother is nursed on a postnatal ward, her partner is at home and their baby is on NICU. At such a time of crisis the family needs to be together for support and strength. Hearing the cries of other babies on the ward is very emotive for a mother with a sick baby, and many mothers are happy to be discharged home as soon as possible.

With commitments at home and work, parents are inevitably going to be apart from their baby for long periods of time. A UK Government Report in 1978 stated that 'It must be one of the principal duties of the staff to help the parents through this difficult time [of separation].' They should be given telephone numbers for the unit, and encouraged to phone to check on their baby's condition at any hour if they are upset or concerned. Even in NICU the parents and baby are physically separated by the incubator, intravenous infusions and monitors. It is very hard for parents to get to know their baby amidst this intimidating array of obstacles. Research has suggested that where strong attachments have not been made between parents and babies on NICU, subsequent non-accidental injuries are most common (Klaus and Kennell 1982).

Congenital Abnormalities, Handicap and Disability

At some stage in the pregnancy most parents briefly consider the chance that their baby may be born with an abnormality. Unless evidence of such a condition is discovered antenatally, these fears usually subside as the excitement of having a baby takes over. At delivery one of the first questions parents ask is 'Is he alright?' Thankfully in the vast majority of cases the answer is 'yes', and the family celebrations can begin. For some, however, the answer they receive re-enacts their worst fears, as they are told of an abnormality or handicap.

We need to be clear of the meaning of the words 'abnormality' and 'handicap' ourselves, and our interpretation of them, in order to be able to explain them clearly to parents. Abnormality generally refers to physiological differences from what is seen as the normal body structure of a baby e.g. a baby born with a heart which has a hole in the septum. However, we need to remember 'abnormality' acts as a label on the baby and in reality we are only talking about a difference from the majority of babies. Handicap, for many people, is a term which evaluates a person and indicates that they are disadvantaged physically, emotionally or socially. Again it can act as a label to a baby or family. Terms which are more positive and accurate are 'developmental delay or disability' where a baby or person has impairment of activities which are part of everyday living. Sometimes the term 'special needs' is used to indicate that a child or person needs extra help in everyday living. Detailed physiological discussion of this range of conditions is outside the scope of this book, which is concerned with bereavement. The reader is referred to *The sick newborn baby* by Kelnar et al. (1994).

How can health workers help to prevent or detect these?

The aetiology of many of these conditions is not fully understood. There have been great breakthroughs in reducing the incidence of certain others with preconceptual advice. Examples of this are periconceptual vitamin supplementation to reduce the risk of neural tube defects (Czeizel 1993) and preconceptual folic acid taken to reduce the risk of first time, or recurrence of, neural tube defects.

Genetic counselling and screening can be helpful to predict the risk of recurrence in parents who have already had a handicapped child, or have a known family trait of a certain condition.

National campaigns of vaccination against rubella and polio have had great success in ensuring that most women of child-bearing age are not susceptible to these conditions, thus preventing damage to the unborn fetus from these illnesses. Inevitably some people slip through this very comprehensive immunisation programme, and immigrants from countries who do not vaccinate against these conditions also pose a problem.

Antenatal screening tests for certain conditions are now routine in many areas. Amniocentesis may also be offered to women who are identified as being at high risk of having a baby with Down syndrome. If an abnormality is detected, a termination of the pregnancy may be offered to the parents. The various screening tests available are becoming more and more accurate, and are covering many more conditions than previously. They are aimed at allowing a diagnosis to be made as early as possible in the pregnancy, to allow an early termination should this be the wish of the parents (see Chapter 2).

Reactions at birth

There is no good time to receive news that your baby is in some way different. However, the period following birth is a time when parents are emotionally and physically drained, thus rendering them particularly vulnerable.

The way in which they are informed is of great importance and has long-lasting impact. The terminology used to describe their baby's condition should be carefully considered; it may shape the way in which they perceive and relate to their baby in the future.

Immediate parental reactions depend on many factors. They will be influenced by the type of disability, its visibility, severity and their degree of knowledge of the problem. The attitudes and reactions of the staff caring for them are of great significance, and it is important for staff in such situations to be aware of their own feelings on this topic.

The initial feelings at this time are of shock, disbelief and sorrow. Denial is common, whereby the parents convince themselves that the doctors are wrong in their diagnosis. Many parents are totally numbed by the news, feeling that their world has fallen apart complete with all their dreams of parenthood. Rejection is also common. Time is needed for the parents to consolidate their feelings. A small number of families of babies with congenital abnormalities totally reject them, taking the difficult decision to place the baby for fostering or adoption. Some change their minds after some time away from the baby, but whatever the outcome they will require a great deal of support (see Chapter 5).

In cases of disfiguring defects, parents have described finding their baby 'disgusting', 'shocking' and 'repulsive' to look at. They also express guilt about feeling this way, and need reassurance that these are natural, honest and common reactions in such circumstances. Sometimes the most immediately distressing conditions for parents are those that can be reversed cosmetically, e.g. cleft lip and palate. Raphael-Leff (1991) points out that 'Professionals must bear in mind that what at first may appear as rejection of the baby, is at this point an inability to accept it.' This changes over time. In addition, emotions and responses vary according to cultural expectations of difference and handicap (see Chapter 9). As in all areas of bereavement, individuals and men and women respond to situations differently (see Table 2.1). In a relationship that is already under stress, the arrival of a handicapped baby may be the last straw (Gath 1985). With time, the tension may reflect the responsibility that mothers generally bear in the everyday care of the child (Cooke and Lawton 1984).

In addition to this range of intense emotions, there is the possibility that the abnormality or handicap may require the baby to be admitted to NICU. This may serve to reinforce feelings of denial and rejection, as the parents are separated from their baby, which makes it more difficult and prolongs the period over which relationships develop between them. The implications of separation are described above.

How can health workers help?

> There is no good way of telling parents that their child is mentally handicapped, but there must be ways of telling them so that a bad situation is not made worse, and of not adding to suffering that is already bound to be considerable. (Hannam 1975).

This applies to all children with disabilities or differences from what parents have expected their child to be.

The way in which the parents are informed of the problem, the timing and the terminology used are vitally important. If the baby has already been given a name, we should use it in the conversation. Most parents would prefer to be told together, with the baby present (perhaps being cuddled by one of them), and as soon as possible. We need to be aware of ourselves with regard to our own views and fears. As professionals we also feel a sense of responsibility if a pregnancy does not go quite right in our care. Being honest with ourselves and parents is a key concept.

The initial explanation should not be too lengthy, as the parents will retain very little of the information given at this time. For this reason it will need to be repeated several times over the next few days, using language appropriate to the family. The parents should have time alone with their baby, and be given lots of opportunities to ask questions when they feel ready. Leaving them with some leaflets or written explanation may be useful. The actual words used are also important. In the case of Down syndrome, for example, the parents should be told that their baby 'has Down syndrome', not that 'he is a Down's baby'. The former retains the baby's identity, whereas the latter classifies him as a disorder.

Most of these babies will need further investigations, maybe over a long period of time, before a full and clear picture of its extent is known. There are wide differences in the abilities of children with the same condition, so we should try not to be too specific over such details early on. It is difficult to strike the balance between being overoptimistic and painting a very negative picture. However, if the parents are kept fully informed, it enables them to work through each piece of news sequentially, allowing them to adjust gradually to the changing picture.

Health workers can help parents to begin and continue with grieving, by bridging the gap between the dream and the reality. This means that how we touch, hold and talk about the baby will make the parents aware of their child. If we can honestly draw their attention to the positive and negative aspects, it is helping them to move towards a real perspective. It means encouraging hopefulness and assertiveness in parents, helping them attain the position where they feel in control again.

It is vital that there is rapid, accurate and effective liaison between the hospital and community health workers, to avoid any unnecessary distress to parents if staff caring for them are unaware of what has happened.

Emotional effects

With their dream of a normal child shattered, the parents need to grieve the loss of the baby they expected. Only when they have relinquished this baby will they be able to start to adapt to the needs and problems of their real baby. Initially, they will only see the way in which their child is different and may find it hard to relate to the baby as an individual character. Unless they are helped through this stage, the baby's practical needs may take priority over the recognition of its unique personality.

Parents experience a similar range of emotions to those who have a preterm baby, with grief, anger, guilt, a sense of failure and disappointment. With most preterm babies, however, the parents have the knowledge that they will mature and develop normally in the future, whilst a baby with a congenital abnormality will have this condition for life. This is another aspect that parents need to come to terms with, but with the ever-changing physical demands and needs of the child, this will not be achieved quickly (Solnit and Stark 1961). Total acceptance may not come for several years, if at all.

Mothers and fathers often react and behave differently, which can be a cause of conflict and added pressure if not confronted. Overprotectiveness is also common, with parents checking their baby more frequently than siblings, and guarding them from everyday occurrences. If continued to the extreme, this can be damaging for both the child and parents.

Disabilities not found at birth

Many disabilities, although present at birth, may not manifest themselves for several weeks, months or even years. In a sample of 4-year-old handicapped children, only seven out of 82 were diagnosed at birth (all had spina bifida or Down syndrome). The remainder were diagnosed at various times over the following years (Chazan et al. 1980). Other handicaps may develop as a result of a severe illness or circumstances associated with extreme prematurity.

Babies of lower birth weight and earlier gestation than ever before are now surviving. Unfortunately, the price for survival for a few of them is some form of physical or mental handicap. The severity of these varies considerably, but the impact on the families is the same. The trauma they endure with sick or preterm babies often spans many months, during which time their hopes are raised and dashed numerous times over not just the health, but the survival of their baby. To be told finally that the end result of months of emotional and physical trauma is a baby with developmental delay, is a tragic ending.

The initial reaction is one of intense denial. In young babies in particular, evidence of mental handicap may not be obvious, and it is not uncommon for the parents to ask for another opinion as to the diagnosis. It is difficult for us to be specific about the prognosis for most babies, and parents find this unknown element very distresing. This 'wait and see' situation is extremely difficult to cope with, as its vagueness does not give the parents a tangible condition to come to terms with. The grief they subsequently feel is for the real child they have formed a relationship with, unlike the parents of a sick newborn baby who mourn the imagined baby they expected. They will need a great deal of support to accept their baby in this new light, and time to create new relationships.

How to tell family and friends

As a society we are not very good at coping with difficult situations, and many people simply avoid them instead of confronting and working them through. Similar to adoption and abortion, disability or difference is made an invisible loss in our society. Hall (1987) points out that at least the death of a child is acknowledged by society and grieving is 'allowed'; for parents of a child with a congenital abnormality or special needs, there is no space given to grieve, and they have to carry on caring for the child.

Friends and neighbours often do not send congratulation cards and may be afraid to ask how the baby is, for fear of upsetting the parents and out of their own embarrassment. This reinforces the parents' sense of failure and of becoming outcasts of society.

Parents need to reach a certain level of acceptance themselves before they can tell friends and family. They will feel more comfortable with certain people than others and should be encouraged to tell these first. It is helpful to run through the scenario beforehand in some instances, in order to prepare themselves for the reactions of shock and how they are going to cope with them. We should warn parents that they are likely to get some very hurtful comments – usually not intentional – and ways of coping with these could also be explored. One way is to say the hurtful phrase back to the person in a more positive light; for example, if the comment is 'I'm really sorry you had a mongol', it could be returned as 'Yes, we were shocked to find Jenny has Down syndrome, but she is a wonderful baby.'

Ongoing support

If chromosomal analysis has been undertaken, the parents' sense of guilt is heightened, as they apportion blame for the condition which their child has. Genetic counselling is useful in such circumstances, and helps to reassure the parents that such defects are not attributed to events before or during the pregnancy.

Embarrassment over the imperfections of their child may persist for a long time, and many mothers isolate themselves socially from family and friends to avoid difficult situations. Encouragement to continue with the social life they anticipated they would have had with a healthy infant is important. If the parents themselves are not hesitant, other people tend to react better.

There is a great need for long-term support for the families of these babies, not only practically but emotionally. Self-help groups can be extremely beneficial, with the family able to discuss their situation openly with other parents and receive empathetic support and advice. Information and contact numbers for local and national support groups may be given to the parents at an appropriate time. Written resources may also be recommended for the family, such as those mentioned in the book list at the end of this chapter.

At the earliest opportunity, in the UK, the family should be referred to the District Handicap Team, or District Child Development Team. It is important that parents are made to feel a part of this team, and are not isolated from the professionals (Rouf 1983). The Warnock Report (1978) recommended the identification of a key worker for the family, often a health visitor. This person can help them overcome the difficulties many parents face in obtaining information, and in liaising with numerous support agencies. This report also pointed out that the parents live with their child every day and are therefore the experts on their own child. As such, they should be regarded as partners with the professionals.

Conclusion

Situations such as those discussed in this chapter are extremely traumatic for everyone involved. We need to be aware of our own emotions in these circumstances, in order to support families effectively. Burnout in NICU and in those caring for families with handicapped children is a very real phenomenon. We need to identify where we go for support and debriefing, and how we survive (see Chapter 10). We also need to take a proactive role and increase the awareness of our society in general about these issues.

> **Key points**
> - Recognise that individuals grieve differently
> - Consider religious and cultural needs
> - Prepare families in advance wherever possible
> - Be honest and present realistic expectations
> - Use appropriate language
> - Repeat information several times
> - Allow time for questions
> - Be available to just listen
> - Consider the needs of extended family members
> - Ensure effective liaison between health workers
> - Make sure that resources for families are available

References

Blackburn S, Lowen L. Impact of an infant's premature birth on the grandparents and parents. *J Obstet Gynecol Neonatal Nurs* 1986; 15(2): 173

Budin P. *The nursling.* London: Caxton, 1907

Chazan M, Laing A, Bailey S, Jones G. *The early education of children with special needs.* London: Open Books, 1980

Cooke R, Lawton D. Informal support for the carers of disabled children. *Child Care Health Dev* 1984; 10: 67

Czeizel A. Prevention of congenital abnormalities by periconceptual multivitamin supplementation. *Br Med J* 1993; 306: 1645

Gath A. Parental reactions to loss and disappointment – the diagnosis of Down's syndrome. *Dev Med Child Neurol* 1985; 55: 343

Government Report Health Circular 28. *Family links and prevention of abandonment.* London: Department of Health, 1978

Gyulay J. The forgotten grievers. *Am J Nurs* 1975; 75(9): 1476

Hall M. But what do we tell the parents? *Health Vis* 1987; 60: 110

Hannam C. *Parents and mentally handicapped children.* London: Minds Specials, Pelican Books, 1975

Harris C. In: Alderson P. *Special care for babies in hospital.* London: NAWCH, 1983

Holmes TH, Rahe RH. Social readjustment rating scale. *J Psychosom Res* 1967; 11: 219

Kelnar C, Harvey D, Simpson C. *The sick newborn baby,* 3rd edn. London: Baillière Tindall, 1994.

Kenner C. Caring for the NICU parent. *J Perinat Neonat Nurs* 1990; 4(3): 78

Klaus MH, Kennell JH. *Parent–infant bonding.* St Louis: C. V. Mosby, 1982: 151–226

Lindemann E. Symptomatology and management of acute grief. *Am J Psychiatr* 1944; 101: 141

Minde K, et al. Self-help groups in a premature nursery – a controlled evaluation. *J Pediatr* 1980; 96: 933

Raphael-Leff J. *Psychological processes of childbearing.* London: Chapman & Hall, 1991

Rouf C. Parents care too. *Health Soc Serv J* 1983; xcII: 415

Sluckin W, Herbert M, Sluckin A. *Maternal bonding.* Oxford: Blackwell, 1983

Solnit A, Stark M. Mourning and the birth of a defective child. *Psychoanal Study Child* 1961; 16: 523

Swan Parente A. Psychological pressures in a neonatal unit. *Br J Hosp Med* 1982; 27: 266

Taylor P. Promoting parental care of high risk babies. *Aust Nurs J* 1986; 15(8): 31

Townshend P. Impact of intensive care. *Midwiv Chron* 1987; 1193: 194

Troy P, Wilkinson-Faul D, Smith A, Alexander A. Sibling visiting in NICU. *Am J Nurs* 1988; 88(1): 70

Valentin L. The problem of grief and separation in the Special Care Baby Unit. *Nurs Times* 1981; Nov 4: 11

Warnock Report. *Report of the Committee of Enquiry into the education of handicapped children and young people.* London: HMSO, 1978

Resources for Parents and Health Workers

Organisations

For preterm and NICU

Action for Sick Children (National Association for the Welfare of Children in Hospital, NAWCH)
Argyle House, 29–31 Euston Road, London NW1 2SD, UK

BLISSLINK (Baby Life Support Systems)
c/o BLISS, 17–21 Emerald Street, London WC1N 3QL, UK

The Child Bereavement Trust
1 Hillside, Riversdale, Bourne End, Buck, SL 8 5EB, UK

National Association for Maternal and Child Welfare
1 South Audley Street, London W1Y 6JS, UK

NIPPERS (National Information for Parents of Prematures: Education, Resources and Support)
49 Allison Road, Acton, London W3 6HZ, UK

Twins and Multiple Births Association (TAMBA)
41 Fortuna Way, Aylesby Park, Grimsby, South Humberside DN37 9ST, UK

For congenital abnormalities and handicap

Action Research for the Crippled Child
Vincent House, North Parade, Horsham, West Sussex RH12 2DA, UK

Association for Children with Hand or Arm Deficiency (REACH)
13 Park Terrace, Crimchard, Chard, Somerset TA20 1LA, UK

Association for Spina Bifida and Hydrocephalus (ASBAH)
22 Upper Woburn Place, London WCH 0EP, UK

Cleft Lip and Palate Association (CLAPA)
1 Eastwood Gardens, Kenton, Newcastle upon Tyne NE3 3QD, UK

Contact a Family
16 Strutton Ground, London SW1P 2HP, UK

Down Syndrome Association
12/13 Clapham Common Southside, London SW4 7AA, UK

National Association for Families of Children with Congenital Abnormalities of the Lower Limbs (STEPS)
15 Statham Close, Lymm, Cheshire WA13 9NN, UK

Network for the Handicapped (law and advisory centre for the handicapped and their families)
16 Princeton Street, London WC1R 4BB, UK

Royal Society for Mentally Handicapped Children and Adults (MENCAP)
MENCAP National Centre, 123 Golden Lane, London EC1Y 0RT, UK

Books

Bowlby J. *Attachment and loss*, Vol III, *Loss, sadness and depression*. London: Hogarth Press, 1980.

Cunningham C. *Down's syndrome: an introduction for parents*. London: Souvenir Press, 1982.

Cunningham C, Sloper P. *Helping your handicapped baby*. London: Souvenir Press, 1978.

Kelnar C, Harvey D, Simpson C. *The sick newborn baby*, 3rd edn. London: Baillière Tindall, 1994.

Mental Health Foundation. *Directory of self-help and community support agencies in the UK and Republic of Ireland*. London: Mental Health Foundation.

Millard DM. *Daily living with a handicapped child*. London: Croom Helm, 1984.

Redshaw M, Rivers M, Rosenblatt D. *Born too soon*. Oxford: Oxford University Press, 1985

Personal experiences

Boston S. *Will my son – life and death of a mongol child*. London: Pluto Press, 1981.

Featherstone H. *A difference in the family – life with a disabled child*. London: Harper and Row, 1980.

Millard DM. *Daily living with a handicapped child*. London: Croom Helm, 1984.

Leaflets

Leaflets on bereavements in these situations from '*An ache in their hearts*' resource package, see details below.

Chapter Seven

Caring for the Bereaved

What we call the end, is often the beginning, and to make an end is to make a beginning. The end is where we start from.

(T.S. Eliot)

Introduction

As this is essentially a practical book, this chapter is divided into two parts. For those of you working in hospitals, you will meet newly bereaved parents either in the Maternity Unit, Neonatal Intensive Care Unit (NICU), Intensive Care Unit or the Accident and Emergency Department. It is you who will have to deal with the rawness of grief as it first dawns on the parents. This is a very different situation from the longer-term bereavement care that is more likely to fall on the community team.

How the death is handled from the outset can have long-lasting effects on the parents. Finlay and Dallimore (1991) found that parents really appreciated unhurried and private interviews, where the informant had an understanding and caring attitude and had time to listen to the parents' questions. Leon (1992) endorses this by saying that the caregiver participates in a vital way in the healing process, not with a flurry of activity but by listening unhurriedly, understanding the meaning of the loss to the bereaved family and helping the parents express their painful and conflicting feelings in words.

Short-term Management

The sudden death of a baby at whatever age from whatever cause is a devastating experience, mostly for the parent(s) but also for those around. Telling relatives of a death has often been assumed to be something that only physicians can do. However, in the study of Jones and Buttery (1981), parents they interviewed indicated that they would rather be informed by a nurse, who seemed to care that their loved one had died and who seemed to understand that the deceased was someone important, than by a physician, who was knowledgeable as to why the person had died but who seemed not to care that the death had occurred.

Shock appears to be a universal feeling following any death, but it may last for months when the death is sudden and unexpected. The purpose of shock is initially to protect a person from the harsh reality of death. A person experiencing a sudden death does not need or require in-depth counselling as they are too numbed to respond. Counselling will come later when the shock has diminished. According to Johnson (1987) there are two forms of shock: tranquil and hysterical. In tranquil shock people are aware of what is happening around them, but are detached from it. They are unable to speak, experiencing a 'calming' or 'numbing' effect. In hysterical shock people may wail, cry, yell, scream, feel nauseated and pound their fists. As professionals, this type of reaction is more difficult to deal with as it makes us feel uncomfortable. However, we need to acknowledge that for some this reaction is normal and part of their grief response to a tragedy.

Whenever possible, bereaved people should be able to react in their way in a place of privacy, supported and cared for by a professional (Friedman 1974). This is not always easy on a busy ward or Accident and Emergency Department, but it should be given a high priority.

Wright (1993) found that nurses responded more easily to people who cried, sobbed or wept, but had greatest difficulty with those who withdrew into themselves. It is not easy to sit with someone who does not respond. It increases our helplessness, but it is important to remember that our physical presence is the most important factor. Physical contact can be very reassuring for some bereaved people, but others may shun such closeness. We need to develop an awareness of telling the difference.

Many bereaved people say 'I can't believe this is happening to me.' The enormity of the situation is too great for the person to take fully in the reality. This is known as *denial*. There is no way in which we can change the situation; there are few, if any, words to say that will make any real difference. Our care and concern will come from non-verbal signs – our eyes, if we care, will show compassion, our hands gentleness. These are the things that bereaved people remember. Jones and Buttery (1981) noted that those who had traumatic experiences in the Emergency Department as the result of poor emotional support had haunting memories which interfered with the resolution of their grief.

Dealing with *anger* is not easy. If it is directed at the staff, our defensiveness may make matters worse. Wherever the anger is directed, we need to acknowledge it, try to diffuse it by allowing them to talk about it and continue to stay with them.

Guilt is not uncommon in parents whose baby has died, especially those whose baby has died suddenly and unexpectedly (Smialekz 1978). However reassuring we try to be, it will not really assuage the guilt, but we do need to listen without judgement and allow people to verbalise their feelings. It is in this way that their guilt will be eased. It is likely that guilt will continue for many months.

Points to ease later grief

We now realise that there are certain practical procedures that can help parents:

1. Seeing and holding the dead child for as long as the parents want to. It has now become more common for a child to be taken home before the funeral and after the postmortem. Many parents are unaware of this option. In everything, parents need to be told of the choices available so that they can make informed decisions, which will help them to feel more in control of the situation.
2. Offering parents the opportunity to wash and dress their dead baby after the death and before a postmortem. Parents may wish to do this on their own, or may feel more comfortable with a nurse in attendance. This can be a very therapeutic experience as it will bring home the reality of the death. Physical contact is healing – to be able to wash their baby for the last time can bring much comfort. It also allows for any mystique to be taken out of so-called 'last offices'.
3. Refreshments and a telephone should be available to parents.
4. A play area for other children in the family allows parents to have some space for themselves.

5. Equipment for taking photographs, footprints and hand prints should be available so that parents may have positive proof of their child.
6. Arranging for transport to take parents home, if required, can make life much easier. Parents in a state of severe shock need to be cared for.

Before parents go home, it is important to give them a clear picture of:

• *Where* their child is, e.g. hospital mortuary.
• *What* will happen to their child, e.g. when the postmortem will take place, what is involved and how their child will look after it.
• *What* will happen to them (the parents). This is especially important after a cot death as the police (or Coroner's officer) will wish to make contact with them. Parents also need to know when they can plan the funeral, which will be dependent on the postmortem.
• *Whom* they can contact for information and to see their baby again, as well as whom they can contact for informal support, e.g. a self-help group or a counsellor (if available).

As there is so much information to give, it is advisable not only to tell parents but to give written information for reference. (A list of available leaflets is given in Appendix 10.)

All the above points will help parents to feel special and cherished. They will not take away their pain, but will help them start the bereavement journey in a positive way.

Longer-term Bereavement Care

It is hoped that when a baby dies, whether at home or in hospital, the GP, health visitor or midwife will visit the family as soon after the death as possible. Parents may need help with practical issues, such as registering the death, arranging the funeral or practical help with the other children in the family (see Chapter 8). Equally important is the nurturing of a relationship with the family so that they begin to trust the healthcare professionals. Research has shown that most families require support after sudden and unexpected death of their child (Cornwell et al. 1977; Tudehope et al. 1986).

It would appear that there is some confusion as to what is meant by 'follow-up' in bereavement. Perhaps some see a 'one-off' visit after the death as sufficient, some will go several times and some will continue visiting for many months. There is also some confusion as to who does the visiting and what coordination (if any) goes on between the professionals or voluntary agencies. In my own experience, I have found that bereavement visiting is done on a very ad hoc basis depending on the level of skills of the healthcare givers. People with physical illnesses seem to take priority over the bereaved, so that grieving families may be left in isolation.

It is only recently that we have realised the need for an assessment tool for bereaved families. We are unlikely to visit someone with a physical illness without carrying out some sort of assessment. Our future care will depend on our findings. We recommend the need to have a key worker identified for bereavement care so that each family is assessed and helped appropriately. Unless this is done, families may be left to cope with their grief totally unaided. Sometimes a telephone call is sufficient. A follow-up visit 6–8 weeks after the death with their GP, paediatrician or pathologist to discuss postmortem findings is particularly helpful to many parents.

Although bereavement is not an illness, I believe we need to have certain guidelines that will help us to plan future care of the bereaved family. Parkes (1975) has identified the following as leading to a more difficult grieving pattern.

1. *Type of death*. If the death was from an illness, even if it were sudden, it is likely to cause fewer problems than traumatic death. Death by injury or death that damages the body is more likely to be thought of as causing suffering and as being an injustice.
2. *Nature of attachment*. Although most mothers and fathers love their babies, there may be times when the death may give some relief, e.g. families where yet another child would mean financial hardship, babies who have died because of congenital abnormalities or where the parents did not want a baby for whatever reason. All this can mean that there is a somewhat ambivalent relationship to the dead baby. This may lead to excessive feelings of guilt.
3. *Past unresolved griefs*. If parents have not confronted other past losses, it is likely that the present death may well compound the situation and make grieving more difficult.
4. *Type of personality*. People who are more vulnerable from past painful experiences, especially in childhood, those who are more dependent and those who tend to see life negatively are more likely to encounter difficulties in bereavement. Bereaved people who avoid feelings of helplessness, who perceive themselves to be strong, and therefore do not cry easily are also at risk of having a prolonged grief reaction.
5. *Social support*. Some parents may well be very isolated in their grief, having few friends or family around to support them. Others may seem to have support but perceive it as insufficient. In some families a conspiracy of silence is adopted where members act as if the death had not happened.

Nicol et al. (1986) found that three factors related to a more difficult bereavement for mothers:

(a) those women who reported a crisis during pregnancy (death of a loved one, family illness, marital problems, general family tensions about the pregnancy);

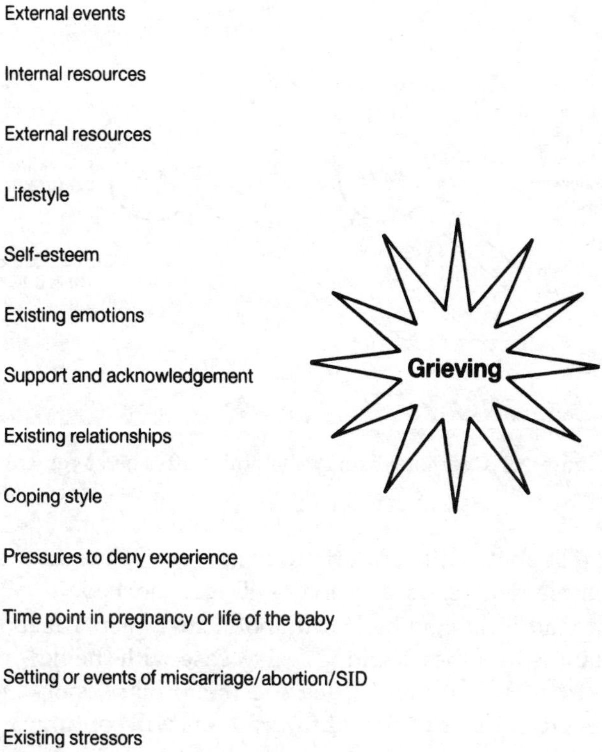

External events

Internal resources

External resources

Lifestyle

Self-esteem

Existing emotions

Support and acknowledgement

Grieving

Existing relationships

Coping style

Pressures to deny experience

Time point in pregnancy or life of the baby

Setting or events of miscarriage/abortion/SID

Existing stressors

Figure 7.1 Individual reactions to bereavement depend on personal resources, experience and stressors.

(b) those who did not perceive their husband and/or family as supportive;
(c) those who saw, but did not hold, their baby after it died.

Not all families will require care in bereavement, but unless a proper assessment is made, we have no means by which we gain an understanding of where a parent is and how he/she got there. It is important that we document our assessment as part of any professional code of conduct. Whilst doing this, we can point out sources of support and explain about changing family dynamics. This can be done pictorially and shown to the families (Fig. 7.2). In this example, the mother and siblings are a cohesive unit with different sources of support. The father is not sharing with the family and has tenuous contact with the GP and health visitor, which leaves him very isolated and at risk. It may also result in a breakdown in the marriage.

Few lay people understand what grieving involves and how long it lasts. They may be unsure as to the purpose of your visit, how long it should last

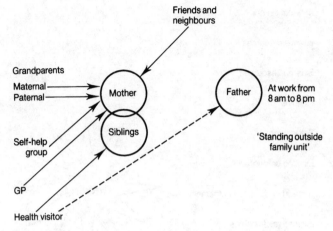

Figure 7.2 Changing family dynamics after bereavement.

and what to talk about. It is important, therefore, that some guidelines are given in a simple manner as they may still feel shocked.

At the first visit little may be learnt about their deeper feelings. What is more important is that they begin to feel at ease with the new carer so that they start to trust that person by sensing their compassion and care, and reassurance is given that caring and future visits will continue if that would help them. By allowing them to choose they will have more control. If after explaining what is available they still feel it is unnecessary for further visits, for whatever reason, a telephone number should be left so that they can make contact at some future date.

At the second visit it will be easier to assess the situation. It is important that an account of the death as they perceived it is obtained. The following questions will help to build up a picture of the bereaved and enable an assessment to be made of those more at risk by using the guidelines of Parkes (1975) and Nicol et al. (1986). The questions may seem blunt but if they are asked with sensitivity, and time given for answers with good listening, the grieving person may have much to say and great deal will have been learnt.

- Was the death expected?
- Were they present at the death?
- Was it a peaceful or violent death?
- What did they feel about the actual death?
- Did they hold the child after it had died?
- Were there any family problems during the pregnancy?
- How did they feel about having another baby?
- What sort of person were they before the death?

- Have they suffered any other major deaths in the past? How did they cope?
- What support do they have from family/partners?

From this evaluation parents most at risk from complicated grieving can be identified. They will require more visiting than those less at risk. A plan or 'Contract of care' can then be drawn up as to how often to visit. This could be weekly initially for several weeks, reducing to fortnightly, then monthly, depending on the progress.

Contract of care

The contract of care can be given verbally, but it may be worth writing it down for the family to digest in their own time.

1. Who are we:
   Credentials/why we can offer this sort of care, either informal or formal experience
2. What can we offer:
   Support – now
              – in the future
              – for how long
              – how often
   Information – relevant to the present, e.g. registering the death, arranging a funeral
              – in the future, e.g. pregnancy
              – self-help group
   Referral – formal agencies, voluntary agencies
3. Where do we come from:
   Our base
   Our telephone number and hours of availability

Bereavement visiting is time-consuming and may be difficult to do with a busy case load. However, prevention is better than cure. In the longer term, frequent visits to GPs, psychologists and psychiatrists may be avoided if good bereavement care is given initially.

How long should a visit last?

A bereavement visit should not be longer than 1 hour. For the bereaved this is long enough to dwell on painful issues. For the carer it is long enough to concentrate fully on what the bereaved person is saying. From the outset of the visit, the carer should make it clear that she/he will be staying for 1 hour and during that time they will concentrate on the grief. Making boundaries is useful both for the carer and the bereaved. If the situation arises where the bereaved person wishes to detain their carer, either by words and/or tears, then the carer must gently say they will continue next time where they left off. It is a good idea to ring later in the day to find out how she/he is and to arrange a further meeting. (Some people can be quite manipulative, especially if they do not wish to be left on their own.) By keeping to time limits the carer is able to go to his/her next visit on time, but will still be seen as caring. Quality visiting, not quantity visiting is the key.

It is this point that visiting takes on counselling dimensions so it is worth considering what this means.

Counselling and supporting families

Today the word 'counselling' is used in many different contexts. It is beyond the scope of this book to delve deeply into this particular aspect as it has been covered by many other authors, but, in order to help someone through their grief, it is necessary to have a basic understanding of what counselling is.

As young nurses and medical practitioners in training we are taught to listen to our patients and to observe. Those basic skills form the foundation for counselling so, although nurses are not generally seen as counsellors in the true sense of the word, they can develop skills to enable them to assist bereaved people through their grief.

The British Association of Counselling gives the definition of counselling as 'an interaction in which one person offers another time, attention and respect with the intention of helping that person to explore, discuss and clarify ways of living more resourcefully and to his or her greater well-being'. Nurse (1980) sees counselling as 'concerned with healing, with health and with wholeness . . . it is to do with strength and awareness for growth . . . it demands certain qualities and skills from the practitioner'. Tschudin (1987) believes that 'counselling is made up of three elements: the client and his or her problem or reason for seeking help; the counsellor and his or her skills; and the relationship between them'.

As carers, all three definitions affect us in our work. We, as the helpers, will inevitably come into contact with 'clients' whom we wish to help as effectively as possible. 'Counselling is not giving out advice but listening and, having listened, talking in such a way that the bereaved person can find his or her own solutions by listening to himself as he talks. The helper, the carer, has enhanced another person and in so doing finds that she is enhanced herself. That is the essence of caring' (Tschudin 1987). From what Tschudin says, counselling is about caring – a characteristic that is attributed to nurses.

Roach (1984) has identified five C's of caring: namely, compassion, competence, confidence, conscience and commitment. Hopefully, we will have compassion, conscience and commitment. Competence and confidence will be gained with time.

It is important to recognise that we are not providing a formal counselling service as in therapy, but are there to be supportive through the grief. Developing good listening skills enables clients to talk so that they may begin to work through some of the phases of grief. Egan (1986) has given us a simple model of helping which forms the acronym, SOLER:

S = sit squarely in relation to the client;
O = maintain an open position, i.e. be accepting of the client, not judging, giving permission to the client to talk of what he/she will;
L = lean slightly towards the client;
E = maintain reasonable eye contact;
R = relax! (I have found that taking a few deep breaths, using the lower abdomen, helps to ease tension.)

It is important for the client to know that we are listening, so nodding, smiling, even grunting occasionally, will reinforce this. During our listening, it is also important that we are quite sure of what is being said. Checking for understanding and reflecting or paraphrasing can help both carer and client. Reflecting is repeating what the client has said, which may sound odd when you are not used to practising it. However, it is a very useful tool, which allows the client to see him/herself as he/she is. For example:

Client: Once the children and Bill have gone off in the morning, I just don't know what to do with myself.
Helper: It seems as if you find it very difficult to be on your own.
Client: I hate being on my own and can't settle to do anything. I know I should do the housework, but don't seem to have any energy.
Helper: It sounds as if you get very tired.

The helper, through the client, has identified two major points: (a) the client finds isolation difficult; and (b) gets tired easily. Both points can then be worked on to try to improve matters. No questions have been asked. Indeed, questioning words such as why, what and how are very inhibiting and should be avoided, if at all possible.

Heron (1976) has described six ways of helping. These are:

1. *Supportive* – giving complete attention, being caring and loving as well as affining and appreciating the other person.
2. *Informative* – giving simple, straightforward information.
3. *Prescriptive* – it is always important that the client stays in control, but a carer can gently direct by suggesting, proposing, persuading or even commanding.
4. *Catalytic* – the carer can enable the client to change things by reflecting, asking open questions and checking for understanding.
5. *Confronting* – here the carer can challenge what has been said with sensitivity so that the client can understand his or her behaviour. If

this is done too gently or too harshly the client will not understand, or will become defensive.

6. *Cathartic* – this allows painful emotion to be expressed such as anger, guilt, sadness or despair. Touching, holding or hugging can be used if the client feels comfortable with this.

What is support?

All of us at some stage in our lives will require support – a prop – to help us to cope with a difficult situation. Human beings need human beings, probably more so in bereavement than at any other time. There is no substitute that works as effectively. A fallen rose needs a stake to hold it up so that it can grow more easily. The stake does not do any of the growing – it is merely there. Its presence is sufficient to allow the rose to blossom. So it is with human beings in bereavement. A physical presence who genuinely feels and cares can bring immense support.

Today, in our changing, more mobile society the old family framework of support has gone in many areas, especially in towns and cities. Most people understand little of the process of bereavement or the length of recovery, so grieving families are too often left on their own to cope with the pain and isolation. It therefore falls increasingly to the healthcare professional to be a caring support, encouraging, showing warmth and sometimes confronting and challenging. It does not mean that we can do grief work for parents. They must do this for themselves but in a framework of trust and understanding. Sometimes they will need permission to start grieving as society has taught us to hide our real feelings. Sometimes they will need help to stop grieving and start living again.

The following is a list of feelings that were expressed by various groups of bereaved parents that I have worked with. It is a formidable list, but worth showing as it demonstrates the wide range of reactions. There were different feelings in each group but *isolation* and *vulnerability* were common to them all:

Intolerance	Forgetfulness
Loss of pride	Unable to go into wide open spaces
Emptiness	Need to have constant
Isolation	companionship
Changed values	Lack of concentration
Irritability	Thinking of oneself only
Loss of expectations	Mood swings
Unable to be close to husband or	Not being the same as others
other children	Not enjoying oneself as others
Loss of role as a mother	I would rather have died
Questioning God	Feeling brittle when seeing other
Loss of feeling – numbness	children achieving

Overprotecting other children
Change in character
Change in physical state
Loneliness
Losing love
Feeling guilty
Blaming oneself for the death
Blaming other people
Not relating to others unless they
  have encountered loss
Despair
Extrasensitive

Feeling suicidal
Overwhelming tiredness
Depression
Aimless existence
Vulnerability
Horror/shock
Still worrying about dead child
Where have they gone?
How are they coping?
Feeling the baby move inside them
Hearing the baby cry

Working with the same groups, I asked what helped them most and what helped least. This is the parents' list. Listening came top of the helping list for everyone. Again isolation was mentioned and again it was experienced by everyone.

Bereaved parents were helped *most* by:

- friends and relations who listened often and attentively;
- God – through talking to their Vicar;
- work – by losing themselves in it and forgetting the pain temporarily;
- finding compassionate friends – especially the first contact people;
- reading about other bereaved parents and feeling a common bond, and a feeling of normality;
- an interesting hobby, or a full-time commitment;
- taking up some new interest;
- having the other children;
- not being alone – having a rota of friends to be with;
- having help with correspondence and practical issues.

Bereaved parents were helped *least* by:

- being isolated – feeling a social 'leper';
- others changing the subject to avoid talking of the dead child;
- people not mentioning the dead child's name;
- having to take the initiative when feeling bruised and sore;
- being avoided by people;
- not feeling part of society;
- people not knowing how to help;
- God didn't help at all;
- waking up early in the morning and realising the loss and the awful thought of getting through another day;
- lack of sleep, constantly irritable and tearful, out of control.

As isolation and vulnerability are so common, perhaps the first task of a bereavement helper is to demonstrate to the grieving person that she/he, the carer, will continue visiting until the pain eases and life becomes more bearable. A helper will inevitably be involved in discussion of practical, social and family matters, all of which impinge on, and influence, recovery, but the principal task is concerned with the emotional features of bereavement. A grieving person is thrown back on personal resources and the helper's task is to put the bereaved person in touch with these and help strengthen them. A carer is involved in helping with the painful and gradual task of acceptance and adjustment.

A carer needs to retain a realistic sense of hope. Bereaved people, although devastated by their loss, have the potential to recover. In the early or most painful days of grief it is hard to believe that life will ever be good again. Reassurance can be conveyed, but not impatiently or falsely, nor in such a way that the pain and suffering is undervalued or denied. Helping in bereavement is demanding and complex. It calls for patience and persistence. Listening is basic to the work. A bereaved person needs to talk of the anger, guilt and sadness, perhaps on many occasions. Ventilating strong feelings of anger and aggression and admitting to feelings of guilt are not easy, so it is important that the carer listens in a non-judgemental way and reassures that the secrets that have been shared will not damage their relationship. The helper needs to create a safe environment so that the bereaved person feels free to talk openly.

There is a tendency to want to fill silences as they can be threatening to the composure of the helper. A silence does not necessarily mean that nothing is happening. Probably many thoughts and feelings are crowding into the mind of the bereaved person. A carer needs to respond with sensitivity and patience and feel comfortable with silence.

It is often difficult for a grieving person to see beyond their own grief. Sometimes they are unable to appreciate the grief of others in the family. A helper can do much to point this out and to encourage them to share their feelings.

Differences between fathers and mothers

Until recently, more attention has been focused on grieving mothers. Women find it easier to talk of their feelings to other women. Men tend to think it weak to cry or show emotions so, rather than risk either, keep their feelings to themselves. Fathers are reported to feel an obligation to 'stay strong' and support their wife following the loss of a child (Helmarth and Steinitz 1978; Standish 1982). It has been believed that fathers have less grief and fewer symptoms of depression than mothers (Wilson et al. 1982). It has been supposed that they experience the loss less deeply and have a shorter grieving period than mothers (Cornwell et al. 1977).

However, the study by Dyregrov and Matthiesen (1987) has shown that the level of distress in fathers is considerable. They state that the cause of differences in mothers' and fathers' reactions is unclear. They believe that they (a) may be caused by a difference in the amount of attachment or 'bonding' to the child; (b) may reflect different reactions to stress or different methods of coping in men and women; (c) may arise because men fail to acknowledge emotions and reactions; or (d) may reflect the different social situation the two sexes experience following the loss.

Verbrugge (1985), in her review of the area of coping in general rather than coping with the death of a child in particular, has suggested that preferences in terms of coping styles may be associated with gender. She concluded that women prefer to use social support and emotionally oriented coping styles, whilst men prefer active problem-solving and tension-reducing ways of coping.

It is important that fathers are not overlooked. It is more difficult to talk to them as frequently because they are working when healthcare professionals visit.

How can death affect a relationship?

It could be assumed that when two parents have suffered the death of their child, the experience would draw them closer together. For some couples this is the case, but for many others the opposite is true. Instead of becoming closer, they draw further and further apart until they end up so polarised that they decide to part.

> Suddenly and frighteningly, this couple, this two wedded into one, has a basic truth thrust upon it. Once again they are two. Each must bear his or her pain and a mate cannot bear it for you, nor can a mate shield you from it. The couple, unlike when they laughed together, holidayed together, shared downfalls together, suddenly finds at the time of the greatest tragedy in their lives – and at the time of their greatest need – that each is an individual. They must mourn as individuals, separately. (Sarnoff Schiff 1977).

I have found that one of the difficulties encountered by parents is that mothers want to talk of their dead child, whilst fathers do not. This can likely be attributed to the fact that fathers must be stoical, therefore any mention of the dead child will unsettle the determination to remain in control and be strong. It takes a lot of energy to constantly be on guard and restrain feelings of pure grief! It is therefore important that both are encouraged to talk of the dead child and other issues of concern. As in all things, communication is vital. However, moderation is the key.

I have found that it has helped grieving couples to set aside a specific time each day to talk of their feelings, the dead child and their sadness. Every day has to be got through, however difficult, but if they each know that there is a time to share and unload, it can make life more tolerable for both of them.

Marital and sexual problems are not uncommon after the death of a baby. Parents may feel embarrassed to talk of such problems with family or friends so it may be up to the care giver to gently broach the subject, or be aware of who might assist if the parents would like further help.

Anniversaries

Most of us enjoy celebrating the dates of our birthdays, weddings and other significant life events. It is often a time for meeting with family and friends to remember the day, by having a special meal and relaxing and laughing together. For parents whose baby has died, there are two significant dates to be remembered: the day of birth and the day of death, both memorable but bringing much sadness instead of the usual joy and happiness. In the first year, most parents will dread the coming of both dates. There is little to celebrate and the reminder of what might have been is so very painful and overwhelming. Some parents, however, find that the actual date becomes an anticlimax. They have waited for the special day, dreaded its coming, and then find that the day itself is just nothing. Others find that when the day dawns, it is often far worse than they imagined.

For us, as carers, we have no way of knowing how parents will react. We can help to plan ahead with them, to consider how they will spend the day, and listen to their fears and pain, which are evoked by the coming anniversary. Perhaps our most useful role can be in remembering – by sending a little card, by telephoning just before or after the day, or actually being there with a hug, if that is what they would like. Our actions will say two things: 'I remember that this is a special day' and 'I care enough about you to want to share your pain.'

We have found that for some families lighting a candle in remembrance of the dead child can be very healing. One family I know baked a cake, taking one piece to the grave where the birds could enjoy it. This for them was like a little pilgrimage, not just for the parents but for their two children. Although it was a painful experience for all of them, they shared something special together and that in itself brought a degree of healing. I know of a mother whose dead daughter's school friends clubbed together to buy a magnolia tree. Years later she still visits the tree on the anniversary of her daughter's death, when amazingly each year the tree is in bloom.

For some parents subsequent anniversaries can be as, or more, painful. They wonder what their child would look like now and what they would be doing.

Christmas, too, can be a very difficult time. For many of us who have children, it is a time of filling stockings, of giving presents and watching the wonder on children's faces. For those that have lost a child there is the painful reminder that a child is missing and these little delights for them or their child will never be.

Celebrations, Christmas and birthdays will come despite your best efforts to avoid them. And they are horrendous times for many years. Their pain cannot be minimised. But they still must be faced. (Sarnoff Schiff 1977)

Grandparents

For grandparents whose grandchildren die, the loss is experienced acutely. Not only have they lost someone special to them, but they have also witnessed the awful suffering of one of their children. In their own grief and search for an explanation, they may comment on the way the baby was cared for. This can be very hurtful for the bereaved parents who may feel even more guilty. Such a situation can leave both parties in isolation. Furthermore, a grieving mother may desperately want to talk through her feelings, only to be told by her parents that it is unhealthy to do so. It is not surprising that grandparents who have been closely involved with the dead child go through full mourning responses to the death (Cornwell et al. 1977).

It is not easy to follow-up grandparents, who may live in the same health district but could be many miles away. They are not essentially ill, although are greatly at risk to become so. Who should tell their GP? They or the healthcare professionals? Sadly, it would appear that few get help. Perhaps offering the parents a leaflet on grandparents' grief to give to their parents may be the first step in recognising their pain.

Family and friends

In some instances, friends and family will rally round and be very helpful and supportive. However, from the families I have worked with, the opposite appears to be nearer the mark.

Most couples feel desperately abandoned and isolated, which brings more hurt and pain. For fear of upsetting the parents by saying the wrong things, and probably for fear of getting upset themselves, people tend to shy away or even literally cross the road to avoid any contact. One mother whose child had died a few weeks previously had to wait for her two other children to come out of school. Previously she had enjoyed the camaraderie of the other mothers. She now found she was standing alone with no-one to speak to. She felt angry and wanted to shout out, 'OK, so my baby has died but why can't you treat me normally?' Not only was she feeling guilty and alone but now had to cope with being ostracised. Sadly, she was the one that took the initiative by talking to a mother she knew quite well, not about her dead baby, but about something related to the school. From then on she was drawn back into the circle of mothers, some of whom were able to ask her about her awful tragedy.

Voluntary agencies

Perhaps the need for bereavement agencies has arisen because of our changing society and the somewhat erratic care offered by the statutory sector. Most, if not all, agencies were started as a result of a perceived need by people who themselves had been bereaved. Over the years the main organisations have grown to national acclaim with branches in most areas of the country. Many run support groups for similarly bereaved people. It can be very comforting to meet others who have suffered as a result of death, where feelings can be shared, problems discussed and where support and friendship can grow. Most bereaved people feel very isolated, so self-help groups can fill a gap and go some way to alleviating these feelings. Befriending rather than counselling is offered by bereaved parents to newly grieving parents in many areas of the UK.

Parents find it a comfort to talk to someone who has suffered a similar tragedy. However, through my work with CRUSE, whose members have not necessarily been bereaved, I have found that a helper with the necessary skills, empathy and understanding has much to offer grieving parents.

Hopefully, most of you who read this book will not have lost a child through death, and yet I hope you will feel able to support and help families through bereavement by extending your skills and understanding.

Perhaps the ideal situation is to have a combination of help from both the voluntary and statutory sectors. It would appear that at present there is little coordination or working together in health districts to give parents the benefits of both available services. From my current research I am finding that many health carers are unsure or vague about which voluntary agencies function within their districts. There is a tendency, when referral is made, to then discontinue visiting, leaving the voluntary agency to carry on with the caring.

Earlier in this chapter we advised that a key worker should be identified to help bereaved families. Such a person could help considerably in providing families with all available resources within their district, and also bridge the gap between the voluntary and statutory sectors. A list of the key agencies and the leaflets they produce is given in Appendix 11.

Key points
- Bereaved people need sensitive non-judgemental listening
- Their feelings should not be denied
- A loss, especially a death, can change family dynamics
- Doing an assessment, appointing a key worker and making a contract of care should happen automatically for any bereaved family
- Grandparents and fathers should not be forgotten

- Voluntary agencies
- Listening and enabling are the keys to good caring

References

Cornwell J, Nurcombe E, Stevens SL. Family response to loss of a child by sudden infant death syndrome. *Med J Aust* 1977; 28: 1

Dyregrov A, Matthiesen SB. Similarities and differences in mothers' and fathers' grief following the death of an infant. *Scand J Psychol* 1987

Egan G. *The skilled helper*, 3rd edn. Belmont, California: Wordsworth, 1986

Finlay I, Dallimore D. Your child is dead. *Br Med J* 1991; 302: 103

Friedman J. Psychological aspects of sudden and unexpected death in infants and children. *Pediatr Clin North Am* 1974; 21: 103

Helmrath TA, Steinitz EM. Death of an infant. Parental grieving and the failure of social support. *J Fam Pract* 1978; 6: 785

Heron J. *Dying*. Harmondsworth: Pelican, 1976

Johnson SE. *After a child dies – counselling bereaved families*. New York: Springer, 1987

Jones W, Buttery M. Sudden death: survivors' perception of their Emergency Department. *J Emerg Nurs* 1981; 7:

Leon I. Perinatal loss – a critique of current hospital practices. *Clin Paediatr* 1992;

Nicol MT, Tompkins FR, Campbell NA, Syme GJ. Maternal grieving response after perinatal death. *Med J Aust* 1986; 144: 287

Nurse G. *Counselling and the nurse*, 2nd edn. Aylesbury: HM&M, 1980

Parkes CM. *Determinants of outcome following bereavement*. Omega, 1975: 308–323

Roach MS. *Caring – the human mode of being – implications for nursing*. Toronto University, 1984

Sarnoff Schiff H. *The bereaved parent*. Souvenir Press (E&A) Ltd. London 1977

Smialekz J. Observations on immediate reactions of families by SID. Paediatrics 1978; 62: 160

Standish L. *The loss of a baby*. Lancet, March 1982

Tschudin V. *Counselling skills for nurses* (2nd edn.) London: Ballière Tindall, 1987

Tudehope D, Rodgers D, Gunn A. Neonatal death – grieving families. *Med J Aust* 1986; 144: 290

Verbrugge L. Gender and health – an update on hypotheses and incidence. *J Health Soc Behav* 1985; 26: 156

Wilson AL, Fenton LJ, Stevens DC. The death of a newborn twin: an analysis of parental bereavement. *Paediatrics* 1982; 70: 587

Wright B. *Caring in crisis*. Edinburgh: Churchill Livingstone, 1993

Chapter Eight

Children in the Family

A child can live through anything, so long as he or she is told the truth and is allowed to share with loved ones, the natural feelings they have when they are suffering.

(Eda le Shan)

Within this chapter

1. Children's understanding of death
2. The effects of death on children
3. How parents can help
4. Viewing the dead child's body and attending funerals
5. How carers can help in the hospital or community

Introduction

Perhaps one of the most difficult tasks in bereavement is to know how to explain death to children and how best to support them. For many years we have believed that children do not understand about death and do not grieve.

We tend to assume that the life of a child consists of little more than the gathering of memories that in later years can be recalled fondly. In reality, nothing could be further from the truth, as childhood is, and always has been, a time of trial and loss. (Morgan 1991)

Parents naturally want to protect children from the harsh reality of death but, in doing so, may suppress their children's grief, which may manifest itself many years later (Pincus 1974).

Furman (1974) has shown that when a person is unable to complete a mourning task in childhood, he either has to surrender his emotions in order that they do not suddenly overwhelm him, or else he may be haunted constantly throughout his life with a sadness for which he can never find an appropriate explanation.

The death of a baby or child in the family may or may not directly affect a child but the suffering of the parents and the way in which they handle their grief will doubtless have an effect on how a child will cope and react. In bereavement, parents have a dual role – to cope with their own grief and to support and help their children – one of the most difficult tasks they will face.

Suddenly they are thrust into a role almost beyond what may reasonably be expected of a human being. It means groping to find the right words and attitudes to comfort a living brother or sister . . . Parenthood now becomes walking and talking and listening and hearing someone else at a time when it takes everything just to think or function for oneself. (Sarnoff Schiff 1977).

Following the death of a baby, parents need to be reassured that they can continue to be good parents to surviving offspring. Perhaps our professional role is to help them to help their children so that they can regain some confidence. It is surely one of the greatest achievements for them to know that they have supported and helped their children through a close death. It must be one of the most valuable gifts that parents can pass on to their children.

Children's Understanding of Death

We are now able to understand and appreciate better the impact of death on adults, but it is more difficult to define the effect of death on children. It is assumed that children are unable to express themselves as directly as adults, but perhaps they are not encouraged to do so because of fear of confusing them and fear that painful feelings will be unleashed with which we feel unable to deal.

Not long after her little brother had died, a 5-year-old girl went shopping with her father. In one of the shops, where the assistant was known to the family, the little girl was asked how she was. She did not answer.

Father: Aren't you going to answer the lady?
Daughter: What should I say?
Father: Tell her you're fine.
Daughter: What if I'm not fine?
Father: Tell her you're fine anyway.

It was not so long ago that we approached adults in the same way (and many people still do so). An added difficulty arises when we are unsure of what children's perception of death is, and we are fearful of not providing neat answers to difficult questions. There is the unwritten assumption that adults know all the answers!

At the age of seven my older son's first mouse died. We buried it in a satin-lined matchbox in the garden, laying flowers on its little grave. My son asked where the mouse would go and I glibly said 'to heaven'. I felt I had dealt with the situation rather well until a few days later my son came in from the garden, crying bitterly and shouting at me that I had lied. I eventually heard between sobs that he had unearthed the matchbox and found the mouse still there!

In talking with dying adults we have learnt not to give answers but to listen to what the patient tells us. Perhaps this, too, is the key to understanding children. However, children's development plays a part in understanding the finality of death. It is important to be aware of the stages, but it is more important that children have the opportunity of being listened to and of voicing their feelings, fears and anxieties than rigidly adhering to age constraints.

There are many influences on children's understanding of death other than age. The openness and honesty that parents create is perhaps the most important. Children naturally ask questions and will continue to do so following a death if that is an established pattern of family behaviour. The opposite is also true. Consider the following poem by A.A. Milne:

Elizabeth Ann said to her Nan –
Please will you tell me how God began?
Somebody must have made him, so who could it be, 'cos I want to
    know.
And nurse said 'well'.
And Ann said 'well?'
I know you know and I wish you'd tell.
Nurse took pins from her mouth, and said –
Now then, darling, it's time for bed.

Past experiences of death, whether good or bad, will have made a lasting impression on a child, which will inevitably affect the present death. Some years ago I cared for a family where the grandmother was dying at her daughter's house. The daughter had two girls aged five and seven. I learnt from the grandmother that the girls never came into her room, which greatly distressed her. On gently asking the girls' mother why this was, she told me that the girls had seen their grandfather die from an epileptic fit. She did not want the children to suffer again and so forbade them from entering their grandmother's room. Through quiet discussion with the mother and the two girls we were able to talk about the grandfather's death and how upsetting the situation was for all of them. Gradually the mother saw how important it was for her girls to see their grandmother and vice versa. Some months later the grandmother died peacefully with all her family beside her.

Television and videos are a central part of most children's lives. It is unusual to see death on the screen as something beautiful and peaceful. Violent deaths are commonplace. It is not surprising, therefore, that children believe death to be something horrific. The fact that an actor dies in one film and comes back in another must also give children the impression that death is not fatal.

If a faith, Christian or otherwise, is practised by a family, then the meaning of death, relevant to that faith, may well have been, or will be, passed on to the children. I was lucky enough to know Anna, a 15 year old who was dying of cancer. Anna's Christian faith was very real to her, as it was for her mother. Both believed strongly that when Anna died she would go on living. In the same hospital was a 2-year-old girl who was also dying. Her parents were obviously extremely upset. On one occasion Anna went up to them and told them that she knew they were both dying but there was no need to worry as she, Anna, would look after their little girl when she got to heaven. Although the parents had no faith, they were deeply moved and comforted.

Peers, schoolteachers and other family members also play a part in fashioning a child's interpretation of death.

It follows, therefore, that we cannot measure a child's understanding by age alone. Studies carried out in the USA by Nagy (1959), Spinetta et al. (1973) and Blue-Bond Langner (1978), and in the UK by Bowlby (1980) and Lansdowne (1987) have all shown similar patterns.

In infancy

This age has no understanding of death, but the baby will react to the fear of separation from its mother. Babies need a warm, loving, caring presence. If a twin has died, then the mother will be grieving, and because babies are very much affected by parents' anxiety levels, the reaction of the baby may be one of irritability and clinging. It is likely that the baby will cry more, probably increasing the mother's tension. It is helpful to encourage the mother to talk of her feelings to release the pent-up emotion. So that the mother can spend time with her baby to keep the feeling of security intact, friends and relatives should be encouraged to help with practical issues. If at all possible, the child's routine should be as consistent as possible.

Under 5 years

Children at this age have little understanding of time. Time is man-made. Even to talk of tomorrow to small children is little understood. It follows therefore that 'forever', as in death, means nothing. They can distinguish between a moving, live animal and an inert dead one, but death is more like a sleep or going on a journey. A little girl asked after her grandmother had died, 'Can we visit Grannie in heaven? Is it further than Manchester?' It is important not to tell children that someone who has died has gone to sleep as the child will relate this to themselves and may be fearful of going to sleep for fear of dying. At this age children are very involved with the basic physical side of life, such as eating, sleeping and excreting. They are often very curious about what will become of the dead body and may well ask questions about how the dead person will drink and urinate. Parents could well be thrown by the blatancy of such questions at a time when they are grieving themselves.

From 5 to 8 years

This age is beginning to understand the irreversibility of death. 'When you are dead, you are dead.' But in their minds, death happens to other people, not themselves. Death is usually seen in the guise of a frightening person whom they can avoid if they are careful. Before they go to bed they will look under their beds and check the wardrobe! They avoid the lines on a pavement in case the bogeyman catches them! Death is usually considered as violent (?television), and when it does happen in their lives they may believe they are responsible, and hold the guilt to themselves unless encouraged to talk about it. David was seven when his little sister died of a brain tumour. Following the death he became withdrawn at home, but was very aggressive at school. His parents could not believe his reaction was anything to do with his sister's death as they considered him too young to understand. In time, I discovered that David was convinced that he had caused his sister's death. Three weeks before the brain tumour was discovered, he had thrown a stone at his sister's head, which had resulted in a large bump and bruise. It took great courage for him to admit this. For nearly 2 years he had held the guilt within him.

At this age children become fascinated by the rituals surrounding death. Unless they see the reality they will imagine things far worse. Cremation can take on frightful proportions if it is not explained carefully that the body is no longer needed. I remember accompanying an 8-year-old boy to his younger brother's funeral held in a crematorium. The parents did not feel that they could look after him as well as cope with their own emotions. I knew Matthew well. He was quite happy to hold my hand as I carefully explained about the coffin and how the body would be burned. I was somewhat taken aback when he asked to see the fire and what happened. After the service I asked the parents if I could take Matthew to see the furnace. They agreed and with the help of very understanding staff we waited for the ashes. Matthew held them proudly eventually – something I am sure he will always remember.

From 9 years

Around this age children are aware that death is inevitable, irreversible, universal and final. They begin to understand that they, too, will die. References are now made to logical or biological reasons for death. For example, 'Not living is when your heart stops beating, you have no pulse and can't breathe.' It is perhaps hard for many parents to realise that a child as young can understand so much. It is also humbling to think that as adults we know little more about the mysteries of death than they do!

Teenagers

There is little published research on the concept of death at this age. Although teenagers are not yet adults, it is difficult to see the differences between their understanding and those who are already adults. Inevitably there will be a wide range of ideas from 12 to 19 years of age, dependent on past influences. Jersild (1978) states that the adolescent tends to fantasise about death, believing that if faced with it, he or she will be rescued at the last moment. Kastenbaum (1967) believes that brighter adolescents think a great deal about death, while others shy away from it.

We see, therefore, that from an early age children have some understanding of death, even if it is not talked about openly. There is a good analogy between learning the facts of life and the facts of death! In some families there will be open discussion of both; in some, little or no mention of them. Children will pick up snippets of information about both as they develop, sometimes correctly, sometimes wrongly.

> Children have to learn about death and the processes often provide the onlooker with amusement . . . but the fears and anxieties of children, since they are not unlike those of grown-ups, are less amusing to the onlooker. (Enright 1992)

How Are Children Affected by Death?

In this book we are dealing mainly with neonatal and sudden death in infancy. Miscarriage, stillbirth or neonatal death may mean that other children in the family have not seen their new brother or sister as a living baby. No doubt they will have been told about the impending birth, only to be told (or to guess) that the new baby is dead. Younger children may believe that it has just gone away but will inevitably be affected by the grief of the parents. When an older baby dies suddenly, children will be affected not only by the parents' behaviour but by the loss of a sibling who had become part of their lives.

The grief pattern that was described in an earlier chapter applies equally to children. We know that shock, numbness, anger, guilt, sadness, searching and despair are feelings that children also will experience.

Common reactions in children

- Some children may become listless and withdrawn for weeks or months after the death. Depression is common in adults after a major bereavement. Children, too, become depressed as they have also suffered a loss.
- Alternate outbursts of anger, crying and irritability are normal and should not be suppressed.
- Minor ailments and illnesses are common. Bedwetting, fear of the dark, recurrent nightmares or dreams may be experienced.
- There is likely to be a decline in concentration, so school work may be affected for quite some time.
- Remembering things and having difficulty in organising themselves may last for months.

Many of these stem from the need for security and evidence that the world has some stability and boundaries.

How Can Parents Help?

It is never easy to break the news of a death to a child. If the child is not told, he or she will be left confused, possibly imagining things worse than the reality. It is important, therefore, that:

- A child should be told as soon as possible after the death by a parent or someone known and trusted by the child, remembering that touch is all important and the most comforting in times of crisis.
- Simple, factual and repeated explanations are given using 'dead' or 'has died' to avoid confusion in the child's mind. Euphemisms such as 'going to heaven', 'dying in his sleep' or 'God took him for His own' can be quite frightening and misleading to a child.
- Time should be allowed for questions. However simple or even unconnected, children's questions need attention. 'Who will take me to school now that Mummy is so sad?' is a very real question for the child. 'Did Sarah die because I wanted her to?' shows that the child may well feel guilty. 'Can I go out to play now?' may seem brutal, but perhaps the real meaning of what has happened has not really registered. 'What does dead mean?' is not an easy question to answer. Children know about dead flowers and animals, so using nature to explain may be acceptable to them. If a question is asked and you do not know the answer, say so. A child will appreciate honesty.

Should Children See the Dead Baby?

- Like adults, children, even small ones, need to make choices after gentle preparation. Children have rights the same as adults.
- Children may well have seen dead animals so death is not wholly strange to them.
- It is understandable that parents may want to protect their child from the reality of death. However, it is difficult to accept that someone has died if we do not see them in the dead state.
- It can be a very healing experience to have the chance to say 'goodbye'.

We have learnt that it is important for adults to see the dead body as long as they feel comfortable. It reinforces the 'dead state' and confirms that the dead person is no longer living and breathing. To say 'goodbye' reinforces the finality of death.

The child may want to place a favourite toy in the coffin, write a letter of farewell or put flowers in the coffin. I know one family where a well-loved grandfather died. The grandmother helped the three grandchildren to pick buttercups to go in the coffin. Years later the children still remember how healing that was for them.

It is natural to say goodbye to people who are leaving us. Why should death be any different? It may be easier for a child to say goodbye to a baby brother or sister in the hospital where he or she died. Just as it is important for parents to hold the dead baby, children, too, should be given the opportunity of having a last cuddle. If this is done in the presence of the parents, the child will feel included and special.

Should Children Attend the Funeral?

A funeral is a special family occasion, which marks the end of someone's life and gives children the opportunity of seeing others grieving. There may well be opposition from friends and relatives who feel that children should be protected from the sadness of a funeral. Parents who feel that their children should be included, if they wish to, face a dilemma. There is no evidence to show that children who go to funerals are harmed. In fact, the opposite is true. There have been many people in my workshops who felt really angry and excluded because they had not been allowed to attend a family funeral as a child. Many years later they still feel cheated.

A child with language should be given simple explanations of what will happen at the funeral by someone known and trusted, and an assurance that someone close to the child will remain with them throughout. For these children the choice should be theirs. If they choose not to go, it is important that a trusted adult should be with them while the funeral is taking place. Perhaps the funeral service could be taped, for use at a later date, so that the child could know what went on.

Parents may feel that many young children could be disruptive and will mar their chance of concentrating on the service, or that they will be so upset that coping with a demanding toddler will be too much for them. In both cases, someone known to the child could either care for the child at home or throughout the ceremony. By excluding a child from seeing the dead person or from participating in the funeral, by hiding their reactions or by shutting the child out from the adult world in other ways, adults can make a worse situation that is already difficult for children.

One of the most moving and healing funeral services that I attended was that of a lovely West Indian girl. The service was in a church, completely packed with family, relatives, friends and schoolfriends of the dead girl. There were many children; younger ones running around, older ones looking very sad. Part of the service was in walking past the open coffin and saying goodbye to the dead girl. I doubt if there was a dry eye in the church. Through all our tears we shared in the family's sadness and came away the richer for the experience. We have much to learn from each other's cultures.

After the Initial Crisis

Just as adults are confused and hurting, so are children. It is important to acknowledge their loss, as well as the parents.

Children need opportunities to share their thoughts, feelings and anxieties. Guilt and anger are normal feelings, which, if expressed at this stage, can reduce long-term effects. Talking of the dead baby is natural and helpful. Answering their questions may be difficult, but should not be dismissed. They may be the same questions that they asked when they first heard of the death; they may be different ones. Just like the facts of life, it is wise to answer only what is asked. A child will come back to ask more, once they have assimilated the first answers. Like adults, children like to be listened to and heard. It is well known that grieving adults respond well to an understanding listener. Children are no different. As a child develops, so they will reinterpret the death. Children may continue to ask questions years after the death because of their changing perceptions.

Ways that parents can help

- Children need to know that anger, sadness and guilt are normal feelings and won't last forever.
- Informing schools of the death and asking for the support of individual teachers can help both the child and the parents. This is vital if schools are to have a realistic expectation of the child's behaviour over time.

• Birthdays and Christmas may provoke feelings of upset and uncertainty in both parents and children. Doing something special in way of remembrance may bring comfort to the whole family. Many families find comfort in lighting a candle on birthdays, or doing something special to remember the dead baby, e.g. planting a tree or flower.

• Everyone in the family will grieve in different ways at different times. Like adults, children, too, will have bad days when they will need gentleness and sensitivity.

• Open and honest communication should be practised if at all possible, but children need to go at their own pace and in their own unique way.

• Providing books about death can be useful, but they are no substitute for talking of feelings. Care needs to be taken in choosing books suitable for the child's age and development. It is often helpful for parents to read the book with the child so that any questions may be dealt with at the time. (An annotated book list is provided in Appendix 11.)

How can Professionals Help?

In hospital

Following the death of a baby, parents inevitably will feel shocked and numb. It is likely that any children in the family will be at home or with friends. Parents may not have considered involving the children, either in an attempt to shield them from the pain or because their own pain is so overwhelming that they can think of nothing else. It may be up to the nurses to suggest that the children are brought in to see the dead baby. If possible, the parents should be helped to see the importance of involving the children. Parents may need guidance on what to say. Simple practical explanations using 'dead' or 'has died' will be less confusing. No child should be forced to see the dead baby, so allowing them to choose after explanations are given is important. If they choose not to, then having photographs to show at a later date may bring home the reality. Encouraging children to come to the hospital may also be a great comfort to the parents. Children need to give, as well as to receive. Perhaps we do not always appreciate this.

There is a lovely story about a little girl who had just been next door to console someone whose daughter had just died. Her mother asked: 'Goodness, what did you say?' And the little girl said: 'Oh, I didn't say anything, Mum, I just crawled on to her lap and cried with her.'

If parents choose not to involve their children at this stage then they may need help either in what to say when they return home or whether to allow the children to attend the funeral.

In the community

As in hospital, the focus of our attention after a cot death is naturally directed at the parents, especially the mother. It must also be a devastating experience for a child to witness the death of a previously healthy baby who may have been well loved. Even if there are ambivalent feelings towards the baby, a child may be overwhelmed and confused.

In all the turmoil and activity following a cot death, it is easy to see how other children could be left out. It is likely that neighbours or friends have been asked to care for the children during the crisis. Once this has passed, it is important for the children to return home so that they can be with their parents. It is difficult for parents to consider the needs of other children when they are so shocked themselves, but, ultimately, it will help the whole family to share their awful pain.

It will be important to assure children that no-one is to blame for the death. In the weeks and months ahead, children will need to talk of the dead baby and to share their feelings and anxieties with someone trusted. Again, parents may need to be helped to do this.

Sibling Groups

In some parts of the country, groups have been set up for bereaved brothers and sisters with good effect. Most cater for those whose sibling has died from a life-threatening illness. There seems no obvious reason why others should not be included. Some voluntary agencies also run groups for bereaved children so that they can meet and share experiences.

Each family will have different needs. Our role is to assess those needs and to tailor our help to meet them. If we can help the parents through their grief, then we will also be helping the children in the family. Children today will be the adults of tomorrow. By helping them to grieve we are preventing complications later on and helping society to change its attitude to death.

Key points
- Children, like adults grieve in their own way
- Age is not the only pointer to how much a child understands
- Children need to be listened to and to be given simple, straightforward information, avoiding clichés
- Children, like adults, need to be given choices whenever possible
- Children can give, too, in bereavement
- Acknowledging children's grief may avoid difficulties in the future

References

Blue-Bond Langner M. *The private worlds of dying children.* Princetown University Press, 1978

Bowlby J. Pathological mourning and childhood mourning *J Am Psychoanal Assoc* 1980; 11: 500

Enright DJ. The Oxford book of Death. New York, Oxford University Press, 1983

Furman E. *A Child's parent dies. Studies in childhood bereavement.* New Haven, Yale: 1974

Jersild A. *The psychology of adolescence.* New York: Macmillan, 1978; 260–1

Kastenbaum R. The child's understanding of death: how does it develop? In: Grollman E (ed) *Explaining death to children.* Boston: Beacon Press, 1967

Lansdown R. The development of the concept of death. *Curr Iss Clin Psychol* 1987; 8: 2

Nagy M. The child's view of death. In: Feifel H (ed) *The meaning of death.* New York, McGraw-Hill, 1959

Pincus L. *Death and the family.* New York: Pantheon, 1974

Sarnoff Schiff H. *The bereaved parent.* London: Souvenir Press (E&A), 1977

Spinetta JJ, Rigler D, Karen M. Anxiety in the dying child. *Paediatrics* 1973; 52: 841

Books for Parents and Health Workers

Wells R. *Helping children cope with grief.* London: Sheldon Press.

Resources for Health Workers

An ache in their hearts resource package; details as per page 104.

Books for Siblings

Althea *When Uncle Bob died.* London: Dinosaur, 1988.

Johnson J.M. *Where's Jess?* Nebraska: Centring Corps, 1982.

Sims A. *Am I still a sister?* Louisiana: Big A, 1986

Stickney D. *Water Bugs and Dragonflies.* London: Mowbray, 1974

Varley S. *Badger's Parting Gifts* London: Collins, 1985.

Wilhelm H. *I'll always love you.* Sevenoaks: Hodder & Stoughton, 1985.

Chapter Nine

Multiracial Issues

The multiethnic nature of our society will give rise to a range of social, cultural and religious needs. A standard pattern of service will not meet these needs.

(Royal College of Midwives 1987, in Alibhai 1988)

Within this chapter

1. Reflecting on your own culture
2. The impact of culture on care of the dying and last offices, autopsies, burial and cremation, and grief reactions
3. Cross-cultural counselling
4. Genetic counselling and cosanguinity
5. The importance of effective communication, and using an interpreter

---

Introduction

The multiracial, multicultural, multilingual and multifaith nature of our society is widely reflected in most towns and cities. Health services are dealing with increasing numbers of users from a variety of minority ethnic communities. Like many other institutions in Britain, Health and Social Welfare agencies have tended to develop an inflexible structure of their own and many aspects of the services are specifically geared to the needs of the dominant white majority culture. This has contributed to an inadequate response to the needs of black and ethnic minority people, many of whom will have experience, priorities and expectations that differ from the white majority population.

Health workers in any part of Britain's health services cannot go through their careers without having to think about the kind of care they offer to people of a different race or skin colour – whether that is black or white. The need for ethnic-sensitive and appropriate approaches in providing support for bereaved families has been brought into sharper focus by the higher rates of perinatal, neonatal and infant mortality in this section of the population. Many midwives, health visitors and general practitioners are committed to providing such services from a multiracial perspective, but find it difficult to turn commitment into practice.

This chapter will explore some of the issues relevant to providing bereavement counselling and support to families and individuals from black and ethnic minority communities. It will also present an opportunity for service providers to examine their own attitudes and skills in this area.

The Impact of Culture

Reflecting on your own culture

Bereavement, whether due to death of a baby, termination of pregnancy or the inability to have children, will be a distressing event in any family. Ways of dealing with bereavement due to death in particular have varied throughout history and according to current customs and religions. In Britain in the latter half of the twentieth century there has been a decline in the ceremony and formal display of mourning which was common in the nineteenth century. The decline has been variously explained as caused by a weakening in established religious influence, by people living much longer and by fewer people dying at home, so that death has come to be regarded as a problem for the welfare state. Death may be seen as a failure and may therefore be treated as a marginal concern and a taboo subject in majority British culture. Bereavement is therefore often viewed as a personal, private affair involving only close family and friends. Despite a great improvement in recent years, it is against the backdrop of this legacy that services to the bereaved are delivered. Service providers, however, can fail to appreciate the influence of their own cultural and social background on their professional practice. They can unwittingly accept their way of doing things as the norm. The expectations and norms described above, however, may not be the same for all communities in multiracial Britain and many black and ethnic minority people confronted by these attitudes may view them as callous indifference.

Although attitudes are gradually changing, it is essential to be aware that all communities and their established religions have been, and still are, essentially pro-natalist and anti-abortion. The more orthodox within any religion (including those ethnic minority faiths) may be more likely to experience feelings of guilt and isolation, because the women may be unable to talk about their experiences to anyone within their communities.

Having explored their own culture and values, and the professional norms that determine their practice, practitioners who are from a different cultural group to their clients will be better able to appreciate and handle cultural information to the benefit of clients.

Care of the dying, the last offices, autopsies, burial and cremation, and reactions in grief are areas where there can be most need for information because, under stress of the moment, parents may find it difficult to ask the right questions or express their wishes on these matters. These two areas will therefore be discussed below. It is essential, however, to exercise caution in acting on the information about cultural practices as presented here. It must be remembered that whilst there are group values and beliefs, culture is neither static or inflexible; people will respond to their environment (including their culture) in singularly personal ways. An approach, therefore, that stereotypes patients also results in relieving staff of their responsiblity to get to know people as individuals. The patient and their family are the best people to provide this type of information and to advise you. The following information is therefore being presented not as a formula but as a starting point from which to develop a rapport with the client. It would be not only unprofessional but potentially harmful and offensive to use it in any other way.

Care of the dying and last offices

In many ethnic minority communities, when death is imminent relatives may seek comfort through religion and ceremonial rites, and from the company of relatives and friends. It is important to find out if relatives wish the child to be visited by, and receive the rites and offices of, their minister of religion. For example, Roman Catholics who are seriously ill will be offered the 'last rites' of the church in the hope that their lives may be spared or (in the case of death) their soul will be blessed. For Hindus, the priest or 'pandit' or a Hindu friend will attend. The leader of the Gurdwara will attend a Sikh, with readings from the holy book. Rastafarians will have prayer readings from fellow Rastafarians. Orthodox Jews will expect a Rabbi, who reads verses and prayers. For Muslims, friends or relatives will recite prayers. Family members may wish to gather around the cot at the time of the baby's death. Some may wish to hold or cuddle the baby.

At the time of death it is important to take into account any religious rites concerning the baby's body. In some religions the nurse will be able to perform this last duty with respect and dignity. Family members themselves will be able to advise on this. However, in the case of Jews and Muslims, for example, it may be appropriate only for someone of the same faith to touch the body. In some communities family members may wish to stay with the body and some may wish to prepare the body ceremonially themselves. It is important to provide an environment within the Neonatal Intensive Care Unit where these rites may be satisfactorily carried out. Others may want to take the body to a religious establishment, such as a mosque or Jewish Society, for this preparation.

Autopsies

An autopsy may not be readily acceptable to some ethnic groups unless it is on strict medical grounds. Where this is indicated there should be full discussion with families in order to ensure that no religious requirements are violated. For example, Hindus may wish that all the body organs be replaced after a postmortem.

Burial and cremation

There will be differences in expectation regarding burials and cremations. The Jewish and Muslim faiths both require that burials take place reasonably quickly and preferably within 24 hours. Staff should do all they can to facilitate this. People in the Vietnamese community may wish to choose the date for the funeral by consulting the deceased's horoscope. The position and alignment of the grave are specially determined, but this will not be practicable in a British cemetery. Muslims would prefer the body to be buried facing Makkah. It is possible that legal requirements could conflict with the customs of some religious groups and this may increase the distress of bereaved relatives. Buddhists and Sikhs are usually cremated, and the Christian denominations also allow this option. For Afro-Caribbeans, Africans and in particular Muslims, however, cremation is less likely to be an option. The cremation of small Hindu children is also extremely uncommon

In some situations relatives may face an unknown healthcare system and what may appear as a formidable amount of bureaucracy. Regardless of how long they have lived in the UK, they will not necessarily fully understand the institutions, traditions and laws. It will be important to explain the formalities concerning things such as the death certificate, a special certificate for cremation if requested, and where necessary the circumstances in which a Coroner's postmortem examination is required.

Reactions in grief

Reactions in grief and bereavement will be affected by individual as well as cultural and religious factors. Not all cultural groups feel the social pressure to contain their grief. Some people may rely on the therapeutic value of the expression of strong emotions to help them come to terms with their loss. They may also rely on the 'supportive grieving' of others concerned. Health visitors, midwives and GPs, who may be more accustomed to families trying to hide their feelings and tears, may find this distressing and not know how to react appropriately.

There may be some situations when the response of families to the death of an unborn child or a very young baby is more subdued. For example, if a very religious Muslim mother attributes her miscarriage, stillbirth, perinatal or even infant death to 'the will of Allah' or a religious Afro-Caribbean mother takes solace in the belief that 'the Lord giveth and the Lord taketh away', this should not be construed as an indication of an absence of any feelings of loss or bereavement. Service providers from the white majority community may share philosophies of life with their Church of England or Catholic patients, but there may be fewer shared beliefs between them and their Muslim or Afro-Caribbean bereaved parents. If such assumptions are not challenged then the very coping mechanisms traditionally adopted by these communities could result in an added source of stress and anxiety for bereaved parents. Such expressions should be taken for what they are: people with a strong religious faith will find solace in their beliefs, which will be instrumental in helping them to come to terms with their loss. The myth of 'their tendency to be fatalistic' should not be used as a reason for not offering support to people whose philosophy of life a health professional may not quite understand.

Cross-Cultural counselling

Dispelling the myths

It is likely that formal counselling, as it increasingly exists in Britain, may be new to many people, including some from black and ethnic minority communities. It is therefore important that the counsellor's role and expectations are made clear and that the family is given the opportunity to clarify their expectations and understanding of what they hope to receive from the relationship.

However, there are several myths that further complicate this process. Firstly, it is often assumed that certain ethnic minority groups are psychologically more robust and therefore do not require 'verbal therapies'. Secondly, whilst the emphasis in counselling is enabling the person to reach their own conclusions about the actions that are required, it is often assumed that black and ethnic minority people want directive, rather than non-directive, support. If counselling is to work to the benefit of black and ethnic minority people, these commonly held myths must be challenged.

Whilst the importance of inter-racial/cross-cultural counselling has been receiving more attention in recent years, there is little research or information in Britain regarding counselling young bereaved families from this section of the population. The literature on cross-cultural counselling in general suggests that religious requirements for modesty may mean that some women from black and ethnic minority communities may be unable to benefit from the services of a male counsellor. Such situations will need to be thoughtfully discussed and suitable alternatives arranged.

It is also important that families and individuals are seen as a whole and not in isolation from their life experiences. Counsellors must demonstrate an appreciation of the disadvantaged position of black and ethnic minority people in our society and convey an understanding of these experiences. In situations where there are close community networks and where the counsellor is from the same community as the client, families will need to be reassured of complete confidentiality.

During the process of counselling, some service providers may feel that they should exercise discretion by avoiding or minimising any reference to the deceased. This tendency may reflect a traditional desire in white majority Britain to deny death. This could, however, appear to some individuals from ethnic minority groups as an inappropriate and insensitive response. Many families, for example, would welcome open discussion about the deceased, as it acknowledges that the person was part of their existence. To deny death is to deny the existence of part of oneself. For the same reasons some mothers may find it helpful to have a photograph of their deceased child.

Genetic counselling and consanguinity

The issue of consanguinity will also need to be handled sensitively where the death of a baby is linked to a handicap which is believed to be related to a genetic disorder. Families should rightly be offered genetic counselling to enable them to make an informed choice about future children. A study of the experience of ethnic minority parents of children with learning disabilities (mental handicap) suggests that younger Muslim couples (especially those who grew up in Britain) are aware of the disapproval of cousin marriages in the wider majority culture. When a handicapping condition or a perinatal death occurs, some bereaved families may already be nursing guilt as a result of thoughtless comments by staff. They may experience feelings of anxiety, discomfort, lack of trust and confidence, which may result in reluctance to accept help, or confide in a white counsellor. Another obstacle to appropriate genetic counselling services for young black and ethnic minority families is whether the particular methods used are appropriate. For example, can all families relate to the 'flow chart tree' method which is usually used to explain genetic inheritance? Most parents will find the concept of an autosomal recessive condition – where non-handicapped parents can produce children with a handicap – one that is likely to baffle anyone without scientific training.

Communication

Effective communication is an essential element in bereavement counselling: the bereaved parents should be able to get over their wishes and feelings and to gain information from those offering support. In addition to the usual communication difficulties that exist in such circumstances, the communication barriers facing many black and ethnic minority people may be compounded by racism and by cultural differences in non-verbal signals.

Of paramount importance is the need to recognise that notions of racial and cultural superiority are unfortunately still part of British culture and can present the biggest barriers to communication. Such attitudes, for example, can also result in black and ethnic minority patients and their relatives being deprived of the touch and physical contact that may be otherwise forthcoming from professionals to their white counterparts at this time. Midwives, health visitors and GPs will need to seek the opportunity to work through such negative attitudes.

When counselling someone from a cultural background which is different from your own it is especially important to be aware of the possibility of misinterpretation of body language and other facial gestures. They should endeavour to ensure that expressions of anger, fear and fright and other such emotions are recognised. It may be necessary to ask, and not to rely solely on non-verbal cues.

An interpreter will be required to communicate wherever the person does not speak English well or where their ability to do so is affected by illness or stress. When using an interpreter it is essential that good practice is maintained. It is bad practice to rely on relatives and friends. Interpreters should be trained and experienced. They should be fluent both in English and the bereaved person's mother tongue and be able to understand and interpret medical terminology and fine shades of meaning. Despite the involvement of a third person, every effort should be made to ensure that communication is always directed at the person, and that they are responded to directly. The health worker and the interpreter should have a good working relationship where each contributes to each other's understanding. Time will be needed to listen to what is said, assess it and to translate it. Two to three times as long should therefore be allowed for a conversation. It is also best not to interrupt when the person and the interpreter are talking.

In conclusion, cross-cultural counselling can only be successful when the professionals involved are aware of their own attitudes, personal expectations, values and prejudices and how these affect their behaviour. It is not possible to generalise for individuals or groups and there can be no blueprint for the counselling and support of parents and relatives through bereavement. Service providers should work consistently to the following standards, which will go a long way to ensuring that bereaved parents and their relatives are offered emotional and spiritual comfort.

Key points
- Make a habit of examining assumptions and stereotypes before acting

- Question your own cultural norms
- Procedures regarding death and dying for the relevant local ethnic groups should be available in the Neonatal Intensive Care Unit
- It is important to check with the parents before following such procedures
- Give careful explanation to families who are unfamiliar with the procedures surrounding death in Britain, or ensure that someone else does so
- A trained interpreter should always be used where there are language differences
- In genetic counselling it is essential that there is a non-judgemental attitude towards cousin marriage
- Beware of the possibility of misinterpretation of the parent's body language and other non-verbal signals

Bibliography and further reading

Alibhai Y. Maternity care – Black women speak out. *New Society* 1988; April 1

Community Relations Council. *Muslim burials*, A policy paper. Community Relations Council.

Green J. Death with dignity: Islam. *Nursing Times* 1989; 85: 5. (Jennifer Green's 'Death with dignity' series continues with Hinduism (85: 6), Sikhism (85: 7), Judaism (85: 8), Buddhism (85: 9), Baha'i (85: 10) and Funerals Abroad (85: 11).

Henley A. *Asians in Britain – caring for Muslims and their families: religious aspects of care.* Cambridge: National Extension College, 1983 (In the same series are *Caring for Hindus and their families; Caring for Sikhs and their families*)

McGuiness S. Death rites. *Nurs Times* 1986; March 19: 28

Nadirshaw Z. Therapeutic practice in multiracial Britain. *Counsell Psychol Q* 1992; 5: 257

Sampson ACM. *The neglected ethic: religious and cultural factors in the care of patients.* Maidenhead: McGraw-Hill, 1982

Resources

Organisations

Commission for Racial Equality
Elliot House, Allington Street, London SW1E 5EH, UK
Tel: 071–828 7022

London Bereavement Project Group
68 Chilton Street, London NW1 1JR, UK
Tel: 071–388 0241
Offers counselling on bereavement and Jewish counselling.

Lorreene Hunte Foundation for Black Bereaved Families
11 Kingston Square, London SE19 1JE, UK
Tel: 071–761 7228

National Council for Hospice and Specialist Palliative Care Services
59 Bryanston Street, London W1A 2AZ, UK
Tel: 071–611 1153
Have appointed a worker responsible for identifying the issues related to black and ethnic minority communities.

Stillbirth and Neonatal Death Society
29–31 Euston Road, London NW1 2SD, UK
Tel: 071–833 2851
They have appointed a worker who is responsible for looking at the needs of ethnic minority people.

Audio-visual material

An introduction to Buddhism, and *An introduction to Hinduism,* containing two audio cassettes, study guide and reading material. Open University, 1984. Available from the Learning Materials Service, PO Box 188, Milton Keynes MK3 6HW, UK.

Grief, a film distributed by Concord Films, 201 Felixstone Road, Ipswich, Suffolk IP3 9BJ, UK. Tel: 0473–76012. Talks about different cultural reactions to grief and includes a sequence on a Vietnamese soldier being returned to his village for cremation. Good for starting a discussion.

The right to be understood, by Jane Shackman. A video and training pack on the employment and training of community interpreters. Available from the National Extension College, 18 Brooklands Ave, Cambridge CB2 2HN, UK. Tel: 0223–316644.

Chapter Ten

Relevant Issues for Health Workers

Experience without theory is blind. Theory without experience is folly.

(Kant)

Within this chapter

1. Difficult visits
2. Complicated bereavement
3. Clues to recognising complicated bereavement
4. Options available for referral
5. Confidentiality
6. Dependency – how to recognise it and deal with it
7. Endings
8. Support for ourselves – available options

Difficult visits

Inevitably there may be occasions when families refuse our help for whatever reason and do not wish us to visit further. This can be hard to accept. However, this is their choice, which must be respected. In such cases it is worthwhile leaving a telephone number for use later, if required, and pointing out that there are other available sources of help for them to draw on. We have found it useful to consider the various options with the family in a pictorial way (Fig. 10.1).

There may be other times when, despite our best efforts, we do not seem to be helping the bereaved person to adjust to their loss. We may be overwhelmed by all the facets involved, have no idea which way to go and end up feeling frustrated and inadequate. At such times it is all too easy to give up visiting, especially when we have other duties and responsibilities.

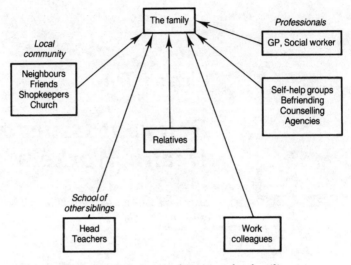

Figure 10.1 Sources of support for families.

It may well be that the bereaved person actually needs more experienced help, which you are unable to offer. Bereavement can be a very complex process. It is important to understand what bereavement is, but it is just as important to recognise when we are out of our depth, to seek help or refer to someone else.

I am always amazed how unsupervised most bereavement visiting is; health carers are expected to deal with the complexities of bereavement care without having someone available who can give valuable insights, advice, encouragement or support. We would not consider this a suitable arrangement for a patient with a physical illness! We would like to think that in future all bereavement visiting is supervised. I know from my work with CRUSE that counsellors have found it invaluable to have a supervisor who is there on a regular basis to advise, support and encourage.

Different Grief Reactions

In Chapter 7 we considered issues that would make grieving more difficult. Different names have been given to grief that does not appear to follow a so-called normal pattern – where the bereaved person seems to have become 'stuck', where the grief goes on longer than usual or where it appears to be exaggerated. The names used are: pathological, unresolved, complicated, chronic, abnormal, delayed or exaggerated. The definition that Worden (1983) gives is:

> The intensification of grief to the level where the person is over-whelmed, resorts to maladaptive behaviour, or remains interminably

in the stage of grief without progression of the mourning process towards completion . . . It involves processes that do not move progressively toward assimilation or accommodation but instead, lead to stereotyped repetitions of extensive interruptions of healing.

If we take a detailed history from the bereaved person from the start of our visiting we are in a good position to identify those who are more likely to fall into this category. We can then be prepared to expect more difficulties in the months ahead and arrange a programme of visiting accordingly to deal with the difficulties. Alternatively, you may see the path ahead as too difficult and may want to refer on at this stage. It is less painful for a client to lose you at this point than later on when you have established a relationship, thereby creating another loss.

However, you may feel well able to deal with some areas by gently confronting the bereaved person and stating the situation as you see it. That in itself may help the grieving person to assess the situation and make changes. Other areas may seem too complicated and difficult and may require reference to other agencies. The following are guidelines as to how some people can be held up in their grieving process.

Belongings

It is always difficult to know the 'right' time to dispose of clothes, toys, etc. belonging to the dead child. Perhaps both extremes are a clue to telling us something of the state of the bereaved person. To get rid of belongings immediately after the death and turn the bedroom into a different room or to hang on to them for many months, keeping the room exactly as it was, could both be signs that something is wrong. However, if several children occupied the dead child's room then clearing away the deceased's belongings may just be a practical step in creating more space. Turning a room into a shrine can be an indicator that the mother (more usual than fathers) has become 'stuck' in her grief process and is unable to accept that the child is dead.

Photographs

Asking to see a photograph of the dead child or baby can be a good starting point when first visiting. Absence of any photographs could either mean that the parent(s) find it too painful to remind themselves or that, in the case of a baby, they have no pictures, although, hopefully, this is less common. I have visited homes where there are many, many pictures, both large and small, displayed throughout the house so that everywhere was dominated by the dead child. I have found that the parents have tended to idolise the child that has gone, which can prevent them from moving through the grieving process. Other children in the family could possibly be deeply affected by this kind of display by holding in resentment, and even bitterness, and feeling less favoured and loved by their parents.

Several losses

Where families have had to endure several losses in quick succession, there may be 'complicated' grieving. Each loss needs to be acknowledged and worked through, which can take much time and expertise on the part of the helper.

Disasters

In the case of a disaster where there have been multiple deaths, it is not uncommon that the grieving process will be more protracted and difficult for the survivors.

Uncertain death

Just as it is important for us to have a diagnosis when we are ill, it is also important for parents to know why their child died. Parents who do not have this knowledge are constantly looking for answers, and in searching may avoid working out their own grief.

Graves

It can be a very healing process for family members to spend time quietly at the graveside of their dead child. However, with some mothers especially, it can become an obsession where the visiting takes precedence over caring for their other children, homes or husbands. This can be a sign that they are not accepting the death, especially if it is months afterwards.

Moods

Depression is a normal part of grieving. When it lasts for many months without any change then referral to another agency may be required. Where there is a history of depression before the death then the present grieving process may be held up. Again, expert help may be needed.

Changes in lifestyle

Any bereaved person who makes considerable changes in their lifestyle following the death of their child and who excludes former friends and family members may well be hiding behind unresolved grief.

Having determined that the person you are visiting needs further help, where do you turn? Perhaps the first step is to discuss the situation with your GP. If you feel this would not be helpful, then CRUSE may be able to offer some guidance. Many of their trained counsellors have valuable experience and would be very happy to help. It is vital that you seek the client's permission to do this beforehand. It does not necessarily mean that the agency will take on the client, although this is a possibility.

What Other Options Are There?

* Bereavement care is generally low on the list of priorities for Health Districts. However, in some areas *bereavement counsellors* are employed who are a valuable source of help. Places such as the Alder Centre in Liverpool, UK, which offers help to anyone affected by the death of a child, are rare but increasing. It is worth finding out what is available within your own area.
* *Referrals to psychiatrists* can only occur through the GP. Even today some people are very reluctant to visit for fear of the stigma that they believe exists.
* *Psychologists* can do much to help but are in short supply for adults. It is normally children who are referred to them, and, again, through their GP.
* *Private therapy* is an increasing option but is not cheap (in the UK approximately £20–£30 per hour). It is wise to check out the reputation of any counselling agency before referral.
* Voluntary agencies in the UK, such as FSID, SANDS and Compassionate Friends, provide support and befriending but do *not* offer help with complicated bereavement.

At present, there is little to offer those whose bereavement pattern takes on complications. As a result, we believe there are many people who live with their grief and consequently are unable to lead full lives. We would like to see more centres such as the one in Liverpool, UK. However, in the present financial climate it is unlikely that such organisations will abound unless they are funded by the voluntary sector, and they, too, have limited resources. Bereavement counsellors in each Health District would be ideal, but, again, their appointment is governed by available monies.

Confidentiality

Anyone who is bereaved is in a very vulnerable position. As carers we are in a unique position to hear many hidden secrets, which the bereaved person may not have shared before. It is only in a relationship of trust that such confidences can be mentioned. Confidentiality means keeping secret any information that has been entrusted to us. It is probably difficult because of our human frailty, staff discussions and professional sharing to stick rigidly to this. However, once again, it is important to make boundaries so that the bereaved person understands fully that there may be times when we have to share our knowledge with others. With this in mind, at the outset of our listening, we should explain that we may discuss the bereaved person's problems with other professionals – more as a back-up for us and our caring, than to gossip about their difficulties. When a client thereafter specifically requests confidentiality about a particular disclosure then this must be respected. There are two exceptions to this, namely (a) where confidentiality has to be broken because of the law; and (b) where there is a danger to a client's life, e.g. the client taking steps to end his or her life. It is important to inform the client that you need help in order to find the right solution. It is important that the client makes choices for him/herself, and therefore it is not appropriate to refer the client to another agency, e.g. a bereavement group, without the client's prior permission. (Whenever possible clients should be encouraged to do this themselves.)

Before discussion takes place with another family member, the client's permission should be sought first. Note-taking should be kept to a minimum and only shared with authorised personnel who would also be bound by confidentiality. If the carer takes notes during an interview, a practice that should be discouraged as it detracts from listening and could put the client off, then the carer could offer to show what has been written.

There may be times when a bereaved person may feel embarrassed or becomes less open as a result of sharing a difficult confidence. At the next session it may be appropriate for the carer to acknowledge this possibility and to reassure that what has been said has not shocked or made any difference to the helping role.

Dependency

I believe that, for many of us, dependency is considered as an unfavourable situation where a bereaved person relies too heavily on our resources and therefore cannot detach his/herself sufficiently in order to adjust to life without our support and encouragement. However, especially in the early stages, dependency is important. Without some dependency a helping relationship can hardly exist. We need to bear in mind that inability to show or accept dependency also blocks any effective help with grieving. If, as the weeks and months go by, the dependency develops into an *over*-dependency, then there may be a problem.

We should also be aware that dependency is not only a characteristic that clients bring into counselling but one that may be the carer's problem. Both client and carer eventually contribute to the level of dependency in the relationship, though usually not consciously. When a carer has strong but unspoken needs to look after people, it may be difficult to discontinue the caring role. Let us consider different levels of dependency.

Insufficient level

If the client denies help, sees it as a weakness or does not trust the carer, and if the carer is emotionally detached, has a lack of reliable commitment, or is unable to contain the client's distress without becoming overwhelmed, then grief counselling is impossible.

Optimal level

If the client seeks help, remains in charge of his/her life and accepts frequent visits from the healthcare worker, and if the carer is able to offer skills and commitment appropriate to the client's needs, enabling rather than taking over and engendering trust, as well as setting limits, then effective grief counselling will result.

Inappropriately high level

Where a client has a history of clinging dependency in key relationships, lacks social skills, seeks a new dependent relationship and is resistant to limits being set, and where the healthcare worker is unaware of being cast in an unrealistic role, is drawn to looking after people and feels guilty about setting limits or saying 'no', then grief counselling will be threatened by dependency problems.

Avoiding or reducing dependency

From the outset it is essential that a risk assessment of the bereaved person is made by the healthcare worker. This will give some indication of whether dependency may become a problem, and in anticipating this, the carer is in a better position to avoid the situation occurring. The keys to remember that can cause dependency are:

- dependent behaviour with surviving relatives;
- helplessness as a personality style;
- social isolation, absence of family support;
- chronic illness or disability

There are also other pointers to possible dependency:

- a marked interest in the carer's background or private life;
- preference for carer's help rather than that of others;
- tendency to prolong interviews by introducing a new topic;

- anxiety expressed at any mention of longer intervals between visiting;
- more than usual warmth in greeting or in parting.

Steps to take when dependency threatens

1. The more signs there are for dependency problems to arise, the more the carer must be responsible for being explicit both with oneself and the client about the reason for visiting and the limitations of care. To set unrealistic expectations can be damaging for both parties. There may be times when carers feel guilty or uncomfortable about setting limits, but unless we do, either the bereaved person will become confused and is more likely to become reliant, or the carer will be overwhelmed, trying harder and harder to make sense of the situation only to end up feeling frustrated and inadequate or too involved.
2. It is important to realise that a bereaved person's needs, whilst not being met, need not be ignored. By giving permission to grieve, i.e. enabling expression of felt needs, and by listening in a sensitive and non-judgemental way, much help can be given.
3. It helps to *acknowledge* the message conveying the client's needs or feelings by putting them into words, e.g. 'It seems to me that you are asking me to take over and do it for you.'
4. It helps to *clarify* the message, e.g. 'I'm wondering if all your family have been avoiding you.'
5. It helps to *accept* what is actually being said. It then becomes easier if the reality of any request within the counselling relationship needs to be challenged in discussion, e.g. 'I can see how very worried you have become about this but . . . '
6. *Advice* is only helpful when the need has been clarified and the advice is designed to enable the bereaved person to take positive steps, if at all possible. The carer can suggest relevant agencies that may give appropriate help. Giving information, e.g. about what self-help agencies exist in the area, is different from giving advice.
7. Occasionally, romantic or sexual attraction can be felt by the bereaved person towards the carer. Again it is important to acknowledge this in a gentle but definite way and allow time for discussion. In this way a difficult situation can be averted.
8. A reality of grief counselling is that it is time-limited. Because of this it is important to plan visits, but also to enable the client to realise that your support will not go on indefinitely. It is best to discuss this early on rather than later, so that no unrealistic expectations are built up and there will be less risk of overdependency.

Endings

Ending a relationship with a client can be as difficult as, or more difficult than, beginning one. If you have planned well, then the bereaved person will be aware that your visits are gradually coming to an end. It is important to explain this to the client so that he/she has time to adjust and therefore will be well prepared before the end. It is important, too, for you to withdraw and recognise that your task is almost completed.

To talk of endings, you will have realised certain changes in the bereaved person. The following is an 'endings' check-list both for you and the client.

- Has the finality of the death and the reality of the loss been accepted?
- Have expressions of anger and guilt been expressed and dealt with?
- Has the bereaved person accepted responsibility for her/himself?
- Is the bereaved parent able to talk of the dead child without being overwhelmed by emotion?
- Has the parent learned that when something triggers off painful feelings, they will pass?
- Is the person beginning to enjoy life again and making plans for the future?
- Are they sleeping and eating well and taking care of their appearance?
- Have they coped with an anniversary and birthday of the dead child and can plan ahead for other difficult times?
- Has the bereaved parent been able to see the needs of others and is not concentrating wholly on him/herself?

Although this will be the end of formal visiting, it is advisable to leave your telephone number. We have found that parents do not abuse this, but just having it is a comfort and a safeguard.

Gifts

Some parents may want to show some appreciation of the help you have given them. Do, by all means, accept with gratitude what they have bought for you. It is their way of giving something back. If the gift is in the form of money, it is best to suggest that it is put into some fund that will benefit other bereaved parents.

Support for Ourselves

Bereavement care can be very demanding and draining. Listening intently requires energy and concentration and seeing and hearing someone's mental pain and despair can take its toll on our resources. It is likely that most of you who read this book have many other duties to perform other than bereavement care. It is important that we recognise the need to care for ourselves, that we take some responsibility and take steps to prevent ourselves from being worn down by the pressures of our jobs and the pain we inevitably meet. Many of us may rely on our *partners* and *friends* to be a sounding board for our problems, fears and worries, but there is a limit to how much we can use them to unburden ourselves. We should have other resources to turn to so that they are not saturated or overwhelmed by our work.

Peer support

Peer support is probably the most common type of support that is easily available and more informal. Reciprocal support works best between people who feel, and are perceived as, equal in terms of hierarchy within the organisation. However, there may be times when such support is not enough and meeting for the sake of meeting does not seem sufficient.

Some, but not all, hospitals have *staff counsellors* who are trained to listen and can allow exploration of deep feelings in a safe environment. Hospital chaplains can be a valuable source of support for staff as well as patients.

Co-counselling is one way in which carers can help and support each other by taking it in turns as client and counsellor. It should be arranged that the couple have the same or similar skills and in a way where each has, say, half an hour to explore feelings, hurts or ideas with the other person, and then change roles. It is important that both parties have an equal part to play. By working in this way, problems can be examined and solutions worked through.

In the workshops that I have run, I have found that nurses especially expect support from their *managers*. Indeed, this is right and proper, but perhaps we have to examine what is truly meant and how realistic this is. A manager is a person who hires and fires, whose job is to ensure that each employee in his/her care is meeting required standards and demands, and is being trained and encouraged to grow and expand to meet their potential. He/she also has to consider skill mix and personality balance within the team, meet deadlines and live within a financial budget. It is therefore difficult for a healthcare worker to share painful inadequacies, to show vulnerabilities and to confide at a deep level for fear of being seen unsuitable for the job. I have learnt from nurses and volunteers that what they require is someone who listens carefully, who can be trusted to keep certain confidences, who does not judge and who can give constructive criticism or encouragement when needed. Only we ourselves will be able to choose such a person if we feel that this is the sort of support we need. Having found someone that meets these requirements, meetings can be arranged on a regular basis for an agreed length of time, probably an hour.

Facilitator-led groups

From my own experience I have learnt that for such groups to work well, certain factors need to be considered. Without forethought, meetings of this kind may end up as a disaster and a waste of time.

Points to consider

1. *Is there sufficient interest to start a group?*
   A group with more than 10 and less than six could raise problems.
2. *What are the main aims of meeting?*
   Group meetings can be arranged for many reasons but a group concerned with bereavement will probably meet for emotional support, advice and sharing.
3. *Considerations in setting up a group*
   - Who should attend?
   - How big should the group be?
   - Should it be 'closed' or 'open', i.e. should there be a set number of people or is it open to anyone to come and go? I have found that it is easier to have a closed group so that people can get to know each other and begin to build up relationships of trust.
   - How often should the group meet?
   - Where is the best place
   - At what time should the group meet and for how long at each meeting?
   - How long will the group run?
4. *Who will lead the group?*
   This is an important issue as the wrong person can put people's backs up and get the group off to a bad start. Ideally, the group should be led by someone who is perceived as having some authority which qualifies her or him to lead the group. A good facilitator will seek to share the leadership gradually and aim to make him/herself redundant. It is worth drawing up a list of possible candidates to consider whether they have the necessary qualifications, skills, commitment and time!

Caring for ourselves

There are certain things that we can do for ourselves without relying on others for support. However, they are included to alleviate stress and should be used in conjunction with the other available options and not used in isolation.

- Have regular, well-balanced meals, taking time out from work, where work issues are not discussed.
- Take regular exercise, in the open air whenever possible.

- Take up a hobby that is relaxing and creative, e.g. gardening.
- Smile and respond cheerfully when meeting others and try to walk, talk and speak at a slower pace.
- Be aware of your own stress signals, e.g. tightening shoulders, snapping, doing everything in a hurry, and take stock.
- Remember you have choices, at work and at home.
- Know your limitations and do not expect too much of yourself.

We started and ended this book with ourselves, which seems appropriate. Unless we are well equipped to help grieving families, many will miss out on the care and help they deserve. It is time we recognised that bereavement care is just as important as care in illness and take steps to offer a first-class service to enable people to return to a quality of life and a life worth living.

Key points
- Recognise our limitations and refer when necessary
- Understand confidentiality and keep within the boundaries
- Be aware of client dependency as well as our own
- Recognise the need to care for ourselves and use others to enable us to do this

---

Reference

Worden JW. *Grief counselling* London, Tavistock Publishing, 1983

Appendices

Appendix 1: Suggestions for Health Workers about Mementos for Parents

Why are memories and mementos important for grieving? They give us something solid and concrete to acknowledge as having been part of our lives and now is absent from our lives. *Memories* are those feelings and mental pictures that parents have about their baby and which make the history book of their lives. Of seeing, touching and being with their baby, of registering the birth or going to the funeral. *Mementos* are tangible items that can be taken out, looked at, and put away again. They may last for years acting both as evidence of a real baby or pregnancy, and as reminders that trigger memories.

Suggestions for *mementos* for any family whose baby has died as a miscarriage, stillbirth, cot death or whose baby has been adopted include the following. Some ideas will need to be adapted to the size and gestation of the baby, e.g. it will not be possible to take a lock of hair from the head of a 12-week fetus.

Photos of the baby

Should we always take photos? We need to recognise that this may be equally important for a family whose baby is perfectly formed and still-born, or whose baby is anencephalic, or whose 'baby' is only tissues that are the products of conception. At any stage in the development and death of a baby, photos are tangible mementos. However, it will depend on cultural beliefs and personal preferences as to whether parents want, or will allow, a photo to be taken. If there are no cultural restrictions, it can be valuable to take photos, regardless of whether the family want them at the time. They can then be stored in the medical records of the mother and retrieved months or years later if the family want them.

Taking polaroid photos of the 'baby' gives parents an instant picture of their child or pregnancy. We need to remind parents that polaroid prints will fade over the years of daylight exposure and that a photographic shop will produce a long-term copy, from the polaroid photo, which will last indefinitely. Taking a whole roll of 35 mm film (24 or 36 exposures), which the parents can have and develop when they want, ensures that some photos will be good ones. Photos might be of the baby with the parents, cuddled by them, wrapped and placed in a cot, or undressed. Or photos might be of a fetus or body tissue, lying in the palm of the parents – it is whatever the parents want.

Where a baby is known to be dying soon after birth, it is equally important to take some photos of the baby alive. See Appendix 2 for examples of photos and points to consider when taking them.

Footprints and handprints

We can take these from any baby who is sufficiently physically developed to have a formed hand and foot. Again, before taking a print we need to be sure that there are no cultural requirements that would preclude making them. Prints can be taken by pressing the hand and foot firmly against an ink pad and then against a piece of card. By steadying the card against the firm, flat surface of the closed ink pad it is possible to hold the baby's arm or leg in the other hand and to get a flat contact with the hand or foot on the card. This gives a good print. Preferably, the print should be on to a card that is folded in half and opens with room for the name and date of birth and death of the baby. Think about doing both hands and both feet, so that parents have a record of the pair.

Wiping the ink off hands and feet is important. Especially with babies of early gestation, this needs to be undertaken gently, in order not to damage friable skin. Generally an alcohol wipe, followed by cotton wool with warm water, will remove the ink staining.

What are the other options for obtaining a memento of the baby's hand or foot? One midwife, caring for a mother who was visually impaired and whose baby died as a cot death, arranged for the orthodontists to produce a mould of the imprint of the baby's foot in the mastic usually used for dental imprints.

Lock of hair

Again, before we undertake this we need to think about cultural beliefs, and suggest to parents that they may **like** a lock of hair. They can then refuse or accept on religious or personal grounds. We need to be aware that to take an item of the body without consent can constitute bodily harm. Many babies, even at 6 months of age, have little hair. If it is not possible to cut a lock then try using a razor to shave the downy fuzz, which most babies have. Think about where to put the hair. Placed in a plastic bag it can get separated; in a folded piece of paper, which is stapled into a packet, it remains as a lock.

Records

We need to offer copies of pregnancy and labour notes. They can be a large part of the baby's life and could include any photos taken at ultrasound scan or items such as cot card or name bands of the baby. The notes need to be accompanied with a debriefing of what happened, what the notes mean and any medical terms used such as 'fetal distress'. Otherwise, the notes can be a source of mystery or confusion, if parents wrongly interpret that something 'caused' the baby to die.

Place and people

To some families it is very important to be able to remember *where* their baby died. It can help to have photos of the room in which the family were or names and photos of the staff who cared for them. We need to be aware that parents might like this and feel unable to ask.

Having a keepsake

Depending on the gestation or age of the baby, the family may have few or no items, such as clothing, toys or bedwraps, which are associated with their baby. For a fetus who miscarried or a baby who is stillborn, parents might like to keep a piece of clothing or wrapping which has been worn by, or been in contact with, the baby.

Caring for their Baby

It is important that parents have the opportunity to care for their baby – it will leave them with a memory of being parents and might be recorded by photos. Many parents are glad of the opportunity to dress, wash or bathe their baby. They may wish to do this privately or with the support of a health visitor.

Appendix 2: Taking Photos of Babies and Families

In this appendix there are a number of photos, for which we thank the families who have kindly given permission for them to be used as a learning resource. If you are in the situation where you are working with families whose baby dies or pregnancy ends please take time to read through this appendix and to look at the photos which will give you ideas for your own practice.

There are various things which we need to think about if we want to take a photo which will provide a lasting memento for the family. Do not ever think that you need to be whizz-kid of a photographer. These tips are for the everyday person who can recognise a camera but does not know about photography. Beware of using black and white film unless you are familiar with it. Colour will give you, as an everyday photographer, a success with the detail and vibrancy in the photos.

Firstly, there are few second chances in this situation, unlike everyday life when if a photo of someone does not come out, you can go back and take some more. This may not be possible if the baby is buried or cremated. So think about taking **lots** of photos. Polaroid photos give an instant result which shows what you have achieved. However, they do not give the detail, nor do they last long-term, in the same way as with other cameras using film which is developed later. With the latter, try taking plenty of photos (e.g. one or two films) in different positions and lights to ensure that some photos are successful.

Secondly, think about the **surroundings**. Is the room in which you are taking the photos friendly? Or is it white and clinical? If the latter, then it is likely to create glare if you use a flash. It is also unlikely to be a very babyfriendly setting, whereas a room with wallpaper, ordinary (not hospital) furniture can appear much more relaxed and homelike. It may be that the family would like to take pictures of the baby outside, in a garden or in the sunshine. Again, these surroundings are often much more what we normally expect to see babies in. Whatever the setting take a number of photos from different angles/positions in the same surrounding so that you have a variety for the family to keep. Included in surroundings of the baby is anything that the baby is lying in e.g. a cot. Again the aim is to make the photos appear natural and normal, so the cot needs to be the right size for the baby. Otherwise, a small baby in a large cot, has an incongruity which prevents families from focusing on their baby. This means that small babies or fetuses need to be in a small basket e.g. dolls size. For very small fetuses of 17 weeks gestation, it may appear more natural for them just to be resting on some material or held in the palm of a hand, because their perfect smallness makes cots and baskets appear too crude and big.

Thirdly, **the baby**. This means when you take photos being aware of the baby you are photographing and seeking to provide the best looking photos and the ones which reflect some meaning to the parents. Think about the following points.

What will the baby wear? Is it something that the family would like the baby to wear, that has significant meaning for them? Consider taking photos in several outfits of clothes or using several types of surrounding bedding, looking in particular for colour contrast. For example, some babies are very pale when they have died and wearing white clothes in white bedclothes means that the baby can appear very indistinct in the photo, because there is no colour contrast. It may be more effective if the pale baby is lying on sheet which is light blue, pink or green. Be wary of using clothes and bedding with a heavy pattern on it, since this too may detract from the baby. With some small fetuses at 16–17 weeks gestation, there is no possibility that they can wear the clothes chosen for an older baby. However, the contrast of the background material on which they are resting, which might be a piece of coloured satin, a scarf from the mother, a handkerchief from the father can provide colour and also significance of what the baby is resting on.

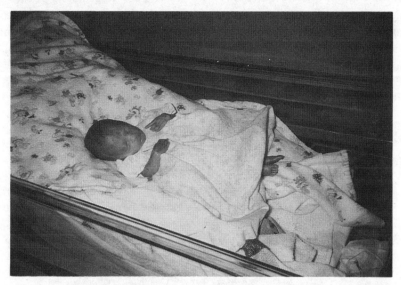

Sophie Chalmers, daughter of Robert and Karen. Sophie was 23 weeks gestation and this photo was taken on the delivery suite at Wycombe General Hospital. Robert and Karen chose Sophie's dress and appreciated seeing the beauty of her little feet. (Reproduced with kind permission of Robert and Karen Chalmers).

How is the baby lying? This needs to reflect the fact that babies when dead can lie in very floppy body attitudes or be very rigid if there has been rigor mortis. As far as possible whatever the gestation of the baby think about arranging the baby to look as much like a sleeping baby as possible. This may be a baby lying on their back with hands outside the coverlet. Or it might by lying on their side or tummy with head turned to one side and the photo taken from above or from the side at the same level as the baby. Or a small fetus it might be lying on their back with head slightly to one side and arms beside their body and legs relaxed perhaps with knees bent. The idea is to avoid a position which is immediately associated with death e.g. lying ramrod straight, because babies just do not lie like this.

The perfection of the baby. Whatever photos we take need to emphasise the perfection of the baby. This may mean for babies who have a deformity e.g. anencephaly, making sure that the deformity is not photographed, but is covered by bedding or clothing. It may mean for all babies taking close-up photos of parts of the baby. Photographs at a distance take in the clothing and the setting the baby is in, but do not give insight into the beauty of the baby. By taking close-ups of just the hands, the feet, the face of the baby, we provide parents with detail of their baby.

Fourthly and most importantly is the **family**. Photographs need to include the baby with the family they belong to. This means photos held by parents, grandparents, siblings, or just in their cot amongst these people. Remember some families may not want to hold their dead baby. What is important is that there are photos of the baby in their family setting, just as photos would be taken of a new live baby.

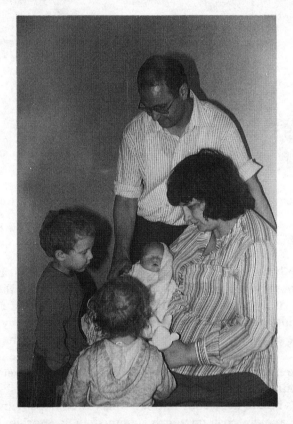

Katie Pearce, with parents Jonathan and Nina, siblings Naomi and Matthew. Katie died when she was a day old. She had Potters Syndrome. This is an important photograph of the family with Katie. (Reproduced with kind permission of Jonathan and Nina Pearce).

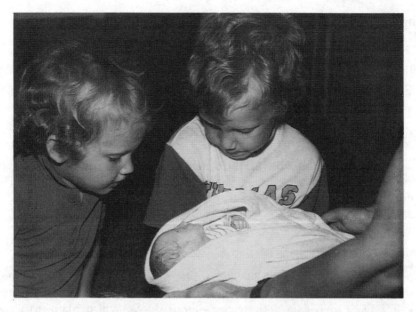

Luke Pearce with parents Jonathan and Nina, siblings Naomi and Matthew. Luke was the second child to Jonathan and Nina who had Potters Syndrome. The pregnancy was terminated at 27 weeks for fetal abnormality. (Reproduced with kind permission of Jonathan and Nina Pearce).

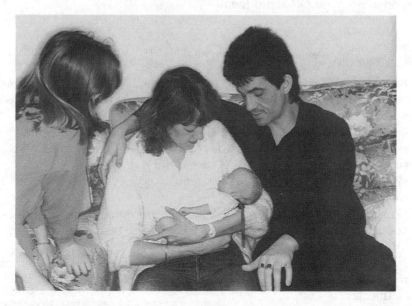

Rikki Poolton, with parents Jane and Adrian and sister Jaycee. This photo was taken in the Bereaved Parents Room on the Special Care Baby Unit, Wycombe General Hospital. Jaycee, and her younger sister Donna, helped to bath Rikki after his death. (Reproduced with kind permission of Jane and Adrian Poolton).

Appendix 3: Handout for Families Going Home after a Miscarriage

This is an extract of a patient handout reproduced with kind permission from Stewart et al. An unfinished story. *Professional Nurse* 1992; July: 660.

After a miscarriage

It is often hard to remember all the things doctors and nurses talked to you about during your miscarriage, and questions often arise later. This handout will give you some useful information.

Why did I have a miscarriage?

It is thought that as many as 20–30% of pregnancies miscarry. In some there is a reason, like an illness or a problem with how the placenta or baby were developing; if there is a definite cause your doctor will explain it to you. Sadly, for most miscarriages there is no obvious reason, which can make people worry whether they did something to 'cause' the miscarriage, but it is extremely unlikely, so try not to feel guilty. If you have any particular concerns, ask your GP about them.

Your physical health

- *Bleeding.* This should decrease in 7–10 days. If it does not, or becomes heavier or smells offensive, contact your GP or midwife. Keep using sanitary towels, not tampons, until it stops.
- *Breasts.* Your breasts may be tender for several days, and depending on how many weeks pregnant you were, they may leak milk. Wear a supportive bra until your breasts are comfortable.
- *Periods.* Generally, if you have a regular cycle this will return in 4–6 weeks.
- *Sex.* You need 2–3 weeks for your body to recover, then it depends how you and your partner feel – it can take time to be interested again. Be loving and understanding about how you both feel.
- *Fatigue.* You may feel tired for a couple of weeks and if so you must rest. If you work, take a week or so off. Your GP can give you a sick leave certificate.

Your emotional health

Miscarriage can shake you and your partner, and you will probably experience ups and downs. Some people adjust quickly, others take a long time; you will find the number of 'good' days slowly increases, but a memory or an anniversary can bring it all back to you. Everyone experiences different feelings, but they can include anger, frustration, despair and bitterness. Some women cry a lot, which may release some of the pain and tension, while some men find it hard to talk about their feelings. You may both have different ways of coping, so be understanding and make sure you have plenty of time together.

If you want to talk to someone who has been through miscarriage and can listen to you, contact the Miscarriage Association, whose local number will be in the telephone directory, or talk to your GP, midwife or health visitor about your feelings.

Your baby

You may want to know the sex of your baby – before 3 months this is impossible to see, but after 3 months babies are more developed. If you have a query, talk to your midwife or GP about it.

If you want to mark the loss of your baby, many hospitals and churches have a Remembrance book, where a page can be inscribed with your baby's name and a verse or message. Ask your health visitor or midwife for details. You may decide to arrange a memorial service or funeral at your church, and again, the Miscarriage Association or your midwife or health visitor can help.

Your family

If you have other children, they may be bewildered at what is happening. If they knew you were pregnant, explain simply what has happened to your baby – your health visitor can give you support and advice on this. Children can get frightened when their parents are distressed or unhappy, so it is important to give them time and attention and stick to familiar routines. Your parents may also be very upset for you. It can help to talk to them and ask their help, perhaps to do the shopping for a week, so they can take some of the strain off you.

Your friends

Many people find one of the hardest things after a miscarriage is meeting people again. You may find you can talk easily to some friends, and that they understand or share your feelings. Others may seem not to care and even avoid you – it may be because they are uncomfortable with death and frightened to ask how you feel or say how sorry they are.

Future pregnancy

There is no fixed time you should wait to have another baby – it is right when you feel ready. It can be a good idea to wait for one period to allow your body to recover and to be sure of dates in the next pregnancy. The chances are that your next pregnancy will be successful – the fact that you had one miscarriage does not mean you are more likely to have another, but it makes sense to get as fit as possible before and during pregnancy, to reduce the risk of miscarriage to the minimum. This means:

- stopping or cutting down smoking;
- eating a sensible diet;
- taking regular exercise;
- avoiding being near people with contagious illnesses.

If you are worried that you need treatment during your next pregnancy, talk to your GP. This is very unlikely unless there was a particular cause for your miscarriage. If you are worried or anxious about the idea of another pregnancy, talk to your midwife or health visitor about your fears.

Help and support

Your GP . . . .   Tel: . . . .

Your midwife . . . .   Tel: . . . .

Your health visitor . . . .   Tel: . . . .

Miscarriage Association . . . .   Tel: . . . .

Appendix 4: Explanation Given to Parents, Whose Baby Died as a Cot Death, about What is Involved in a Postmortem

This explanation needs to be adapted to: (a) your local hospital policy, which varies according to the pathologist undertaking the postmortem; and (b) the gestation of the baby – very small fetuses may be impossible to repair. Speak to your pathologist and then write down the information for other staff.

You might choose to use the words 'your baby', as in this explanation, with parents who had no choice consenting to a postmortem, since their baby died suddenly and there is a legal requirement for a postmortem. Or, you might choose to use the words 'the baby', which does not personalise the postmortem to their baby unless they consent to it. Whilst it may feel uncomfortable to talk about cuts, stitches and replacing parts of the body, in reality what we tell parents is considerably less gruesome than they imagined:

A postmortem is like a surgical operation on your child and it is done with as much care and dignity as if your baby were alive. It involves an incision (cut) to the chest, which is like open heart surgery, generally down the length of the breastbone in the middle of the rib cage. There is also a cut on the head, often at the back above the neck. The reason for these two cuts is to allow the pathologist (who is a doctor) to look carefully at all the parts of the baby such as the brain, heart and lungs, to see if he can find any reason for the death. When the pathologist has finished looking at your baby, they will replace every part of your baby, except for any small pieces of tissue that are taken for laboratory tests looking for infection. Then they sew the baby up again. So, your baby has stitches and generally sticking plaster over the stitches, just like after an operation. Your baby will *look* the same, except for the cuts, and *feel* the same as they do now. Most importantly you can still see and cuddle your baby after the postmortem and take your baby home, before the funeral, if you want to.

Appendix 5: Information for Health Workers about Funerals, Burials and Cremations

We have talked throughout this book of the importance of goodbyes as part of the process of grieving. It is important that we can give parents accurate information about their options; this avoids regrets in the future and disappointments in the present. In the past we have often provided only minimum or substandard care; we should now be striving for *good practice*.

The following information applies to England and Wales and there may be minor variations in Scotland and Ireland. For accurate, detailed information read *Miscarriage, stillbirth and neonatal death – guidelines for professionals* (SANDS 1991) currently being revised, and for babies born before the age of viability, *'Dignified endings'* by Nancy Kohner (1992).

Certificates and registration of birth and death

The process is administrative and often painful to the families involved. We need to make it as smooth as possible by providing accurate information and making parents aware that the choice of funeral or cremation needs to be clearly decided, because different certificates are needed by the funeral director.

For pregnancies that end before the age of viability (24 weeks)

There is no legal requirement for this death to be certified or registered. However, a funeral director organising a cremation or burial will need some form of authority (certificate such as Fig. 2.4, or a letter) from the midwife (if buried) or doctor (if cremated) who attended the delivery, stating that the gestation was pre-24 weeks and that no signs of life were shown. A copy of this pre-24 week certificate should be given to parents as their only record of the birth.

For stillborn babies

A medical Certificate of Stillbirth needs to be completed and signed by either the registered midwife or the doctor at the delivery or who saw the baby after the delivery. This certificate needs to be taken to the Registrar to register the stillbirth (see below) and the parents should have a copy of it. The Registrar will issue a Certificate of Burial or Cremation, which is a *white form*, which needs to be given to the funeral director. In addition, if the baby is to be cremated, the doctor who certifies the death needs to complete Form B giving cause of death.

For babies who are born alive and then die

The following applies to all situations except where the death is under the jurisdiction of the Coroner or Procurator Fiscal. The doctor who certifies the death gives the parents either a:

• *Medical Certificate of Cause of Death*
   Scotland and Northern Ireland all babies
   England and Wales only use for babies dying over the age of 28 days;
   or

- *Medical Certificate of Cause of Death in Liveborn Children Dying within 28 days of Life*
  England and Wales only for neonatal deaths.

The certificates should be given to the parents, with a copy for themselves, to take to the Registrar (see below). The Registrar will issue a Certificate of Burial or Cremation, a *green form*, which needs to be given to the funeral director prior to the funeral. Where the baby is to be cremated, Forms B and C need to be completed by the doctor giving the cause of death and by a second doctor notifying the death.

For babies whose death is under the jurisdiction of the Coroner or Procurator Fiscal

If a doctor is unsure of the cause of death and has not attended the baby in the last 14 days, or there are suspicious circumstances surrounding the death, it has to be reported to the Coroner. This means that a medical certificate is generally not given to the parents and they will need to contact the Coroner for the death certificate. The Coroner has the power to decide whether or not to have an inquest for deaths reported to him. He can also order a postmortem for all cases of sudden and unexpected death. After the Coroner holds an inquest, he sends a *Certificate of Inquest* (within 5 days) recording the cause of death, to the Registrar. A member of the family does not have to register the death in person. To allow the funeral to go ahead the Coroner can issue either a Burial Order or a Coroner's Certificate for Cremation before completing the Certificate of Inquest. If there is not an Inquest, then the Coroner issues either *pink form A or B*, which are notification that he does not consider it necessary to hold an inquest. Form A is when there is no postmortem and the cause of death is taken from the medical certificate issued by the doctor. Form B is after a postmortem and certifies cause of death on the basis of the pathologist's report. These are either collected by parents or sent to the Registrar, and families then have to go to register the death (see below). After a postmortem the Coroner can issue a Certificate for Cremation, or if the parents wish for a burial, the Registrar will issue a Certificate for Burial after receiving pink form A or B.

Registration

Registration takes place in the local registrar's office, which in England and Wales needs to be in the district where the baby *died*, not necessarily the one where they were born or lived. Many hospitals make arrangements for the Registrar to come to the hospital during specified times. Registration needs someone, to go in person, who is a 'qualified informant'. This is normally the mother of the baby or the father, if married to the mother. If the parents are unmarried and wish for both their names on the certificate then this can be done providing both parents register together. The information the parents need to give is the name and sex of the baby, date and place of delivery and details of the parents. For babies who die soon after birth, the parents may register the birth and death at the same time. It is *very important* that we remind parents that their only opportunity to register the baby's forename on either the Stillbirth or the Death Register is *at the time of registration*, unlike the birth register, where the name can be added up to 1 year after the birth.

Babies who are born after the legal age of viability have to have their birth and death registered before the baby is buried or cremated. Exceptions are where a family wish to have their baby buried quickly for religious reasons or there is a holiday period, then the Registrar can issue a Certificate of Burial before registration. This option does not apply to cremation or where the death is under the Coroner – registration has to be completed before disposal of the body.

Stillbirths need to be registered within 6 weeks of birth and not later than 3 months.

Other deaths need to be registered within 5 days of death. For some babies who have lived only a matter of days, this means that the parents will register the birth and death at the same time.

The person registering the birth or death will receive a *short copy* of the entry on the Stillbirth, Birth or Death Registers. They can then obtain a *full copy* a few days later by requesting one and paying the necessary fee (approximately £5).

Organising the burial or cremation

Who does it?

Miscarriages, therapeutic terminations and abortions

Before the age of viability, there is no legal requirement for burial or cremation. For women who experience hospital care during these events, the hospital assumes responsibility for disposal of the baby or body tissues unless parents request to make their own arrangements. SANDS (1991) points out, 'Babies born before the legal age of viability have no legal status. Consequently the law offers no guidance about what may or may not be done with the bodies of such babies.' SANDS goes on to recommend that for babies born before the age of viability there 'should be provision for respectful disposal. What constitutes respectful disposal may vary according to what is lost (especially whether or not there is a body) and more importantly what is appropriate and needed by the parents.' However, the lack of legal requirements means that disposal may be incineration of body tissues or burial/cremation. Small embryos from abortions and fetal tissues have, in the past, been disposed of by hospitals giving them to researchers. The Polkinghorne Report (1989) stated that all parents should give their written consent to this form of disposal of their baby.

For our practice we need to be able to clearly tell parents what is existing policy, so that they know what would happen to their 'baby' if the hospital makes arrangements. They have the choice to make their own arrangements.

Stillborn babies and babies in Intensive Care Baby Units

All hospitals are recommended to provide a service (by contracting to a local funeral director) to arrange for disposal of stillborn babies in hospital, and this may extend to babies who are in Intensive Care Baby Units. Depending on the contract, disposal may be burial or cremation and may include a blessing to make it a funeral. Parents can choose to accept this hospital provision or make their own arrangements by going to a funeral director. Important issues in this decision are.

- Is it burial or cremation?
- When will it be?
- Where will it be?
- Is a blessing said if so by whom?
- Is there a tangible place for the family to go to?
- Can the family have a plaque or other memorial?

Older infants and babies who die at home

Families whose baby dies on the paediatric wards or at home, e.g. as a cot death, have to make their own arrangements, for which they may obtain assistance from a funeral director.

Having their baby home?

We need to make sure that families know about these choices. Parents may make arrangements to have their dead baby brought home directly from the hospital. A release of body form needs to be signed. The funeral director will take the baby from the hospital to the home. Alternatively the parents may ask for the baby to come to their home for the night before the funeral to say their 'hellos and goodbyes'. For babies born before the age of viability, the hospital should provide parents with an opaque, closed lid container to take their baby home in.

Planning a funeral

For families organising the funeral of their baby, the task need not be daunting with the support of a known health worker, the hospital chaplain (who may have a major role) and the funeral director. Choosing a funeral director may be by personal recommendation, from the yellow pages or from a list provided by the health worker caring for them. It can be useful to check if the funeral director is a member of the British Institute of Funeral Directors or the National Association of Funeral Directors (see addresses at the end of this Appendix).

The family need to take time to look at the numerous choices and feel right in what they decide. The importance of these goodbyes means that there can be no second chance for reorganising the funeral. Choices include: burial or cremation; whether to have a service; whether to have flowers or donations; whether to have singing at the service or people saying a poem; whether to have siblings at the funeral (see Table 2.2). Some of these questions which can help families decide are outlined in a booklet we used in Avon, UK (Appendix 6). We also need to be aware that the choices bring conflict for parents about what they want to do and what they can afford. We need to support them to understand that it is what is in their hearts in saying goodbye that counts, not what an expensive funeral shows.

Burial

Churchyards have their own policy as to who can be buried and where they can be buried. This sometimes excludes babies who are stillborn or born before the age of viability (24 weeks), or requires that they are buried in a particular area of the churchyard. Either the pastor of the churchyard or the local funeral director will be able to advise on the regulations that apply. *Crematoria* may have similar restrictions, having a specific area that is allocated for young children with either single or shared plots. Alternatively, parents can choose to buy their own family plot to bury their baby. In either churchyard or cemetery, if parents wish to erect a plaque or headstone to the baby, this needs to be checked, because there are often regulations as to size and placement of these items. Practice has now changed from previous years when many young babies were placed in shared graves.

Cremation

Some crematoria state that there will be no remains of a baby, whether stillborn or an older infant. This is because at the high temperatures used in cremation there is little residue left from young babies. However, with methods such as extra filters and cooling the temperature at the end of the day, it may be possible to have some ashes. Under Home Office regulation 23, parents of babies who die should be informed if a crematorium cannot offer ashes of their baby and have the option to go elsewhere. Most crematoria have the opportunity for parents to place a small plaque in the grounds of the crematorium. In some places there are special Gardens of Remembrance for babies and children. A recent initiative in Wycombe Cemetery, South Bucks, UK, is an appeal to produce a garden in the shape of a snowdrop created by flowers, shrubs and seats.

Costs of a funeral

If the *hospital* organised the disposal of the baby, it will pay the costs of the burial or cremation. Anything extra such as flowers or a headstone remain with the parents. If the *family* organise the funeral, you will appreciate that costs do vary according to locality, options and rising prices over time. Check your local area to be able to advise accurately. Costs to any family may include the following:

- *Funeral.* Many funeral directors offer their basic service (including organisation and coffin) free to families whose child dies under the age of 14 years, unless cars or extra services are required. For those who do charge, there may be variation in costs, so do check around.
- *Cremation.* There may be costs at the crematorium including the chapel for a service. Most babies dying less than 1 year of age are cremated free.
- *Burial.* In a cemetery it means buying either a private plot or having a family plot. Each brings different costs. In a churchyard there may be fees for upkeep and for digging the grave; these are generally less than in a cemetery. In both a cemetary or churchyard there may be costs of using premises for a service. In addition the minister may charge if there is a religious service.
- *Extra costs.* May include flowers, memorials such as plaques and head-stones.

At the time of writing in 1994, burial costs may vary from £185 to £405 and cremation costs are 25–50% cheaper.

In the UK, families receiving any form of income support may be eligible for a means-tested payment towards the costs of the funeral. This can be claimed on form SF200 within 3 months of the funeral. The form is obtainable from the Department of Social Security and funeral directors. If this benefit cannot be claimed, some charitable funds may be found from work social funds or hospital trustees funds.

Finally, even if the family do not want to be part of a funeral, they can still choose to have a thanksgiving service months or years later.

References

Kohner N. *Dignified endings.* London: SANDS, 1992

Polkinghorne Report. *Review of the guidance on the research use of fetuses and fetal material.* London: HMSO, 1989

SANDS. *Miscarriage, stillbirth and neonatal death: guidelines for Professionals.* London: SANDS, 1991

Organisations

British Institute of Funeral Directors
146A High St, Tonbridge, Kent TN9 1BB, UK

National Association of Funeral Directors
618 Warwick Road, Solihull, West Midlands, B9 1AA, UK

Appendix 6: The Importance of Goodbyes

This is an A5 size, pink paper leaflet given to parents in Avon, UK who had a baby die suddenly and unexpectedly. It covers some of the choices families have in planning a funeral. Consider adapting it to suit your local area and needs. (*Reprinted courtesy of Avon Infant Mortality Study, Department of Child Health, St Michael's Hospital, Bristol, UK.*)

Goodbyes

Firstly, we want to say how sorry and sad we were to hear that your baby had died and to meet you today.

At the time your baby died you may have many feelings, including shock, anger, upset and confusion. It can be hard to take in or understand what has happened, what it means to your family and what needs organising. For many families it is the first time they have known a person die. It can be frightening to find out what needs to be decided or organised. The most important thing which we can say is 'take time, don't rush'. There *is* time to decide. The choices you now make for your baby are important both now and in the future for sharing your love and saying goodbye to your baby. However, if you forget something and want to do it years later, such as an inscription in a Book of Rememberance, it is never too late.

This leaflet is about suggestions from other parents on the choices you have. Talk about them with each other, family and friends. Decide what feels right to you. Goodbyes are the memories of the future.

Before the funeral

- You can go and see, touch or hold your baby when your baby is in St Michael's Hospital or at the Funeral Directors.
- Photographs of your baby are taken by the hospital staff and we will look after these until you want them. Alternatively, you may wish to take some more with your own camera. Or you could ask a friend or relative to do this for you. Even if you never look at the photos, you have them there for sometime in the future. Remember the hospital photos on polaroid film will fade after several years, so consider having copies made by a photo shop.
- At the hospital we also take a handprint or footprint from your baby, which we will look after until you wish to have it. You may want to put it in an album. You may also want to take a handprint or footprint in clay or plaster of Paris, which you can keep and have glazed. Some parents

---

'The material in this Appendix is from a public information handout and may be reproduced without the permission of the Publisher or the original source organisation.'

find that they want to have a lock of their child's hair or fingernail clippings to put in a locket. If you would like to do this if you go to visit your baby, then do – if not ask us.

- You may wish to keep a familiar toy with your baby or wrap them in a blanket. You might wish to choose particular clothes for your baby to wear either before or during the funeral. If you would like company when you dress or bath your baby, we, or the funeral director, can be with you.
- You may wish to have your baby home again before the funeral, to be able to share precious moments together as a family in your home. Depending on how you feel, this might be on the morning of the funeral or for longer.
- You, or your other children, may wish to put a poem, picture or letter with your baby as a way of saying 'We love you'.

About funerals

- The practical details of organising a funeral can be done by a funeral director. They care about the pain you are feeling. They can help to make the choices you want and carry it out – it is their job to take away the hassle of arrangements. Or, you may wish to organise all the details yourself. If you choose a funeral director, then go to one who is recommended by family or friends, or look in the telephone book for one who is near you.
- Choosing burial or cremation of your baby will depend on your feelings. If you want cremation then check whether the crematorium can offer you ashes after the cremation. If they cannot and you want to have ashes, ask about another crematorium.
- Whether you choose burial or cremation it is generally possible to have either a stone or plaque as a memorial to your baby. You need to check this with the funeral director, because there may be special requirements in terms of size and place of these items.
- You might wish to go in a car to the funeral with your baby, or carry your baby into the church or chapel yourself.
- You might wish to put toys, photos, poems, letters or something of yours, e.g. a scarf, with your baby in the coffin. You may then wish to keep a duplicate with you as a tangible link to your baby.
- The service you choose does not need to be religious. It might include music, nursery rhymes or a short talk by someone in the family. If you want a minister your funeral director can advise you on one whose tastes may suit yours. You may wish for the service to be held in a church, chapel or even outside.
- As part of organising a cremation you need to think about whether you would like the coffin to remain in the chapel or to move and have the curtains close in front of it.

- You may want to make a collage of photos for family and friends to see at the funeral.
- You may decide to take your other children to the funeral. If you do, make sure that you have someone to look after them, so that you do not feel torn between looking after them and saying goodbye to your baby.
- You might want to keep some flowers from the funeral to press and keep in an album.

Costs of the funeral

The costs of a funeral vary. Many funeral directors will try to show their care by charging a nominal amount or doing the basic funeral free with only costs of hire of cars, etc. The remaining costs will be churchyard or crematorium fees. If you are on income support then you may be able to claim for some of the costs by sending in a form, which the funeral director will have.

After the funeral

- You may want to put a verse or sentence in a Book of Remembrance at the crematorium, church or hospital chapel.
- Some parents want to make a memorial to their baby. This might be fund-raising for charity or planting a tree. There is a special Mother and Baby Dwarf Rose, with deep red flowers, which is sold in aid of the Mother and Baby Trust, based at Bristol Maternity Hospital, which funds research into stillbirth and cot death. The bush costs £3 plus £2.50 postage from John Sanday (Roses) Ltd, Over Lane, Almondsbury, Bristol (Tel: 0454 612195).
- Some families find they want to write a poem or draw a picture as an expression of their grief.
- In Bristol there is a memorial service held annually in the Spring for all parents whose baby has died. Contact us for the time and place.

Things to remember when organising a funeral

1. *Would you like your child buried or cremated?*
   Do you have strong personal or religious beliefs about it? Is there somewhere local or special to the family? If you have a cremation, remember that there may be very few or no ashes of your baby.
2. *Where would you like the service?*
   In a church, chapel, crematorium, elsewhere?
3. *Who will take the service?*
   Minister, yourselves, friends?
4. *What type of service?*
   Religious, music, readings.

5. *What would you like your child to wear at the funeral?*
   Do you have some special clothes? Do you want to put them on?

6. *Would you like particular items with your child in the coffin?*
   Toys, pictures, letters, something of yours? Ask the funeral director to organise this.

7. *Mementos of your child*
   Do you want any photos, lock of hair, handprint?

8. *Will your other children go to the funeral?*
   Who will look after them?

9. *Do you want to see your child again before the funeral?*
   Will you see them alone, with others? Do you want your child home?

10. *Do you want family and friends to stay together after the funeral?*
    Where do you want them to go? Who will make arrangements?

11. *What about payment for the funeral?*
    Is it free for the funeral? Can you claim any benefits?

12. *Do you want people to give flowers or money?*
    Is money for a charity? How will you let people know? The funeral director can put a notice in the paper.

13. *Do you want a memorial?*
    A stone or plaque or tree? Where would you like it?

Appendix 7: Families Seeing Their Baby Again After Death

Families whose baby is in the hospital mortuary before or after having a postmortem, or before going home or to the funeral parlour, often have a need to see their baby again. The issues we need to consider are about providing access and support to families.

- *Access* – can parents see their baby at any time in the day or night?
- *Who* – is the person they need to contact about seeing their baby, and how do they do this (phone number or radiopager)?
- *Where* they will see their baby (in an ante-room to the hospital mortuary or in the hospital chapel)?
- *Company* – who will be there when they see their baby?

Access

Parents should be able to see their baby at any time of the night or day. This has implications for the workload of staff to prepare and accompany families. There may be conflicts if several parents wish to visit at the same time. If so we need to be honest with the parents that there are other families who wish to see their baby – most families are very supportive of each other.

Contact

Families need to be clear who they contact to be able to see their baby. If the mother is still in hospital it might be easy to find the member of staff looking after her. At home families are reliant on phoning or turning up on the off chance. For reasons of preparation and workload most units request families to phone before they come to the hospital to see their baby. If we do this, we need to be sure that they can easily get through to the relevant person and are not left hanging in mid-air by the switchboard.

Where

Ideally, there should be a room where parents can sit with their baby, which is peaceful, furnished with comfortable chairs, tissues and a cot for the baby. It should always be available for this purpose. In some units the hospital chapel is used, which causes problems having access at any time, if this conflicts with the needs of other patients. A bereavement room should be part of a unit's designated space. Any room that is used needs to be large enough for several family and friends who may come.

Company

Having a person to be with them can be very important for parents to feel 'safe' to see their dead baby; it may be the first time that they have seen someone dead. They need company until they feel comfortable to be alone, as a family. In some hospitals it is the practice for the hospital porter to be contacted when a family wish to see their baby. A porter, without training or support, *is not* generally equipped to deal with the family's grief. It is good practice to have a designated person, such as midwife or nurse (especially if known to the family already), to welcome and accompany the family to see their baby. The advantage of having a bereavement room that is placed within a maternity/paediatric unit is that staff can easily come and go, leaving families for some time together without feeling that they are isolated away from a support person.

Preparation

Whoever accompanies the family to see their baby needs to take responsibility for preparation.

- *Preparation of the baby.* Making sure that they are removed from the mortuary fridge, wrapped or dressed and placed in the room where the family will go. Making sure that any accompanying property, such as toys, are there with the child.
- *Preparing the family for seeing their baby.* We can say 'Your baby will be cold to touch and their lips will be blue.' It may include preparing them to see their baby after a postmortem and we can use the leaflet '*Guide to the postmortem examination*' from the Department of Health to discuss this with parents.

Documentation

It is important that there is documentation, kept in an agreed place in the hospital, which records the property of the baby (toys, clothes), any visits by the family and any concerns of family or staff. This means that information is accessible to all health workers involved with the family.

Know the policies in your area of practice and always review them in the light of good practice.

Resource leaflet

'*Guide to postmortem examination – brief notes for parents and families who have lost a baby in pregnancy or early infancy*' by the UK Department of Health, produced in consultation with the National Advisory Body for the Confidential Enquiry into Stillbirths and Deaths in Infancy, SANDS and FSID. Use the leaflet with parents as an aid to discussion.

Appendix 8: Leaflet for Grandparents after their Grandchild has died suddenly and Unexpectedly

This is an A5 size, yellow leaflet for grandparents. If you find that any parts are useful then adapt them to suit your local area and needs. (Reprinted courtesy of Avon Infant Mortality Study, Department of Child Health, St Michael's Hospital, Bristol, UK.)

Grandparents' grief

Firstly, we want to say we are sorry to hear that your grandchild died. This can be a time of sudden change, pain and lots of people coming and going. We have written down some of the things that grandparents have told us. If you find bits useful then hold on to it; if it does not feel right for you then let it go.

Having your grandchild die

Hearing that your grandchild has died suddenly can mean that you are full of feelings, whether sadness, anger, frustration, guilt and helplessness. For you there is a double grief, which may be the worst pain you have felt. Firstly, grieving for your grandchild, the enjoyment you had with them, being able to care for them in a special way yet not having a responsibility for them as a parent. The fun you had hoped to have buying them treats and taking them out for a trip. Secondly, grieving for the pain your own child is feeling. It can hurt you to feel unable to protect your child, prevent them from feeling the pain and grief and be unable to 'make it better'. Whilst you cannot take away the pain of their bereavement there are many things that you can do for your child and any other grandchildren to make it 'easier'.

What is grief?

It is what you and your child and family feel. It is our reaction to the loss or death of someone we love. The feelings change in strength and nature over months and years. It is a normal response to loss and death. Sometimes the feelings can be so strong as to make people wonder if they are losing a sense of reality, but it is a reflection of love and loss. Everyone grieves differently in their own way in their own time, so do not expect that you, your child or your partner will all react in the same way. Some of the feelings that you may hear people talk about in grieving are: shock and

---

disbelief; fear, guilt and anger; sadness and apathy; acceptance and hope. It is important that we hold on to the fact that many people do not have all those feelings, or they may occur in a different order; there is no 'right' way to grieve.

Many grandparents question why they are still alive when their grandchild died. This is called 'survivor guilt'. You may have feelings of guilt and anger at surviving and outliving your grandchild, who was only at the beginning of their life. Do not be angry with yourself – it is important to recognise that we can never know in advance that a child or person is going to die suddenly.

Firstly, what about you?

You need to recognise that you will be feeling grief just as parents do. This means allowing yourself time to think and feel and to recognise that you need support from family and friends. The death of your grandchild may trigger all sorts of memories of losses and deaths you have experienced previously in your life. At some point it may help to talk to someone like your GP or health visitor, to have space to talk about your grandchild. It is often impossible to talk with your child because it upsets them too much and you are trying to be strong for them. So, make sure that you have your space to grieve in.

Grieving is hard work; it involves strange emotions, which are tiring. You may want to go to bed early and wonder why. Take care and be kind to yourself as your body is telling you it is tired with pain, thinking and feeling. It may make sense to look after your energy to help your children. There is always unfairness and injustice about death to those who are left behind. You may have personal or religious beliefs, which give you a strength or an understanding of what has happened. After someone dies we need to reach an acceptance that we have much to offer in our own life and that we cannot barter our lives on the basis of fairness and what we would like to happen. The energy you use being angry is needed to cope with your own and your child's sadness.

What can you do for your child?

Most importantly, you need to show how much you care, *and* you can hug and listen to your child. In times of distress we turn to the people we know and care about; with them we can be silent, cry and get angry. Letting those feelings out is part of grieving, and for you to be able to support your child is one of the most important things you can give them. It is important that we have no *expectations* about when they will cease to be so distressed; each person grieves in their own way.

It can mean being there, helping to run the house, looking after other children, giving them a chance to talk about anything and everything. It may mean helping to organise a funeral, but make sure that the parents make choices about the goodbyes they want to make to their child. Memories are not only feelings and talking, they are the things you can touch. So do not clear out all the baby things and photos in your own or your child's house, unless the parents strongly request it. Doing so is denying the existence of the baby. Put all the things like toys and clothes on one side; shut them in a room or cupboard, and look at them at another time.

Sometimes grandparents feel unable to cope, either physically with offering practical help, or emotionally with the pain and distress of their child. We are all different and need to accept that. If you feel like this, then explain it to the bereaved prents: how you feel and why you cannot support them. This is being *honest*, rather than allowing confusions to arise with your child.

Physical illness in grief

Often strong emotions such as feelings of grief are accompanied by physical symptoms or illness. This may be aches and pains, infection and tiredness. If you or your child have these then do go and see your doctor, tell the doctor what has happened and ask for advice or treatment as necessary.

Questions you may have about a baby dying suddenly and unexpectedly

There are particular features of sudden unexpected death of a baby or child that can add to the pain and grief: the suddeness, the fact that it is a child and the legal requirement to have a postmortem regardless of age for any sudden death. Having some knowledge of sudden unexpected death can help and we have outlined some information below.

What is a postmortem?

This is an examination performed by a pathologist, who is a trained doctor. It will be carried out with as much care, respect and attention as an operation on a living baby will be. By looking at your grandchild very thoroughly the pathologist tries to find out why your grandchild died. As with any operation there will be a stitched cut, which you will see if you look carefully after the postmortem. In other ways your grandchild will not look different and they can be wearing the familiar clothes chosen by the family.

Can we find out about the postmortem?

Normally, someone will let the parents know the results as soon as possible and answer any questions. This may be the GP or a hospital doctor. Ask the parents if you can be there, or if you need more information, talk directly to the person.

If your grandchild dies as a cot death?

Sudden unexpected death of a baby (almost always during sleep) has been recognised for thousands of years and is mentioned in the Bible (I Kings v:16–28). Such cot deaths were for many years explained as overlaying, although there was no evidence to support this idea. Since 1970, the term sudden infant death syndrome (SIDS) has been widely used in the UK. It is another term for cot death and describes the sudden and unexpected death of an infant or young child for which a thorough postmortem fails to find a cause of death. Cot death is not a diagnosis. We do not exactly understand why cot death happens and probably many factors contribute to why the baby died. It is important to discuss this with your GP if you have any questions.

Where can you go for support?

Various self-help groups link parents and grandparents of children who have died for different reasons with other families who have had a similar experience. You can contact either of the national organisations to give you the telephone number of the local person.

Organisations

Cot Death Research
8A Alexandra Parade, Weston-super-Mare, Avon, UK
Tel: 0934–413333

Foundation for the Study of Infant Death
35 Belgrave Square, London, UK
Tel: 071–235 0965

Books

Murphy S. *Coping with cot death*. London: Sheldon Press, 1990 (£4.95)
Lubyn J. *Cot death*. London: Bedford Square Press, 1990 (£6.95)

Appendix 9: Information for Health Workers Planning Care for a Family during a Subsequent Pregnancy

The aim of care during a subsequent pregnancy is to promote the confidence of the family and provide support as needed. In the area where you practise there may already exist a formalised system of care. For example, families whose baby died as a cot death may be part of the Care of the Next Infant (CONI) scheme. This general overview needs to be adapted to: (a) the particular reason for the previous death; and (b) your work area to achieve an organised division of roles and responsibilities between community and hospital staff. The value of continuity of care for families after bereavement is immeasurable. It reduces the vulnerability of being exposed to people who do not know the family's fears and it means that they only have to explain their concerns and feelings to a few people. It is important to have some system of marking the notes so that carers, who may be unknown to the family, are aware that the family has been previously bereaved. This might be a sticker on the notes or notes in red where babies have died. Both methods need to be identified and explained to families.

Antenatally

It can be useful to arrange an appointment with the parents, early in the antenatal period, with the midwife, GP and either an obstetrician or paediatrician. This is an opportunity to:

- review previous events;
- answer any unresolved questions about the death, and postmortem if performed;
- review any measures that might help to prevent a recurrence of death;
- discuss the care that can be offered to families during pregnancy and labour and postnatally.

We would suggest that antenatal care includes:

- an opportunity for extra antenatal and postnatal visits;
- encouragement to phone if there are worries;
- a suggestion to plan the care that they want to have in labour.

Information such as the names of health workers, plan of contact, outline of care, advice for pregnancy and support group contact could usefully be incorporated into a leaflet for parents.

We need to take time during visits to stress that we know it would be unrealistic to expect that they will not worry. Even though the statistical odds mean that this pregnancy is likely to go well, the reality is that telling parents not to worry is like asking them to hold their breath until Christmas. What we can give is TLC (tender loving care) in their time of anxiety. During pregnancy, measures that can help families pass the milestones, which are reminders of the pregnancy where the baby died, include:

- having easy access to talk to health workers;
- discussing what is different in this pregnancy to separate this baby from the baby who died;
- possibly having extra ultrasound scans (USS) to see the baby moving as reassurance (the benefits of this have to be weighed against the unknown long-term risks of USS);
- contacting other bereaved parents in their local self-help group to meet others who have 'successfully survived' having another child.

The value of discussing measures that can reduce the risk of recurrence cannot be overestimated; it is a very important way of giving parents *control* over their lives. For example, after miscarriage or stillbirth we can suggest a balanced diet, exercise and trying to stop smoking as important factors in contributing to the health of the baby. After a baby has died as a cot death, on the basis of the 1991 UK Health Campaign, we can discuss how families can reduce the risk of cot death by quitting smoking, placing their baby supine to sleep and avoiding overwrapping. It means that we need to keep current with research and public health issues to be able to advise our clients on any worthwhile measures to reduce the risk of recurrence.

In labour

The staff caring for the family need to be aware of the previous death and to give the family the opportunity to state any requests that they may have about the labour and delivery. For example, one woman, who had had a stillbirth previously, stated as she came through the delivery suite door that she wanted to be on the move all through her labour, because last time she had spent it on the bed.

Postnatally

After the delivery it is important that the baby is carefully examined by a paediatric-trained professional and that all the findings, whether normal or abnormal, are discussed with the parents. Depending on the baby it may be appropriate to have paediatric follow-up appointments, e.g. for a baby who died as a cot death there may be support with an apnoea alarm. If this involves hospital appointments, there needs to be effective liaison between hospital and community to avoid delays in information arriving. For example, letters are routinely sent from hospital to GP following a clinic appointment. The information may never reach the health visitor, who regularly sees the family, unless a copy is also sent to her.

When parents are at home with their baby they need to know who to contact if they have any concerns. The family may initially need extra visits postnatally from community health workers to develop their confidence that their baby will survive and that they are able to be parents. Their previous experience may have shattered their self-esteem.

Finally, throughout our care we need to value the impact that the previous bereavement will have had on the family. It may have shattered their trust in a safe life and they may fear the outcome of the next pregnancy and the next, and so on. Equally, anxieties are not confined to the repetition of the previous event, e.g. miscarriage. When a miscarriage has not happened, there may be fears of a stillbirth, a cot death, etc. Conversely, other families will accept what happens as happens.

Appendix 10: Information for Health Workers about Adoptees tracing Birth Parents

In the UK, the Children's Act of 1975 has meant that at the age of 18 years, adoptive children have the right of access to their original birth certificates, which contain the maternal name and address at the time of birth and possibly the paternal name. This information can then be used to trace their birth parents. Under this current legislation birth parents are prepared for the fact their child may try to trace them at a later date. However, parents who had their child adopted prior to the Children's Act of 1975 had no expectation of ever seeing their child again. Therefore, there is a requirement for all children of these parents to have an interview with a counsellor *before* having access to their birth certificate.

Application for a birth certificate is made to:

For England and Wales
The Registrar General, Adopted Children's Register, Titchfield, Fareham, Hants PO15 5RY, UK

For Scotland
The General Registrar's Office, New Register House, Edinburgh EH1 3Y1, UK

For further information on tracing, adoptees can contact any of the organisations listed at the end of Chapter 5, such as BAAF, PAC, PPIAS, NORCAP. NORCAP offers:

- tracing agency facilities
- contact leaders nationwide to advise on tracing
- Search-In Days at St Catherine's House, London
- a booklet on searching
- an intermediary service for making contact with birth parents.

NORCAP
3 New High Street, Headington, Oxford OX3 7AJ, UK
Tel: 0865–750554

Appendix 11: Suggestions for Further Reading and Information available from Voluntary Agencies

For further reading

1. *When a baby dies.* Nancy Kohner and Alex Henley (Pandora 1991) The experience of miscarriage, stillbirth and neonatal death, using parents' own accounts.
2. *Miscarriage – women's needs and experiences.* Christine Moulder (Pandora 1990)
3. *Family.* Susan Hill (Michael Joseph 1989) Contains an account of the premature birth and 5 weeks of life of Susan Hill's second daughter.
4. *Mothers writing about the death of a baby* (National Childbirth Trust 1984)
5. *Swimmer in the secret sea.* William Kotzwinkle (Ellis 1976) A short fictional account from a father's perspective on the stillbirth of his son.
6. *Caring in crisis. A handbook of intervention skills.* Boehringer (Churchill Livingstone 1993)
7. *Bereavement. A guide for nurses.* Jenny Pewson (Harper & Row 1990)
8. *The bereaved parent.* Harrient Sarnoff Schiff (Human Horizons 1979)
9. *The anatomy of bereavement.* Beverley Raphael (Routledge 1984)
10. *Grief in children.* Atle Dyregrov (Jessica Kingsley 1991)
11. *Talking about death – a dialogue between parent and child.* Earl Grollman (Beacon Press 1976).
12. *I know just how you feel – avoiding the clichés of grief.* Erin Linn (Publishers Mark 1986)
13. *Helping children cope with grief – facing a death in the family.* Rosemary Wells (Sheldon Press 1988)
14. *Recovering from the loss of a child.* Katherine Fair Donnelly (Macmillan 1982)
15. *After a child dies. Counselling bereaved families.* Sherry E. Johnson (Springer 1987)
16. *The death of a child – a book for families.* Tessa Wilkinson (Julia MacRae Books 1991)
17. *Young people and death.* Ed. John Morgan (Charles Press 1991)
18. *Helping children cope with death.* Hannelore Wass and Charles Corr (Hemisphere 1984)
19. *Crisis intervention with children and families.* S. Auerbach and A. Stolberg (Hemisphere 1986)
20. *Order from chaos – responding to traumatic events.* Marion Gibson (Venture Press 1991)
21. *How teenagers cope with grief.* D. Zagdanski (Melbourne Hill of Content 1990)
22. *On the death of a child.* Celia Hindmarch (Radcliffe Medical Press 1993)

Leaflets available from voluntary agencies

Foundation for the Study of Infant Deaths
35 Belgrave Square, London SW1X 8QB, UK
Tel: 071-235 0965

*Information for parents following the unexpected death of their baby**
Details of the procedure following a cot death, normal grief reactions and
information on further help available – for bereaved parents. This leaflet
should be given to every family bereaved by cot death.

*Support for parents**
Information on help available for parents following a cot death – for
parents and health professionals.

*Guidelines for befrienders**
Guidelines for supporting newly bereaved parents.

Guidelines for GPs when cot death occurs
Advice to GPs on support needs of the family.

Guidelines for health visitors when cot death occurs
Advice to health visitors on support needs of the family.

Guidelines for Accident and Emergency Departments
Guidelines for management of cot deaths in casualty departments.

Grief

Three grief leaflets
Describe reactions and needs of the family. The titles are: Grief of Parents
Bereaved by a Cot Death; Grief of Children whose Brother or Sister died as
a Cot Death; and Grief of the Extended Family When Cot Death Occurs. For
health professionals and bereaved families.

Basic facts

Questions and answers
Answers to 26 common questions on cot death – for the public.

Factfile 1: Cot death: facts and figures
Background information, definitions and statistics of cot death – for the
public.

All leaflets are free to individual parents (please send s.a.e.). For educational
or training purposes or for health authorities and other institutions, the
charge is 25p each leaflet on orders up to five times; then 10p each, unless
otherwise marked. Leaflets marked with an asterisk are free to all – parents,
students, professionals, hospitals, etc. (please send s.a.e.).

Compassionate Friends
53 North Street, Bristol BS3 1EN, UK
Tel: 0272–665202

No death so sad
For newly bereaved parents.

A father's grief

Bereaved parents and the police
For police officers.

Bereaved parents and the professionals
For doctors, nurses, health visitors, social workers and others working with bereaved families.

Coping with special occasions
Birthdays, Christmas, Anniversaries.

Grieving couples

Helping bereaved parents
Suggestions for concerned relatives and friends.

Ministering to bereaved parents
For clergy and their helpers.

On inquests (in England and Wales)

Preparing your child's funeral

Shadow of suicide

Teenagers
A section from 'Helping younger bereaved brothers and sisters', listed above.

The healing process
For bereaved parents, and others, outlining how grief usually progresses.

To bereaved grandparents (whose grandchild has died)

When a Child in your school is bereaved
For teachers.

When an adult child dies

Appendix 12: Contact Addresses in Countries Other than the UK

This list only includes some of the self-help organisations for some of the areas of bereavement which we have written about in this book. If you are seeking an organisation in a different locality or for support for a different bereavement, try contacting the local hospital social worker or one of the organisations listed here, since most have excellent networking links between organisations.

AUSTRALIA

National Association for Loss and Grief (NALAG)
Has a branch in each state and is listed in the phone directory.

Funeral and Bereavement Educators Association
Offer information and support.
Contact address:
722 High St, Kew, Victoria

The Compassionate Friends have chapters in the different states which offer support to bereaved families.
Contact address:
Bereaved Parents Support and Information Centre, Lower Parish Hall, 300 Camberwell Road, Camberwell, Victoria 3124

National SIDS Council Australia
891 Burke Road, Camberwell, Victoria 3124
Tel: 03 882 7022
Has resources for education and research and can link to the parent organisations in each state listed below.

Sudden Infant Death Association ACT (Inc)
PO Box 58, Jamieson, Act 2164
Tel: 06 258 6174

Sudden Infant Death Association NSW (Inc)
PO Box 209, Baulkham Hills, New South Wales 2153
Tel: 02 639 5343

Queensland Sudden Infant Death Research Foundation Inc.
GPO Box 1987, Brisbane 40001
Tel: 07 836 3030

Queensland Sudden Infant Death Syndrome Parents Network Inc
641 Underwood Road, Rochedale, Queensland 4123
Tel: 07 341 1176

Sudden Infant Death Association of South Australia Inc,
301 Payneham Road, Royston Park, SA 5070
Tel: 08 363 1963

Sudden Infant Death Research Foundation Inc,
1227 Malvern Road, Malvern Victoria 3144
Tel: 03 822 9611

Sudden Infant Death Syndrome Foundation Inc,
Lotteries House, 79 Stirling St, Perth, Western Australia 6000.
Tel 09 220 0620

Tasmania Sudden Infant Death Society Inc.,
PO Box 1007, Burnie, Tasmania 7320
Tel: 004 33 0457

Stillbirth and Neonatal Death (SANDS)
Has a branch in each state.
PO Box 204, Curtin, ACT 2650
11 Narelle St, North Epping, New South Wales 2121
PO Box 708, South Brisbane, Queensland
109 Young Street, Unley, Southern Australia
19 Canterbury Road, Camberwell, Victoria 3124
Agnes Walsh House, King Edward Memorial Hospital, Bagot Road
Subiaco, Western Australia 6008

CANADA

Canadian Foundation for the Study of Infant Deaths
offers parents' groups, resources for education and research.
Contact address:
The SIDS Foundation National Office
586 Eglinton Ave, E., Suite 308, Toronto M4P 1P2
Mailing address: PO Box 190, Station R, Toronto, Ontario M4G 329

NEW ZEALAND

The Compassionate Friends
offers support groups for the bereaved,
listed in the phone directory.
Contact address:
9 Welles St, Ranfurly, Otago.

Cot Death Association
offers support groups for parents, education and research
5 Clonbern Road, PO Box 28177, Auckland 5
Tel: 09 524 8597

Stillbirth and Neonatal Death (SANDS)
offers support for parents with local groups.
Contact address:
30 Church St, Palmerston North.

USA

Compassionate Friends
is a worldwide organisation offering support to bereaved people. Local chapters are listed in the telephone directory.

The Candlelighters Childhood Cancer Foundation has parents' groups, resources for education and research worldwide.
Contact address in USA:
Suite 1011, 2025 Eye St, NW Washington DC 20006

National Sudden Infant Death Syndrome Foundation
has parents' groups, education and research resources. There are also local organisations for bereaved families in the different states which the foundation has information on.
Contact address:
8240 Professional Place, Suite 205, Landover MD 20785, Maryland

National Sudden Infant Death Syndrome Research Center
is for education and research.
8201 Greensboro Drive, Suite 600, McLean, Virginia 22102–3810
Tel: 703 821 8955

Glossary

Abortion

Expulsion of the fetus from the uterus before the 24th week of pregnancy (current legal age of viability), where the fetus is not born alive.

Spontaneous. This is the situation where the pregnancy is expelled with no previous intervention. It is commonly referred to as 'miscarriage' (see below).

complete – when all the products of conception are expelled
habitual – three consecutive spontaneous abortions
incomplete – when part of the products of conception are retained in the uterus.
missed – the pregnancy separates from the uterus but is not expelled, it becomes surrounded by layers of blood like a clot
threatened – uterine bleeding, but all the products of conception are retained.

Induced. By medical or surgical means; this situation is commonly referred to as 'abortion'. Grounds for induced abortion, also referred to as termination of pregnancy (TOP), are under the Abortion Act of 1967, which was amended in 1990 in the Human Fertility and Embryology Act:

(a) that the pregnancy has not exceeded its 24th week and that continuance of the pregnancy would involve risk greater than if the pregnancy were terminated, of injury to the physical and mental health of the pregnant woman or any existing children in her family;
(b) that the termination is necessary to prevent grave permanent injury to the physical or mental health of the pregnant woman;
(c) that the continuance of the pregnancy would involve risk to the life of the pregnant woman, greater than if the pregnancy were terminated; or
(d) that there is a substantial risk that if the child were born it would suffer

from such physical or mental abnormalities as to be seriously handicapped.

The everyday usage of the word 'abortion' refers to clause (a) above and often is applied to risk of psychosocial damage if the pregnancy continues. *Therapeutic abortion* (or termination) applies to the other clauses, where the pregnancy is ended to prevent subsequent death, handicap or illness.

Adoption

Adoption is a legal process by which the rights and responsibilities for a child are given up by one set of parents and taken on by another. Legal adoption cannot be cancelled, although it is possible for a child to be readopted by another family. Adoption is for life, for better for worse, for richer for poorer. (Rowe 1982)

Open adoption: 'One in which the birth parents meet the adoptive parents, participate in the separation and placement process, relinquish all legal, moral and nurturing rights to the child, but retain the right to continuing contact and to knowledge of the child's whereabouts and welfare. (Baran et al. 1976)

Adoptee

The person who is adopted.

Adopter

The person who adopts another.

Amniocentesis

Aspiration of a sample of amniotic fluid through the mother's abdomen, for analysis of fetal sex, chromosomal anomalies, congenital abnormalities and maturity.

Artificial Insemination (AI)

Injecting semen into the woman's vagina or uterus by means other than sexual intercourse. Where semen is derived from the husband it is referred to as AIH, and from a donor as AID.

Birth Parent

The other term used is relinquishing parent, the parent who is the biological parent of a child who is adopted by other parents.

Chorionic Villus Sampling (CVS)

A sample of chorionic villi are taken for DNA analysis, karyotyping or enzyme analysis. It is possible to check for conditions such as Down's syndrome, sex of the baby and cystic fibrosis.

Congenital Abnormality

Physical malformation present at birth.

Ectopic Pregnancy

Ectopic means out of place. The pregnancy is outside the uterus, and most commonly in the fallopian tubes. This can become a life-threatening situation when the pregnancy grows and eventually erodes into a blood vessel.

Embryo

Term used to describe the developing offspring of mammals. In the human the term fetus is used after a certain point in development. Under the Human Fertilisation and Embryology Act (1990) the term embryo applies until 14 days.

ERPC

This term means evacuation of retained products of conception. It is a surgical procedure to remove any remaining tissue from a pregnancy which has started to miscarry.

Fetus

Term used to refer to the developing human offspring; it is a period of development that follows on from embryo (see above).

Gestation

Pregnancy (in the human it lasts approximately 40 weeks).

Handicap

This is a value term which refers to any condition that 'for a substantial period, or permanently, retards, disturbs or otherwise adversely affects normal growth, development and adjustment to life' (Court Report 1976: 219).

Infertility

There have been varying definitions of infertility. The World Health Organisation (1975) defined a failure to conceive 'despite cohabitation and exposure to pregnancy for a period of 2 years'. This time period has been shortened by many practitioners to a period of 1 year of unprotected intercourse. The New Zealand Infertility Society (1990) defined infertility as 'inability to conceive after 1 year of trying, or an inability to carry pregnancies to live birth'. This extends the remit, further than conception, to any difficulties getting and keeping a baby in pregnancy.

In Vitro Fertilisation (IVF)

Techniques that are outside the body, which involve the fertilisation of human eggs and the culture of embryos, which are then returned to a woman's uterus.

Miscarriage

See spontaneous abortion above.

Neonatal

Newborn, neonatal death is of a live-born baby within 28 days of birth.

Neonatal Intensive Care Unit (NICU)

Provision of specialist resources for sick neonates who require either life support or basic medical procedures.

Perinatal

At the time of birth. Perinatal death includes babies who are stillborn or who die within 7 days of birth.

Prenatal diagnosis (PND)

Screening tests to detect sex, inherited diseases or chromosomal anomalies early in pregnancy, with a subsequent option for a therapeutic termination to end the pregnancy.

Pre-term

Less than 37 complete weeks of pregnancy.

Stillbirth

An infant born after 24 weeks of pregnancy, who did not breathe after birth, or show any signs of life.

Sudden infant death syndrome (SIDS)

The sudden death of any infant or young child which is unexpected by history and in which a thorough postmortem examination fails to demonstrate an adequate cause of death. (Beckwith 1970).

This is a diagnosis by default, because a cause cannot be found. At present there is debate as to any age limits of SIDS, whether it is 1 year, 2 years or at any age, a sudden death.

Sudden Unexpected Death in Infancy (SUDI)

Where a baby (generally up to 12 months of age) dies for no apparent reason; a postmortem may reveal that there was an unknown anomaly or infection or find no cause of death (SIDS).

Surrogacy

Traditionally, this involves a woman agreeing to act as a surrogate mother for a couple, to bear the child of the husband and give the child to the couple at birth. There are numerous variations with the advent of artificial insemination and IVF. The egg may be from the wife, or a donor, or the surrogate mother. The sperm may be from the husband or from a donor. The sperm may be introduced into the woman's body through sexual intercourse or artificial insemination; or the egg and sperm may meet outside the woman's body – IVF. Under the UK Human Fertilisation and Embryology Act (1991), a court can legalise the adoption of a child from a surrogate mother to a couple, where the gametes of the husband or wife are used to create the embryo, and providing the married couple make application within 6 months of the child's birth and have evidence of agreement. This agreement cannot be given by the surrogate mother until at least 6 weeks after the birth.

Therapeutic Termination

See induced abortion.

Trimester

A period of 3 months (13 weeks).

Ultrasound Scan

Sound waves that are beyond the human detection range, which can be used to resonate and produce a visual representation of the differing tissues on a scan. In pregnancy it is used to detect the growth and development of the fetus.

References

Baran A, Pannor R, Sorosky A. Open adoption. *Social Work* 1976; 21(2):97

Beckwith JB. Observations of the pathological anatomy of the sudden infant death syndrome. In: Bergman A, Beckwith J, Ray C (eds) *SIDS: proceedings of the Second International Conference of the Causes of Sudden Death in Infants.* Seattle: University of Washington Press, 1970

Court Report. *Fit for the future: Report of the Committee on Child Health Services.* London: HMSO, 1976

New Zealand Infertility Society Inc. *Newsletters* 1990;1 (1):2

Rowe J. *Yours by choice.* London: Routledge Kegan Paul, 1982

World Health Organisation. *The epidemiology of infertility.* Report of a WHO Scientific Group, Technical Report Series 582. Geneva: WHO, 1975

Index